INTERACTION:

AN INTERDISCIPLINARY PERSPECTIVE

FOUNDATIONS OF A THEORY OF COMPATIBILITY CONTINUED: EXPLORING COMPATIBILITY

BY

VLADIMIR MOROZOV

PUBLISHED IN ENGLAND

BY

QUICKSTONE PUBLISHING UK

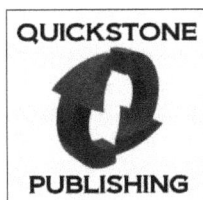

Interaction: an Interdisciplinary Perspective

by

Vladimir Morozov

ISBN: 978-0-9927357-1-5

First published in Russian, entitled
Общество и экономика взаимодействия

(ISBN: 978-5-91292-147-6)

Published in England

by

QUICKSTONE PUBLISHING UK

This book is a continuation of the work Exploring Compatibility: Foundations of a Theory, which the author wrote in 2014, and presents an emerging methodology of compatibility in socio-economic systems that is based on common shared values. This approach relaxes the boundaries of economism and widens the scope for research by considering related non-economic features in the development of the social body. By structuring economic thought around the concept of socio-economic compatibility and the interaction between subjects and objects in decision-making, it makes possible an elaboration of approaches to and the identification of effective mechanisms for an "interaction economy", expressed in a compatible (in terms of needs and values) model of social development and of interaction between sectors of the economy.

The book's central strand is the role of diverse value factors in an economy, factors that shape its overall development vector and that provide social justification for one form or another of socioeconomic organization. Priority areas are identified for the development and reinforcement of compatible states in the subjects and objects that make up the socio-economic environment, alongside cultural-intangible and socio-political institutions. Compatible characteristics for sustainable interaction between subjects are proposed, together with criteria for evaluating the effectiveness of development in a given territory.

ISBN: 978-0-9927357-1-5

CONTENTS

INTRODUCTION

It has become clear that economic science is in need not only of new ideas, but also of a new analytical methodology that would help economics to overcome the fundamentally narrow view of the world inherent in neoliberalism, which tends to be overly focused on purely economic categories (such as market demand and supply, prices, money and capital) to the exclusion of anything else. A newly revamped methodology would be expected to broaden the boundaries of the traditionalist economics approach, broadening the realm of our exploration and bringing in pertinent non-economic aspects of social development to study them in interaction. Speaking of subjective aspects of socioeconomic processes, we have to emphasize primarily the role of values in the development (progress) of society, values that set the overall direction of this development and providing social justification for certain formats of socioeconomic order.

When we consider issues that highlight the unity and contradictions between society, the state (government) and the economy, we note that the current development of the economy and society on the basis of stability and security undermines this basis (both stability and security) because of the rise of extreme mass poverty and an excessive concentration of wealth in the hands of the few; the gradual depletion of the middle class; a lack of access to and failure to accumulate knowledge; the government's inability to ensure universal prosperity because of pressure from the superrich (the oligarchs); society beginning to operate exclusively for the benefit of the chosen few, and similar issues. So how can we achieve the public good, representing spiritual and material values and benefits? According to a group of scientists that includes B. Chicherin, human interests, both material and spiritual, can become public interests, partly through mutual connections among them, because only by joining forces with others can an individual fulfill his purpose.

Society today is driven by trends towards the destruction of traditional values, trends that are "imposed" from above, trends that are based on abstract ideas remote from reality and real life against the will of the majority of the people, who do not accept the ongoing changes or the proposed revision of dearly held values that for many centuries have been the spiritual and moral core of their civilization and of every ethnicity, every nationality. Interaction should be the foundation for a contemporary society with multiple centers of balanced power, including interaction between socioeconomic entities, government agencies and NGOs, political and religious associations, parties and movements, regional intersectoral markets (i.e. those spanning multiple industries), scientific and cultural organizations.

The ongoing economic crisis demonstrates what can happen when all efforts in a society are focused only on economic development and are not tempered by spiritual and moral principles.

This would force us to revise the existing methodology of

evaluating ethical and cultural fundamentals of government administration and the practice, principles and methods of constructing economic policy, their effect on the development of society and on interactions between organizations and other entities. Because organizations are the key enablers and drivers of development of the social environment, we propose to explore issues of harmonious regional development based on exploring and expanding the compatibility of organizations, interactions between organizations of different types and purposes based on shared or similar values and differences of socioeconomic nature.

The purpose of this book is to develop the methodological groundwork for the economics of interaction among the fundamental elements and structures of society based on the shared common cultural values that inspire and energize its life and activity. We pursue this purpose by considering and attempting to resolve the following issues: 1) Development of theoretical understanding and key conceptual approaches to defining the economics of interaction and its role in the life of society; 2) Development of a multi-level compatible structural model of the cyclical development of society; 3) Identifying a foundation for interactions between controlling elements and elements under their control within society using the operations and management of national government agencies, regional offices and companies as possible examples by way of illustration; 4) Laying the groundwork for financial, economic, organizational and technological mechanisms of interaction between organizations based on their common shared cultural values; 5) Development of a set of conditions for, and compatible definitive features of, effective interaction between organizations.

In this book, we present a structural model of societal progress and development and build a multi-level system of interactions among sectors of the economy by using a complex methodology of social and economic sciences that includes dialectic and historical comparative methods, relies on structural, functional and adaptive approaches, as well as principles of multidisciplinary approach and systems compatibility. At the same time, we use situational, systematic, logical, statistical and comparative analysis methods, as well as synthetic, ranking, hypotheses testing and other methods.

In Russia, political and social actors and the powers that be are facing the urgent task of redeeming and rehabilitating a value-based discourse in its own right. Such rehabilitation will be possible when values are not only merely proclaimed, but also backed by relevant institutions, laws, and socioeconomic programs that help to implement these values. Values must be combined with a real economic policy and legislative process, which can be represented as an interaction economy based on both spiritual and consumer values, and on the compatibility of a solid standard of living for the people with the continued development of the state.

CHAPTER 1

THEORETICAL FOUNDATIONS OF INTERACTION

1.1. Interaction: Definition, Varieties and Properties

When we consider interaction as a philosophical category, the essential or inherently important factor is that this interaction reflects the process whereby objects (subjects) act upon each other, upon their mutual determination and the way one of them engenders or produces the other. The dictionary defines interaction as an objective and universal form of movement or development that defines the existence and structural organization of any material system. T.

Efremova in her New Dictionary of the Russian language defines interaction as either (1) the action of objects, or various phenomena in reality upon each other, that determines (brings about) changes therein, or (2) coordinated actions by military units (usually in different service branches) to fulfill a military (combat) objective. Ozhegov defines interaction in his Dictionary of Definitions of the Russian Language as mutual support. Interaction can be understood as a connection between phenomena. Ushakov's Dictionary of the Russian Language defines interaction as a mutual connection; mutual determination and interaction of social phenomena.

The Dictionary of Psychology[1] describes social interaction as a phenomenon in which the behavior of one individual becomes a stimulus for the behavior of another, and vice versa. In statistical interaction, the effects of two (or more) variables are interrelated; for example, the complexity of a task and the level of excitement frequently interact in such a way that an increase in excitement results in greater success in solving simple tasks but reduces the success rate of solving more difficult tasks. Interaction in psychology is the process of direct or indirect influence of objects (subjects) on each other, from which spring their reciprocal determination and a two-way connection between them. Interaction becomes an integrative factor, helping new structures (entities) to form. Studies have identified such varieties of interaction as fellowship, competition and conflict. One would do well to bear in mind that these varieties apply not only to interaction between two individuals; they can take place between parts of groups or between whole groups of people. For example, during interaction between members of a newly-established group, traits emerge that characterize the group as an interconnected stable entity of a certain level of complexity and development, as the material process entails the transfer of matter, impetus (movement) and information: interaction is relative, it takes place at a finite speed within a certain space-time continuum.

---

[1] Петровский А.В., Ярошевский М.Г. Психологический словарь. 2-издание – М.: Политиздат, 1990

However, these limits apply only to direct interaction; indirect interaction formats are limited by space and time to a much lesser degree, only a fraction of the extent of limitations that apply to direct interaction.

Interaction is the combined influence of two or more independent variables on dependent variables when the independent variables act in conjunction with one another. While studying the effects of variables in an experiment, the influence of each one of the variables cannot explain the overall change. Therefore, in situations of this kind, it would make sense to resort to statistical tests, such as dispersion analysis, designed to evaluate the effects of interaction between the variables, as well as the specific effect of each variable.

Interaction in Kant's philosophy is a relational category that is responsible for the unity of things and processes of the world of experience. Interaction is understood metaphysically in occasionalism, in Leibnitz and Lotze's philosophy. In psychology, interaction represents the mutual influence of soul (psyche) and body, the psychological and the physical. According to the "double cause – double effect" hypothesis (proposed by K. Stumf and E. Becher)[2], every physical, neurological process, just like any psychological process, has a dual cause (physical and psychological) and a dual physical and psychological effect. This hypothesis enjoys the benefits of the psychophysical parallelism theory without suffering from its theoretical problems. Proponents of this hypothesis include E. Hartman, W. James, Oswald Kuelpe, E. Becher and A. Wentzel. Interaction is the kind of action of things upon each other that enables them to demonstrate their "inherent" properties, the internal properties of a system. In this sense, Friedrich Engels defined interaction as the ultimate root cause of all existence, a cause beyond which there are no other more fundamental determining properties. In any complete system, interaction is associated with different components or bodies within the system, mutually

---

[2] Губский Е.Ф., Кораблева Г.В., Лутченко В.А. Краткая философская энциклопедия, М., 1994

reflecting each other's properties, a phenomenon that can produce change in these bodies.

Interaction from the system's perspective is a system of mutually determined individual actions connected by a cyclical cause-and-effect relationship, in which the behavior of each participant is both a stimulus and a reaction to the behavior of others at the same time.

In the context of the Dictionary of Economics,[3] interaction is a concept that denotes the action of things upon one another, a concept that is used to reflect the connection between different objects, to describe the forms and formats of a human event, human activity and cognition. The concept of interaction incorporates direct and "reciprocal," or "reversed," influence of things upon one another, exchange of matter, energy and information between different objects, between living organisms and their environment, as well as formats of human cooperation in different cooperative scenarios and situations. Interaction spans direct and indirect relations between or among objects and systems. The classical mechanics deals with examples of direct interactions: this branch of physics considers mutual collisions and the rebounds and bounces that transmit the impetus and motion from one object to another. A possible example from the social realm would be direct communication between human individuals. Interaction is often taken to mean direct, immediate interaction alone: the two are often equated. Using the equation sign here carries the risk of transferring mechanical motion patterns to description of different areas and realms of reality (organic or social), which do not lend themselves to this kind of a schematic approach. Similar simplifications can also arise in social analysis when attempts are made to explain social processes using patterns of direct interaction between people. Using the mechanical approach to explaining nature and the psychological approach to

---

[3] Гацалов М.М. Современный экономический словарь – справочник. Ухта: УГТУ, 2002

describing social evolution is largely the result of erroneously substituting overly simplified concepts of direct and immediate interactions for a detailed description of specific interaction systems. The concept of interaction is, for cognitive purposes, the starting point for defining the notions of movement, change, maturation, development and process. However, the concept of interaction is made specific and tangible through these notions. Interaction becomes specific and concrete as a way to impart or transfer impetus and movement from some objects to others, as a change in properties of chemicals undergoing a chemical reaction, as transmission of messages in human contacts or as a synthesis of different human powers that generates new knowledge, new things or new ways to organize things. Interaction in social processes becomes the points of connection and disconnection of social links. In other words, interaction therefore becomes not the starting point, but rather a recurring moment that supports and ensures the stability of enduring social customs. If we consider precisely this aspect of interaction, we can deal with more than just an individual stand-alone instance of interaction, but rather with series and sequences of interactions, with systems that ensure uninterrupted progress of complex process across not only space, but also time. A single instance of interaction then is only one record of multi-dimensional interconnections between objects or human activities, a still image captured from a motion picture: a still image that represents the interconnection of things or human actions for the benefit of our observation. The simplest analysis of interaction presumes a mutual connection between two objects or two individuals, two persons. For example, many social science textbooks begin the discussion of social interactions by looking at interactions of two or more individuals; the implication here is that even when more than two individuals interact, their interaction is still based on a simple pattern of mutual interaction between two subjects. However, a more careful analysis reveals that "pure" interaction of two subject is an idealized simplification leaving outside the frame the "hidden" intermediaries: the standards, stereotypes, orientations and biases falling outside the scope of direct contact. To describe interactions when analyzing natural objects and systems, one also has to take into account various temporal, group, population relations and cause-and-effect connections that do not get registered within the scope of direct interactions. A person thus becomes involved in chains and series of interactions. It is contact with interacting systems, rather than registering isolated instances of interaction that becomes the focus of his experience (according to V.E. Kemerov in his Introduction to Social Philosophy[4]). In fact, this is the key difference between the contemporary "non-classical" cognitive/learning situation and its classical counterpart that was constructed around separate instances of interaction between things and that presumed a single individual subject dealing with a separate act of registering an instance of interaction. However, the more prominent this distinction becomes, the clearer it gets that describing a cognitive/learning situation as a stand-alone instance of interaction was an idealized approximation that focused on customary and enduring patterns of human experience. The simple experience of human interactions is predetermined, preset and requires explanations that would augment common experience. Direct interactions reveal individual properties of objects but rarely can describe the objects' distinguishing features and characteristics or specific types of movement typical for these objects. An individual can gain a more specific, tangible idea of movement types, of special combinations of interconnected objects and of their qualities by creating measurement tools, the concepts of measures, and obtaining knowledge of event categories and ways to juxtapose and compare them. This experience is registered in cognition, which is commonly described as scientific cognition (learning). However, the latter also helps to establish that even a person's everyday experience is full of patterns that enable him to incorporate generalizing and guiding forms in his perception and understanding of direct interactions.

---

[4] Кемеров В.Е. Введение в социальную философию: учебник для вузов. Аспект Пресс, 1996

From a narrowly philosophical perspective[5], the concept of interaction is one of the most important for identifying the relation between phenomenology and metaphysics. The key question deals with the relation between the situation of one's existence that an individual has to face and the need for the person to step beyond the boundaries of this situation, and consider this need when defining his existence. Interactions are a starting point for different types of cognitive situations, because they help to identify shifts and changes in the states and movements of objects, in positions, actions, and perceptions of the individual. By "revealing" the properties of objects involved in interaction, interaction also indirectly defines the cognitive situation, identifies cognitive capabilities of an individual, his "engagement" in a situation, how involved he is in interaction, thus also defining his inherent properties. Interaction contains a cognitive paradox. On the one hand, it manifests itself because the person who is engaged in the cognition and understanding is "inscribed"[6] into the situation at hand, on the other hand, it points towards factors, forces and reasons beyond the scope of the cognitive situation that are beyond the individual's control and that can become the main reason for mismatched interaction and its detection by the individual. The patent and objective fact (the "givenness") of interaction requires that the individual should make adjustments for its objective properties that are independent of his cognitive mode, his mindset or his influence on the logic of things. This paradox of interaction has to do with the fact that a person exists not in isolated acts of being together with other people and things, but rather in sequences, series, intertwined and dovetailing network of such acts. He constantly has to transition from individual, separate interactions to connected series and chains of interactions, and, as a consequence, he has to modify his cognitive position (the position from which he engages in cognition), his cognitive means and tools. In fact, he has to do this to see indirect interactions beyond the direct ones, to

---

[5] Философский словарь.enc – dic.com>vzaimode jstvie - 359
[6] Современный философский словарь. – М.: Панпринт. Кемеров В.Е.1998

master or create the means that include him in broader systems of interactions than those systems that are immediately available to him. Interaction can mean participation in common work or another activity, cooperation, joint performance of certain operations or (financial or business) transactions.

Let us consider briefly the physical understanding of the structure of the world with four types of interactions. From the perspective of structures found in the world, the world's objects are combined into systems as a result of interacting with one another. Interaction in the narrow sense of the word is understood as processes in the course of which the interacting structures and systems exchange quanta of specific fields, energies and sometimes data as well. Qualitatively different systems of linked objects exist in nature. Atomic nuclei are connected systems of protons and neutrons; atoms are nuclei connected with electrons; macro bodies are an agglomeration of atoms and molecules; the Solar System is a "brace" of planets and a massive star; the Galaxy is a grouping of stars. The existence of connected systems of objects signifies that there must exist something that connects parts of a system into an entity. In order to "destroy" a system completely or partially, one needs to expend energy. "Mutual influence of parts of a system or its structural units is achieved through fields (gravity, electrical, magnetic and others) and can be described by the energy of interaction. It is a commonly accepted belief today that all types of interaction between any objects whatsoever can be reduced to a small class of four fundamental interactions: strong (nuclear), electromagnetic (different source frequencies and corresponding vibrations), weak and gravitational (or universal). It is common to describe the intensity of interaction using the so-called interaction constant, a coefficient, a dimensionless, purely numerical parameter that defines the probability of processes determined by this type of interaction. Strong and weak interactions are characterized by their short duration. Interactions between structures are transmitted through the appropriate field at a finite speed that equals the speed of light in the vacuum. The categories of movement and interaction are similar in their content."[7]

Attaining the level of absolute compatibility indicates that the world has multiple levels. Linearity shows us the visible world, while the multiple levels represent the actual world. Visible does not necessarily mean actual! We must learn to understand that any cognition and exploration process presumes a gradual, stage-by-stage movement from the external to the internal, i.e. from 0 to 1. As the quality level rises, the number of components increases, too. This should not be perceived as a violation of the law of transformation of quantity into quality. Quite the opposite: this confirms the validity of this law. A complete equation of this process looks as follows:

quantity → quality → quantity'
(or, to express the same idea in different terms: external → internal → external')*

This formula applies to a multilevel, non-linear world. As we consider this using a human individual as an example, the meaning of the internal is this: at first, the human being becomes infatuated with the external, consciously reducing the potentially available areas of the internal, substituting the external for the internal, and then, when he reaches the 0.5 level, when the crisis of the external reaches its height, he suddenly opens his eyes to his own infatuation, stops the narrowing process, and then tries hard to recover the lost ground.

The history of interaction of the external and the internal can be presented as an addition of the material lower cone and the non-material upper cone with full (a) and partial (b) interaction of material and spiritual components in the life of society (see Fig. 1):

---

[7] Гусейханов М.К., Раджабов О.Р. Клнцепция современного естествознания: Учебник – 6-е изд., -М.; Дашков и К, 2007

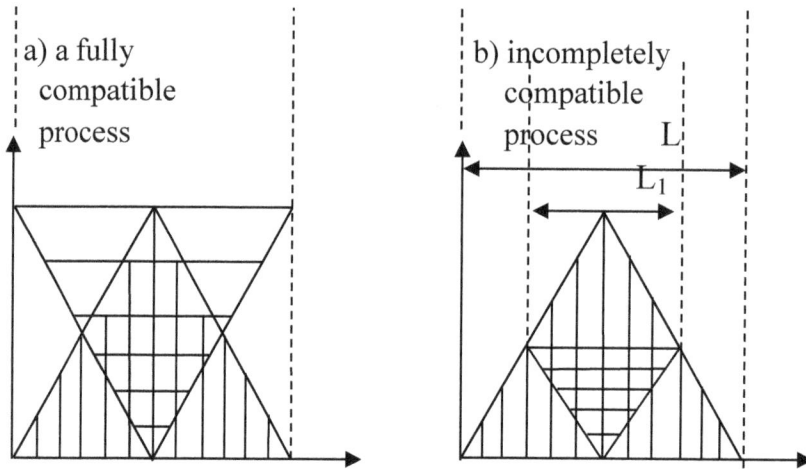

Fig. 1. Explanation for the diamond shape: please note (as regarding an individual) that a person becomes familiar with the external first, and only then does he move away and beyond the exterior shape.

We are looking at what we have within the context of only one cycle of multi-level interaction. Considering that there are multiple internal and external levels, we can reach the conclusion that the form (the external) is vanishingly small, while the content (the internal) approaches infinity.

We will illustrate this discussion below with specific examples of human / social needs and values, as well as examples of interaction between institutional subsystems in an environment and its constituent members (companies and organizations), including the human being.

1.2. Compatibility Theory and the Model of Social Development[8]

The interaction between abilities and needs is associated with one of the deepest contradictions in the human personality which has become more acute in the era of mass manufacturing when the producer is interested primarily in maximizing profit, when life according to possession or the existential principle creates in people different need systems, driving them toward different consumption models. A system of contradictions of the modern personality emerges. [9] Production of life amenities, which allows the human ability to shine, is viewed as something secondary and is taken for granted. This orientation impoverishes the personality and weakens the whole social system.

Ways to oppose this one-sidedness (make it incompatible) are designed through government regulation and legal restrictions on excessively destructive types of activity (enriching oneself by illegally seizing property, drug trafficking, depredation of the environment, etc.), through morality and tradition, family moral education and upbringing, through activity of public association and movements. The ideas of values have a powerful impact on the world of needs.

Society is a combination of people united within it, original and cultural collective groups, interacting and exchanging services with one another. All these collective groups form society on the strength of their existence under a common authority that enforces its control over a territory delineated by borders, supporting and imposing a more-or-less common culture. These factors convert a combination

---

[8] Morozov V. Exploring Compatibility; Foundations of a Theory (Quickstone Publishing UK, England) - 2014.
[9] Фромм Э. Психоанализ и религия. Искусство любить. Иметь или быть? - Киев: Ника-Центр, 1998.

of relatively specialized original corporate and cultural collective teams into a society.[10]

It is culture (values) that is responsible for introducing structure into role interactions, integrating the various roles into a single system, and thereby solving the problem of order, including in other territories of power.

Institutional compatibility of standards and rules is an equilibrium – a state in which, at a given combination of players' strengths and a "given set of contractual relationships … none of the players believes he can benefit from expending resources to restructure the agreements already in place."[11]

Institutions are closely connected and interrelated, and often a change in one institution requires changes in others, too (in the so-called "adhesive effect"). All of this significantly increases the quality of the established institutional order, reflected in the famous path dependency concept.[12]

Social interactions constantly result in social construction of new rules. Interactions in "new situations" do not take place on a completely "clean slate." On the contrary, the actors tend to interpret "new interactions" based on their ideas that became formed on the basis of their previous experience, although these pre-existing concepts change under the influence of "new situations."[13]

An organization's external environment can be described as a combination of factors affecting its operations, including consumers, the competition, government/state agencies, suppliers, financial institutions, sources of labor, as well as technological and scientific

---

[10] Шилз Э. Общество и общества: макросоциологический подход //Американская социология: Перспективы, проблемы, методы. М.: Прогресс. 1972. С. 341, 345.

[11] Норт Д. Институты, институциональные изменения и функционирование экономики. С. 111-112.

[12] Подробнее о концепции «тропы зависимости» в политических исследованиях см.: Pierson P. Increasing Returns, Path Dependency, and the Study of Politics// American Political Science Review. 2000.Vol. 94. № 2.

[13] Морозов В.А. Развитие общественных институтов // Маркетинг, № 2.2012 с.320.

progress (a scientific and intellectual sphere of the environment and some individuals), culture (including global processes, theological and national developments), the state of the broader society (including political and social events and developments) and natural phenomena.

If a company's products are selling, its potential increases (in terms of applicable factors) — including economic, social, sociopolitical (of the territory where the business organization is based), ethnic/national (what ethnic/national group or religious denomination the organization most identifies with), cultural and world-view (because every member of the team, as with the organization as a whole, is striving to achieve the best results required in the relevant areas of operation) and scientific (intellectual) and spiritual (defining creation of new products making the life of society better).

So why are these factors arranged in this particular order? As we look at human needs, we go back to the famous Maslow hierarchy of needs, which puts physiological (lowest) needs at the foundation, and the need for self-actualization at the top.

Speaking of key types of socioeconomic systems, we consider the issues of compatibility and compatible influence taking into consideration system type (1) the external environment (institutions) and system type (2) the object of our inquiry (the organization). We provide a way to visualize the relative positions of organization groups - uniform directions included in the external environment's compatibility levels described above (see Table 1)[14].

---

[14] Морозов В.А. Предприятие и внешняя среда: уровни взаимодействия // Российское предпринимательство, № 8 (206)/4.2012.

	Levels of external environment	Composition of basic functional organizations
1	Product and material	Join-stock companies (with liability of different types) in manufacturing, trade and service industry. Start-ups focused on implementation of R&D. Individual private enterprise. WTO. Associations to manage environmental projects spanning several sectors. Business incubators, R&D-internsive multinationals, corporate universities
2	Financial, economic	Banks, exchanges, investment organizations, IMF, economic and financial organizations (ministries/offices) and the like
3	Social	Social groups (voluntary, national, territorial, special-purpose, professional, youth, women's and men's organizations), social strata (classes, castes) and similar
4	Political	Political organizations, parties. Government organizations (regional, municipal). Inter-governmental military and law enforcement organizations
5	Religious and theologikal	Institutions of major religions, including sects, separate friaries, orders, worship organizations of peoples and ethnic groups. Atheist organizations. Inter-denominational organizatins and similar
6	Cultural, relating to world view	Organizations: cultural and historical; arts. Organizations that educate and look after health (health care). Voluntary associations and societies aiming to integrate different cultures
7	Scientific (cognizant)-spiritual	Global and national (government-run) research institutions and labs, research universities and centers, colleges, private personal research

Table 1. Multilevel external environment and objects through which it operates

Society is presented as a unity of people joined together in a variety of social formats: business organizations, institutions, foundations and foundation-type organizations, associations, which are ranked by their purpose and divided into groups according to levels of their needs. These levels were described in a hierarchical order in the previous sections (see Table 1).

Society is a macrosystem. "Like breeds like." In the context of compatibility, this means that everything that comprises society – all the modifications – essentially, its incarnations, are defined through their compatibility. However, the Universe has a large number of varieties of homo sapiens, which explains the existence of different civilizations, which develop consistently and in coordination according to the laws of the universe. We consider society as a multi-level spatial system, [15] an environment (1) that includes numerous objects with a broad range of different functions (2) with processes (3) going on within and among them. These processes are meaningful because they take place on the basis of targeted projects created (4) by objects – projects of different size and timeframe. The four types of system listed above can be described in terms of the four key processes reflecting operation of a system (including subsystems and their components) in a certain environment.

The internal unity of a system (a society) is ensured by harmonization (1), which defines the coordination of subsystems' operation (compatibility levels)[16] and their development. The second process type is evolution (2), which defines changes in macro environmental properties[17] based on the mechanism of self-organization of objects comprising the macro environment. The third process — reproduction (3) is oriented towards replacement of key resources and preserving a system's properties while protecting

---

[15] Морозов В.А. Экоуправление развития (территории, сектора экономики, человек). – М.: Креативная экономика, 2008.

[16] Level (meso-system) One is the level of products and assets, followed by: financial and economic (2), social (3), political (4), theological (5), cultural and world view (6), and spiritual and learning (scientific) (7) levels.

[17] Macro environment is understood to mean the whole society, while microenvironment is meant to represent individuals objects (organizations).

reproduction (replacement) at lower levels of compatibility. The fourth process reflecting operation within an environment is metabolism (4).

The first compatibility level comprises objects that create products essential for keeping a man alive and operating (food, clothing, technology and tools, living quarters, etc.). **The second meso-system** is the financial and economic level, that is responsible for supporting life and basic operating needs (the inter-relations and interactions on the lower level) and defines the variety of human interactions (both those of independent individuals and members of various organizations) by creating different kinds of securities (with a system for buying and using those securities) which are equivalents of underlying natural products or assets of the first (lowest) level. **The third level** (the third meso-system) of compatibility is the social level, which shapes the product of relationships of a human being and social groups around him, because this is the product of type determination of the human being's engagement with these groups (according to the format of his membership in them). Why do social groups provide context? Because every single human being belongs functionally and is attached to a certain job, a residence, to recreation, participation in indulging in his hobby, as well as other social inclinations and desires. This level, just like others, comprises a variety of objects with their different properties and special features, expressing the unique nature of connections and interrelations. While human society is part of nature, it has a more complex system and organization than natural systems.

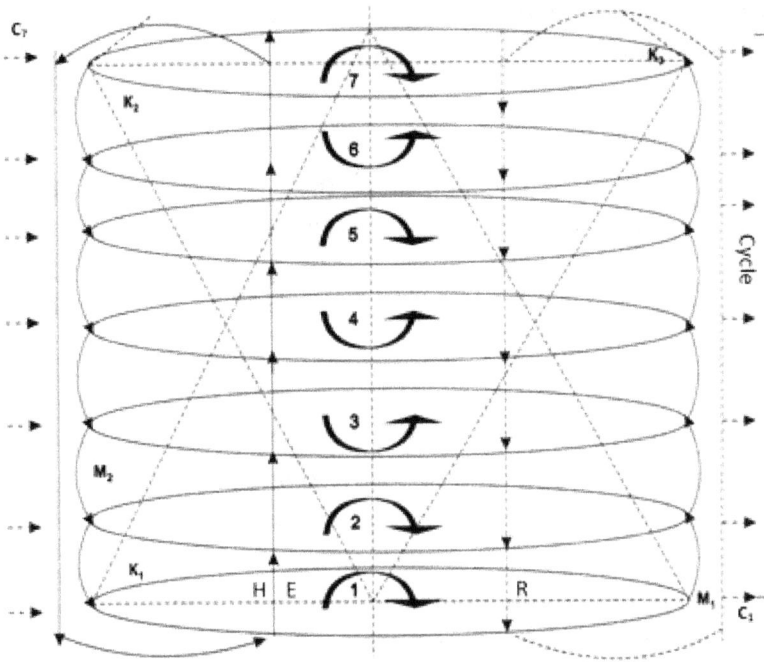

Fig. 2. Life of society – Compatible multi-level and multi-functional macro system

K_1 is a material cone (within Cycle 1); K_2 is the non-material (cognitive-spiritual) cone of the cycle; K_3 is a material cone (of Cycle 2).

S_{1-7} are incoming/outgoing signals (processes) of the external environment.

H stands for harmonizing (including morphogenic) processes that create and reinforce a compatible environment.

E stands for evolutionary processes that ensure self-organization of the meso-system by level (clockwise), and involutionary processes (counterclockwise).

R stands for reproductive processes which provide temporary insurance (protection) for the lowest proximate levels.

M_2 signifies downward catabolic (metabolic) processes, which destroy integrative clusters within cycle development (counterclockwise across levels, just like involutionary processes).

M_1 stands for upward anabolic (metabolic) processes, which shape products of each level.

The main purpose of levels within the structure:
7 — accumulation of integrative knowledge;
6 — globalization (and analysis) of values common to all humanity;
5 — grouping of religious values;
4 — combining ideological behavioral formats;
3 — development of social institutions;
2 — development of financial and economic institutions;
1 — use of material manufacturing facilities.

The fourth level (the fourth meso-system) is that of politics (the political level). It produces a synthetic product – a national common good, generates a nationwide ideology that ensures reproduction of common behavioral patterns and a relatively complete perception of social reality based on common cultural meanings and a system of cultural definitions. **The fifth level** of compatibility is the theological level, which preserves and refreshes value systems and features of these value systems (every system is closely associated with a specific religion) that help a human being find his place in the world by combining his personal interests with those of society. The systems of norms, culture codes, cultural meanings and prescriptions are designed to promote the interests of society where "people need to take care of their soul, their spirit more than their bodies."[18] Only the Renaissance humanistic ideology and scientific worldview of the 16th and 17th centuries was able to take its explanation of human nature (and the origins of human compatibility) further. **The sixth level** of compatibility as a meso-system is the cultural and worldview level, which generates holistic, uniting human values, taking into consideration the nationality, ethnicity and religious affiliation of a human being viewed as a well-rounded individual. The product of this level is spiritual globalization, integration of all five lower layers – compatibility levels, unified within each level, which only stands on the threshold of active integrative events (objects that serve as the content of each level have been discussed above). The next and final (**seventh**) level is focused on comprehensive scientific cognition to understand the universe and society, to develop man's ability to think. (The global spirit "which is more than just a Hegelian concept" has an ineradicable drive for gaining knowledge of, and achieving harmony with, oneself.) The product of Level Seven is the understanding and forecasting of the future path of society's development while reducing conflict and contradictions within itself (starting from lower levels) through universal harmonious development.

Each of the levels (meso-systems) listed above participates, by producing its own product, in adjacent production processes which, for the most part, belong at higher and lower levels. Using more biochemical terms, anabolism (see Figure 2, M1, which is an upward-directed variety of metabolism, trending to making things more advanced and more complex) serves, in the context of the first level – the level of products and proprietary things – as an indicator of financial and economic state (stabilization, growth, weakening) of the next higher level. The state of levels one and two is the necessary condition for implementation of social mechanisms of providing for citizens who belong to various social strata, groups and organizations. This is essentially the necessary condition of the

---

[18] Демокрит. Материалисты Древней Греции. Под редакцией М.А.Дынника. М.,: Изд. Политической литературы.1955 с.160.

prosperity of citizens that gives a human being an opportunity to realize his potential at higher consumer categories (levels). The third meso-system looks at the state of consolidation and dominance of social groups and territories to determine the political platform for their centralization and regulation. The results of state ideology and material benefits adjust the operational vector of Level Five, the theological level. The culture code, shared historic values that define the variety and unity of people also determine (format) the degree of unity in a society (6). The state of globalization, integration and unity of society focuses and concentrates its abilities for speeding up cognition and using the environment in a humanistic and intellectual manner to promote its own unified development. The results of cognition, fundamental discoveries and corroboration of truths that define the development of new multifunctional processes take shape as renewed, nano-modern or more functional intellectual products, applied discoveries in different fields of scientific and humanistic progress, generation of personal, material and intellectual benefits for each human being and for society as a whole.

The second process we look at is evolutionary. When describing a given macro system from the perspective of evolutionary processes, we have to say that changes in the parameters of meso-systems are based on their self-organization mechanism. A volatile external environment makes performing the basic functions at different levels more difficult. This requires adaptation of structural components of meso-systems, i.e. restoration (refurbishment) of the required values of these functions. We introduced two superimposed cones in Section 1.2 (with the lower one representing material systems and the upper one non-material ones), created by the action of centripetal forces. The composition of key organizations described in the previous section for each level creates their own combined product. The product may be regarded as high-quality and complete if all participants in the processes at every level are working together, in a well-coordinated manner. Absence of contradiction and non-constructive conflicts and lack of stagnation make it possible to create a product for each level, defining the operation of self-organization mechanisms. This identifies these processes as most effective (characterized by activity and drive for adaptation), and interaction between organizations at each level in this case makes it possible to identify a common direction vector of movement. Figure 2 shows this vector as arbitrary on the vertical axis: the dextrorotation (clockwise) is shown with arrows E1, E2, E5, E7; while the levorotation (involutionary counter-clockwise rotation) is shown with arrows I3, I4, I6. Dextrorotation of levels is reminiscent of a rising helix, with cycles of forming paired cones. It is necessary to note that as physical conditions (the lower levels) become right, there is an increased probability of active mental progress (beneficial condition of the mind at subsequent, higher levels) for proper cognition of spiritual values.

The reproduction processes in Figure 2 are shown with arrows R1–R7. As we look at these processes through which upper levels affect the lower ones, we discover that the first and second levels are characterized by support from above of the production activities and cooperation of all formats of the product and property level. In turn, at the third and second levels, social institutions benefit from achieving stability and solid productive operation of the financial and economic sector in the course of its development. Government authority, represented primarily by political institutions (4–3), strives, through the mechanisms of pressure and indirect trust, to maintain mutual respect and coordination between social groups and organizations. The theological and religious meso-system (5–4) based on history and culture, moral standards and traditions of spiritual behavior, claims its foundations in the international territories of nations and ethnicities that created this religious denomination, uniting these political forces into a community. Globalization of human values in the modern world (6–5), which is only starting to manifest itself, is oriented towards the preservation and evolution of cultural diversity, the experience of which it can use to build the concept of unified humanistic development of society.

Arrows H1-H7 in Figure 2 denote the harmonization processes which make it possible to achieve solidarity, an orderly, neat proportion and agreement in actions at all levels (meso-systems) of the environment (the macrosystem) in the proper order, i.e. moving from lower to higher levels. Speaking of social processes, we have morphogenic (creative, shaping) processes here that define the fundamental innovations and the state of society, and the higher up the compatibility levels we get, the more deterministic their role becomes. In this case, the product/proprietary meso-system (1) provides a varied multifunctional "nutritional medium" – an environment for its assessment by society and individuals and for all manner of cooperation at the first level through harmonization of financial and economic mechanisms of processing this "environment." The economic meso-system (2) through its general coverage of organizations and individuals and systems of evaluation of the social sphere, ensures the safety of its operation, interaction and contradiction-free development. The social (3) institutional megasystem strives to humanize the fruit of operation of the government and political meso-system (including laws and normative legal acts, moral and behavioral social standards, administrative and monetary solutions and requirements), making every citizen of the country aware of them. Mostly political (4) – for now – state ideologies, regardless of the interests of each individual state (for example, the Russian Orthodox Church and the Roman Catholic Church), implement their solutions to unite groups of states into various communities united by identical or similar religious beliefs (cultural traditions, national/ethnic moral standards, historical values, etc.). The meso-systems of religious culture (5) thanks to accumulated value systems and their evaluations, are based, each in its own way, on truths shaping a uniform understanding of the world and unity (love and respect) of human relationships. The institutional meso-system of general human values (6) harmoniously defines the direction of progress and the place of the "field of knowledge," allowing the human being, based on his elevated spiritual state, to create the thought forms of the next order of knowledge, harmonizing (matching) them within new material knowledge (7) for the benefit of society. Practical understanding of new knowledge, tests and experiments with new products at the very least serve to improve significantly the quality (functionality, reliability, affordability, aesthetic appeal, etc.) of the product(s) itself (themselves), and most importantly create absolutely new intellectual products, which open up new spectra of opportunities (compatibility) and new need levels. In this manner, the cycle repeats itself harmoniously.

In order to understand the ongoing processes holistically, let us consider the systematic analysis of processes at a (business) organization, which helps to shape and fill with meaning all levels (meso-systems) within the environment (the macro system). G.B. Kleiner's Enterprise Strategy discusses the structure of key subsystems of a business organization in detail (Fig. 2.4, p. 178), as well as the business organization's external environment, which is structured in a similar manner (Fig. 2.5, p. 185). As G.B. Kleiner points out, this arrangement of subsystems corresponds to a "certain order of stages in the innovation internalization process" and corresponds to the Nonaka-Takeuchi theory of "organizational knowledge creation." (Makarov, Kleiner, 2007).

We can superimpose the structure of key subsystems within a company, a business organization over a structure compatible with human needs to see that every subsystem of a business organization finds a peer, every layer of one structure corresponds to a level (meso-system) of macro compatibility (compatibility in the context of society).

Table 2. A version of functional correspondence:

SUB-SYSTEMS IN A MACRO-ENVIRONMENT (SOCIETY)	SUB-SYSTEMS IN A MICRO-ENVIRONMENT (BUSINESS ORGANIZATION)
Cognitive (scientific) spiritual level	Cognitive sub-system
Cultural and worldview level	Mental sub-system

Religious and theological level	Cultural sub-system
Political level	Historical sub-system
Social level	Institutional sub-system
Financial and economic level	Imitation sub-system
Level of products and assets1	Organizational, technological, proprietary sub-system

1.3. The Interaction of Economics and Other Disciplines

The contemporary situation with the environment and the direction this situation has been taking pose a great number of new, pressing and complex problems for humanity. Can we honestly say that the full scope of environmental issues is covered exclusively by natural sciences alone, or by social science alone, or by technology alone? The clear answer to that is "no." To solve these problems – both at the level of formulating a unified theory of interaction between society and nature, or the compatibility theory briefly described in Section 1.2, and at a level that involves formulating more specific, more focused questions that we consider in this book – the "economics of interaction" would rely on direct and immediate involvement of scholars working in all of these groups of sciences.

It is absolutely clear that an adequate assessment and finding a working solution for environmental problems would be unthinkable without close interaction and cooperation of absolutely all the sciences and humanities currently in existence; first of all, social science, technical sciences and technology and natural science. Environmental issues – both positive (weather forecasting and weather management, saving resources etc.) and negative (weather, water, air and natural habitat cleanup and reclamation) – all of this requires the maximum possible, planet-wide aggregation of effort.

International cooperation, combining efforts in the different fields of humanities, science and technology is becoming a vital necessity. When an artificial divide is drawn between the various sciences and humanities, and the connection between them is severed, this results in a one-sided approach to an environmental problem, and all sorts of awkward issues emerge as a result.

A comprehensive approach to the study of natural science and social science enables us to see adequately, on the one hand, social formats of engaging and operating new natural processes in the orbit of practical activity, and, on the other hand, the natural-science and technology content of various formats of social interaction. In other words, this perspective enables us to see both a contemporary unity, a merger of nature and society into one entity, and equally the specifics of one and the other. Because this unity is anything but amorphous and indistinguishable. In reality, an increasing unity of nature and society is revealed every time the specifics of one and the other manifest themselves. This, in turn, presumes further delineation of sciences, a widening gap between them, that, in turn, would require them to come together again and form a synthetic unity after some time. It would be completely unacceptable to overemphasize any one of these processes as the key or main one and set it in opposition to the other. Many authors maintain and even demand a total ban on a search for ways to integrate the key concepts and laws of natural science, technology and social science. And yet, we can only develop any science, including social science, independently of others only as far as their relative independence of one another extends. And only to that extent! As soon as we find these boundaries objectively, this particular science can no longer answer the questions arising at or beyond these boundaries. It has to seek the assistance of other sciences. And so, an inevitable "tension of ideas" arises and stays in effect at the boundaries between all sciences and humanities. This tension of ideas is precisely what turns the entire multiplicity and variety of scientific knowledge into one unity, into one science. However, this is the result of more than just the synthetic nature of environmental research. A fact of greater relevance is that each of the group of sciences under consideration not only is a component of the unified system of all sciences, but also has its specific features. These specific features make social, natural and technology-related sciences mutually complementary.

And therefore, as we look at interactions between society and nature, social cognition poses and studies questions about the goals a human being pursues in this interaction, what values serve or should serve as the basis for his transformational activity, what the social consequences would be if the society were to choose a certain course of action in its interactions with the natural environment.

Natural science opens up completely new opportunities for interaction between the human being and nature, while also identifying the acceptable limits of human involvement in development of natural processes (the acceptability of these limits is measured with a range of different metrics). Technology-related sciences, in their turn, are concerned primarily with creating and refining the methods, means and tools for interaction between society and nature, mostly such tools as would be not only efficient economically, but also acceptable for social and environmental reasons.

Therefore, it is clear that to formulate a forward-looking unified (compatibility) theory of interaction between society and nature, to manage this interaction in a rational and sustainable manner, it would be essential for the research means and approaches of social, natural and technology-related sciences to be mutually complementary. It is equally important that this kind of mutual complementarity is necessary too for solving specific and pressing environmental problems – something green economics is beginning to deal with at present.

A similar situation is developing in such a recent and aggressively developing branch of scientific inquiry as ergonomics. Its objective is the holistic design and optimization of labor of the person operating contemporary technological machines and systems. Many scientific disciplines study various aspects of labor. They include the sociology of labor, engineering psychology, technological aesthetics, physiology, biomechanics and labor hygiene. Along with them, many natural and technology-related sciences research and develop tools and means of production such as advanced highly mechanized automatic technology systems. As for ergonomics, it relies on data from all sciences that explore some aspect of labor: social, natural and technology-related. However, it has a special subject for its study: the man-machine-environment system, which it considers in its entirety, observing the interaction of this system's components. This comprehensive approach is a necessary condition for creating new technology and new equipment, which, with its high performance, artificial intelligence, reliability and resource-saving aspects, can promote and ensure positive social outcomes: keeping people's health and promoting their personal development in the workplace, making human activity more meaningful, efficient and higher-quality both in the workplace and elsewhere where human beings have to come into contact with modern technology.

These problems can be integrated as components of such a global and far-reaching problem as managing the progress of scientific and technological revolution. This includes identification and examination of key trends and paths of scientific and technological development, analysis and evaluation of its multifaceted social consequences to be able to predict in advance and neutralize possible negative effects of scientific and technical progress.

More specifically, this is a problem of achieving a comprehensive, holistic, exhaustive, multi-aspect evaluation of technological processes and new types of equipment now being created and designed. This comprehensive assessment would be impossible without close interaction between the key groups of sciences. Social sciences play a central role here, as they help to evaluate technological and scientific progress both as a whole and as a series of specific innovations from the perspective of social and personal development. Development of ergonomics and environmentally friendly technologies are prime examples of how scientists address important social issues while they develop technologies and find solutions to scientific issues that benefit the macro economy. This is a key characteristic feature of present-day scientific inquiry.

Its comprehensive nature is the core characteristic of contemporary science, the sine qua non of an accurate and complete reflection of the object under research, covering all its aspects at the same time, in their interconnection and interrelation. The object of research in contemporary science is usually seen not as its separate, relatively isolated aspects, but rather as a whole. This requires a unifying combination of deconstructive analysis and synthesis. Therefore, all sciences without exception, while exploring different aspects of an object, should presume the object's unity, its holistic character at all times, taking into account the inalienability and cross influence of all its aspects and manifestations.

A study of natural objects through interaction of the various branches of science and humanities applies also to the study of social phenomena. For example, the study of juvenile delinquency as a phenomenon, and revealing the reasons for these acutely negative social phenomena would be impossible through only one branch of social science or through several individual social sciences. These phenomena could be understood, and their reasons could be identified, and ways to eradicate them could only be found through close interaction of all these branches of science. In this particular example, in addition to legal science, other sciences that should be brought to bear are:

- economic sciences to study the material living conditions of underage people;

- pedagogical sciences to explore matters of school education and personality building;

- social sciences to explore their family life and social milieu;

- ethical sciences to explore the moral aspects of the issue, address matters of responsibility for a common cause;

- philosophical sciences to explore the ideological aspect of the issue, study the role of social consciousness in the life of society;

- psychological sciences to study the psychology of adolescents, etc.

Consequently, what is needed here is organic interaction of all the humanities without exception, including social science and its branches, and possibly some branches of biology; for example, genetics. As we consider the connection between economics and other sciences, we must start from the fact that economic theory is the methodological foundation for a whole swathe of sciences: sector-specific (economics of trade, economics of industry, manufacturing, construction, etc.); functional (finance, credit and lending, marketing, management, economic forecasting, etc.); interdisciplinary (economic geography, economic demographics, economic statistics, etc.). Economic theory is one of social sciences, right alongside history, philosophy, law and others. Its purpose is to reveal one aspect of social phenomena in human life and activity, whereas the science of law deals with another aspect, the moral science – with yet another, and so on, and only a combination of theory, social sciences and history is capable of explaining the operation of social life.

Economic theory draws upon the knowledge accumulated and processed by specific economic sciences, as well as sociology, psychology, history and other areas of scientific endeavor, without consideration of which its conclusions could be erroneous.

Economic theory must lie at the foundation of economic policy, through which it would filter through to the field of economic practice and inform its operation. Action (practice) leads to knowledge, knowledge leads to foresight, foresight leads to appropriate action. Economic theory is not a set of rules on how to get rich. It does not offer ready answers to all questions. Theory is only a tool, a way to make sense of economic reality. Having solid command of this tool, knowledge of the basics of economic theory can help anyone make the right choice in many life situations.

Wesley C. Mitchell in his seminal Lecture Notes on Types of Economic Theory (originally published in 1935) insisted that economic problems were connected with non-economic issues, including problems of sociology, culture and other problems and issues that defined the psychology, behavior and motives driving people's activities in society.

Economic theory is closely associated with economic genetics, because economic development contains inherent genetic economic information. Economic genetics is defined today as a science that gives us in-depth understanding of the inner workings of dynamics, relations and interactions of inherited and variable features in the process of uneven cyclical development. Transmission of inherited economic ideas and frameworks is always processed by the human mind and implemented through human labor.

One must draw a distinction between economic theory and economic policy. Economic theory was developed as part of a search for solutions to real-world economic problems, though they are but a tool for understanding economic reality and forecasting its future development, its future dynamics.

Economic policy is a purpose-driven system of actions and measures the government can take in the realm of production, distribution, exchange and consumption of benefits. It is intended to reflect the interests of the whole society, with all of its social groups and serves primarily to strengthen a nation's economy. Economic policy undertakes to look for ways to solve economic problems and set in motion progress towards solving or eliminating such problems. Politicians, while taking advantage of economic theory, should also take into consideration cultural, social, legal and political aspects of the issues they address, if they want their policy to be successful. Achieving objectives of economic policy can result in a transformation of the economic system, its improvement or refinement, which is reflected in subsequent development of economic theory. A course in economic theory is guidance to understanding economic reality without claiming a monopoly on the truth, without claiming that the way it offers is the only possible one.

Every science is related to others in a certain way. There are so-called borderline areas where different sciences come into contact and overlap, where new areas of scientific research and inquiry and new sciences emerge; for example, biochemistry, geophysics, economic cybernetics, etc. As noted above, the economic science is closely connected with sciences that deal with society: sociology and social science, political science and legal studies. Economics is also connected with sciences concerning the human being and nature: geography, psychology and biology. Modern economic science also makes extensive use of mathematical methods. For example, geography is a science that deals with natural and territorial and industrial complexes; the distribution and structure of natural resources, their economic assessment and rational, sustainable use. Economic theory and geography share a common subject of inquiry – land, natural resources and human resources – although they focus on different aspects of this subject. Next we have psychology, a science that deals with the laws and patterns of how human beings reflect the reality around them in their life (using senses, memory, cognitive ability and so on). Just like psychology, the science of economics takes an interest in inner regulators of human activity such as human needs and motives. Biology is a science concerned with the structure and function of living beings, their origins, development and evolution, their connections and relations with one another and with so-called inanimate nature. The knowledge and expertise from specific fields within biology – such as genetics and selection – are used to look for ways to advance agrotechnology and biotechnology, which, from an economic perspective, are a reserve for raising the efficiency of agricultural production. Knowledge of human physiology helps to define the best ways for using its capabilities that people or managers need for rational and optimal organization of management of working teams. Knowledge of environmental studies and ecology, the science concerned with the way of life of human bodies, animals and plants depending on the condition of their environment, as noted above, is used in economics to define the boundaries of industrial expansion or use of certain technologies. Mathematical methods have a broad application in economics. To corroborate this, let us look at one fact. The first winners of the Nobel Memorial in Economics in 1969 – Jan Tinbergen and Ragnar Frisch – received the award for "having developed and applied dynamic models for the analysis of economic processes." We are not going to deal with complex mathematics in this textbook, but we will use some concepts you will remember from your math classes. These are sums, averages, modes and medians, percentages of specific values, growth and functions. If geographers draw maps or create scale relief models to illustrate certain patterns, if physicists and chemists build models reflecting the inner structure of atoms, molecules, etc., economists use plot lines and charts – in the same way that mathematicians do. The purpose of having charts and plots in an economics textbook is to help the reader understand the important links between economic phenomena.

The next sphere, political science (Level Four in Fig. 2) is a science concerned with the nature, functions and branches and agencies of the government through which it wields and uses power. The connection between political science and the science of economics arises from the fact that the government is an important and active player in the modern economy; is involved in economic processes; some of its functions of power are exercised to adjust the economy, among other things; and government revenue and spending (the government budget) and the government sector are the economic foundation of government (state) power. Sociology (Level Three in Fig. 2) is a science that deals with the division of society into different groups (along ethnic, property ownership, age and other lines), interaction and problems of the communal life of people as representatives of specific social groups. The connection between economic theory and sociology is quite obvious: economic relations are an important component of interaction and coexistence between various social groups. Law is the science concerned with the combination of standards established by the state (legal laws), compliance with which is enforced by methods of government influence. The connection between the economy and law is realized through giving legal form to economic relations. Any country has laws regulating property, establishment and operation of business organization, income taxation and many other matters. When creating laws, experts rely on actual economic processes, as if deriving them from economic life. At the same time, once bills are passed into laws, they cause changes in the economic situation. When the country's supreme legislative body passes a law, the question arises how enforcement of this law can change existing relations: distribution of resources and revenues, prosperity of certain strata of society, economic growth, and more. We propose looking at these social, legal and political issues in greater detail below.

Interaction of politics and economics plays a decisive role in the development of any society. As the economic sphere expands, and economic relations become both deeper and more complex, the impact of politics on the economic life of society also increases. The problem of interactions between politics and the economy becomes especially acute when relations within society, the whole social structure with its concepts, perspectives and shared values enters a period of upheaval and turmoil.

Politics is the operation of government agencies, political parties, social movements, non-governmental organizations and their leaders in the realm of relations between large social groups, nations and states and their governments aiming to mobilize their efforts with the purpose of bolstering political power or winning it by special methods.

The intent of politics and policies is not only to be a tool for realization of certain social and class interests, but also to perform the function of regulating and establishing order in social processes and relations, the conditions for material public production and collective labor.

The economy (Level Two in Fig. 2 above) is a historically defined combination of social and commercial and industrial relationships. The key defining element of the economy is the ownership of the means of production and the associated status and relationship of people in the production process, the ongoing exchange of activity and distribution of benefits and responsibilities. The economy is also understood as the combination of the various sectors of the nation's industry, agriculture, services and trade.

Therefore, the economy of a country is a combined economic (commercial) system that spans all components of [public] production, distribution and trade. In other words, the economy and economic activity is the realm of material sustenance of a human being's and society's life and existence by the human being and society themselves.

The economic development of a specific country is measured by such metrics as per-capita gross revenue and distribution of revenues among different population groups – the criteria of the society's political maturity.

People do not live in isolation; they live in a community where they depend on one another as they engage in economic activity. There are three main production factors: labor, capital and natural resources.

People's status in society and their mutual relations with one another are largely defined by their position vis-à-vis these various production factors. Those who own capital have a different social status than those who sell their labor. A majority of political and economic discussions and analyses at all times have focused precisely on this issue: how ownership and use of the means of production divides people into different social classes.

The relation between policy and politics on the one hand and the economy on the other is shaped and defined by class and broader social interests and people's relationships. Political problems arising from the influence of various social strata and groups, political and non-governmental organizations and popular movements, parties, or those arising from competition among these groups – all of these can be ultimately reduced to a relation of economic interests.

Understanding economic relations and economic connections gives us a way to change the conditions we live in, an opportunity to make our lives better. Whether we like it or not, our day-to-day life, our living conditions and status depend on our wages or other income and prices, the cost of accommodation and taxes, profits and investment, unemployment and inflation. These phenomena are the subject of macroeconomics. If we do nothing to influence these phenomena and do not understand them, relevant decisions, decisions that affect us all, will always be made by one or another of the small groups of so called economics "experts." These economists represent the interests of different groups, social strata and classes and are usually at odds with one another.

Macroeconomic processes and phenomena, as well as decisions and actions affecting them, have direct political consequences. Political figures and political movements have an interest in providing economic explanations for their policies, equipping them with "scientific" reasoning.

Taking the economic perspective on the nature of society by asking the question how material benefits are produced and distributed goes to the fundamental core of relations in the life of human beings and societies. And here different people, classes and social groups have different takes on questions and possible answers, because they affect the people's and social groups' vital interests. The intricate relation between policies and politics on the one hand and the economy on the other is most fully expressed in the concept of economic policy.

Economic policy is a system of economic measures taken by the government, by the state authority, a combination of goals, means, objectives and actions that exert directional influence on economic development. Economic policy is the decisive method to support the country's political course.

The government (the state) has always played an important role in the development of the market economy. Even free competition cannot do without the government, without the state, which takes responsibility for organizing money circulation and providing the legal foundation for the free market economy.

State involvement in the economy can be justified from an economic perspective by the inadequacy, failure and imperfection of the free market. Purely free market-based distribution does not guarantee a certain minimum standard of prosperity, without which a democratic society would be impossible. Besides, the market mechanism cannot ensure jobs for everyone able and willing to work. Strategic breakthroughs in science, technology, or structural change in the economy cannot be achieved without the government's involvement, just as regional problems cannot be resolved without the government. Negative consequences of the free market mechanism (monopolism, inflation and others) also require government involvement. Consequently, the market mechanism often needs adjustments that can only be made by the government.

The government becomes involved in the market economy to support economic stability, a macroeconomic equilibrium, to smooth out cyclical economic recessions and booms. But first of all, the government promotes efficient commercial operation of all business organizations and entrepreneurs. To achieve this, the government makes the [free] market mechanism more efficient.

The role of the government and the state in the economy has been growing steadily in the modern world. Signs of this process are increasing government spending and substantial expansion of direct regulation of the economy and economic activities. Total government expenditure today amounts to a significant portion of GDP. The key expenditure items are defense spending, spending on education and health care. In addition to its role in the distribution of the domestic product, the state also acts an independent economic agent, in the so-called government and government-controlled sector of the economy. A traditional understanding of the government sector for societies used to the frameworks typical of a planned economy is as a collection of government-controlled and government-owned companies making products used for collective public consumption, mostly consumption by other government companies and agencies or for government purposes. Government sector employees are currently a major part of the employed workforce. However, one would do well to remember that a swelling government sector carries the risk of replacing free market mechanisms with government administration, government regulation and an excessive expansion in the ranks of government officials – the bureaucrats. Sustained efficient operation of the government sector is also a big problem, as trends arise here towards lower efficiency, reduction in quality and other hazards. This is associated with weaker influence of market forces on government-owned and government-run companies on the one hand and with government support for such companies on the other.

As we come to a conclusion in our discussion of this topic, we need to say a few words about the ways different scientific disciplines interact. Two of these ways are "intertwining" and "centering." An analysis of interaction between sciences at the present time offers the following conclusion: the prevailing trend in the evolution of contemporary sciences since approximately the middle of the 20th century – as the science and technology revolution came into its own–was their movement towards "intertwining" and "centering."

"Intertwining" of sciences denotes a type of interaction between branches of science where several scientific disciplines come into a more or less prolonged contact to find a solution to a complex scientific problem or to develop some area of sciences that involves a multitude of different sides or aspects. These interdisciplinary problems are so complex and have so many aspects that they cannot be solved or explored independently by individual branches of science, and this objective can only be accomplished through interaction of all scientific disciplines relevant to the issue at hand[19].

---

[19] Взаимодействие наук как фактор их развития. Сборник научных трудов» - Новосибирск, «Наука», 1988г., Рузалин Г.И. «Концепция современного естествознания» М. 1997г.)

"Centering" of different sciences complements their "intertwining" and "intersects" it, creating as a result a complex system of different forms and ways in which processes of interaction between contemporary scientific disciplines emerge and develop. Fundamental, intermediate, applied science and technology science begin to "intertwine" with each other in different ways, crossing paths with "centered" sciences at the same time.

The highest form of interaction between sciences is their "formation through multiplicity." Not only sciences in adjacent or similar fields of inquiry interact, but also sciences all across the board. Molecular biology is a compound natural science of this kind. "Formation through multiplicity" as it relates to science is not simply adding together the methods of different scientific disciplines, not simply letting the creation and generation of new scientific constructs and ideas follow the analysis of collected evidence; it is in fact a merging together of sciences to explore and make sense of their shared subject of inquiry.

CHAPTER 2

VALUES-BASED STRUCTURAL MODELLING OF THE ECONOMY

2.1 The Vital-Mind Economy (an Economy of Harmony between Human Beings, Society and Nature)

Once, when I was discussing the hierarchy of different types of economics with the Dean of the Lomonosov Moscow State University Department of Economics, he asked me: "What kind of economics are you talking about when you consider the religious and theological level [of compatibility]?" I replied, "It is about traditional economics." As the question, so the answer. This Section deals with what is probably the core of development of a personality and society. Herein lies perception of the Astral Planes (Subtle Worlds) of deep realization of one's actions and of the material daily product of our activity, which sometimes forces us to sacrifice the essential, the most important, in a sequence of decisive actions of our short lifespan in the material world, actions uninspired by spiritual considerations.

From a philosophical perspective on economics and economics of interaction, we should be talking about the main approaches to classification of values, to formulating a system of values by identifying the practical implications and types of values. There are many value systems (classifications, paradigms) in which values are categorized based on chosen criteria. For example, Max Scheler's or Erich Fromm's; one can also find systematic value categorizations in the works of Vladimir S. Solovyov, Nikolai O. Lossky and Viktor Frankle. We believe that prominent Russian American sociologist Pitirim A. Sorokin offered a fairly comprehensive heuristic categorization of values that also lie at the basis of a classification of different cultural types. He famously identified sensual, ideational or idealistic values as dominant depending on whether sensual and bodily or spiritual values or some combination of the two were seen as dominant. As a general principle, a classification emphasizes specific parameters of the objects or phenomena under consideration largely by definition (of a classification). All classifications are to some extent subjective, utilitarian and accurate on their own terms. Among a handful of classifications that we adamantly do not accept would be one that attempts to divide values into "values of the mind" and "object, or objective values." This dichotomous division would be completely inappropriate and erroneous because of the factors discussed in greater detail above: notably because all the values of the mind are always rooted in the world of tangible things in their ideal content (except for some values associated with psychological emotional turmoil over values) and always tend towards their embodiment, their "incarnation" in the material world of things.

Material objective values are always created and identified by the operation of the mind. On the whole, let us remind readers that the ideal and multi-dimensional nature of existence of values precludes a purely mechanical reduction of these values either to psychological acts of the mind or exclusively to their material objective "incarnation" (to the things that represent the values). We tend to believe that a traditional classification of values drawing on basic human needs and dividing the whole hierarchical "realm of values" into material, social and spiritual ones is not only the simplest and most obvious approach in its rationale, but also a classification that retains its full heuristic potential.

After all, it is the ideal content of values that has priority in the human attitude towards existence – the content that helps these values to be identified first, and then to be embodied. We will also refrain from providing a full list of value categories (or value modalities), and will limit our analysis only to some of them and focus instead on the main formal and structural patterns typical of every level of values irrespective of the specific configuration and content that value modalities take on in the existence of specific individuals, social groups and cultures. The latter, naturally, also have a direct impact on the ordor amoris of their individual members.

At present, we realize that assigning value directly to material things that satisfy our bodily requirements, or implying a purely physical, biological nature (completely devoid of any ideal aspects) to our inner urges would be a serious fallacy. This approach leads to the somewhat typical case of making a fetish, an ultimate value out of objects that help us satisfy our vital bodily needs and our needs for emotional pleasures. This fetishization is the direct source of the ideology of hedonism and blatant consumerism focusing on material things to the exclusion of everything else. Plato was among the first to focus in his analysis on the relationship between bodily needs, which manifest themselves as a desire (a want) in the psychological and emotional perspective, and the object of this need. Plato makes an incisive observation here to the effect that vital bodily needs do not entail a requirement for specific properties in an object that can satisfy these needs; in other words, products and things do not have some intrinsic value in their own right, but they are seen as valuable only insofar as they are capable of satisfying our vital need. "If we have a large selection of beverages, our thirst takes on different flavors (as thirst for different kinds of drinks): we start craving for more and more; and if what we have is simply thirst, we crave for just a little. However, thirst itself will never be a craving for something other than a beverage – something that can slake that thirst, just as hunger itself will never be anything but a natural desire to consume food. A craving for a specific property is external and accidental. In other words, the natural feeling of hunger and the associated desire to eat do not contain a single hint at the objective value of a cake with a lot of cream or of succulent roast beef; an objective need for clothing by itself cannot be used to explain and justify the value of a gown of the finest cloth; while the natural desire to rest while reclining cannot by itself be used to derive the value of a waterbed. The main factor at play in each case is the external and accidental ("brought in from outside," to use Plato's term) ideal content of values – aesthetic, cultural and ritual and others; but much more often the cause of specific desires is simply a fundamental lack of discipline and irresponsible hedonism (which are typical vital anti-values), which combine to result in the trivial cult of consumption.

In the latter case, it is no longer a situation where things satisfy our rational and moderate essential vital needs, but one in which we become slaves to an excess of material things and irrational bodily whims and urges. Having one's mind focused on material things goes hand in hand with a cult of deriving an increasingly more acute/stronger and more sophisticated emotional pleasure, i.e. it is contaminated by a fetishization of the emotional experience associated with values, a fetishization that is never a goal in its own right, but merely a reinforcing consequence in normal situations. Plato may have been a little too categorical when he claimed that "there is thirst for a specific beverage, i.e., craving for that specific beverage, whereas thirst itself represents a yearning for neither copious nor light consumption of beverages, a craving for neither high-quality nor poor-quality beverages; in other words, it does not extend to any specific quality: thirst itself (i.e. thirst in a general sense) is naturally matched with drinking (consumption of liquid) as such." We believe that rational (moderate) vital bodily needs do point at some objective properties of material things, the objects of these needs, somewhat contradicting Plato's statement. These properties would include, among others: (a) the utilitarian usefulness of material things; (b) the need for unconditionally high quality of things and food that satisfy our essential vital needs; (c) the multifunctional nature of things, i.e. their ability to satisfy as many rational "material" needs as possible. Clearly, a fancy-shaped egg-frying skillet or a 300-kilogram Yamaha motorcycle, which are intended for satisfying irrational vital needs, are probably better categorized as the material representation of a content that is antithetical to values.

Let us now consider the nature of our vital desires and urges. At the outset, their nature is not entirely organic, physical or unconscious. They clearly have an ideal dimens.and food chosen by an aesthetically well-rounded person are radically different from the daily life of a person who does not have any spiritual needs or goals. Essentially, superior value-centric meanings (content) are capable of exerting a powerful organizing and structuring influence on meanings of a lower order, up to reducing them to a bare minimum, with the lives of saints and holy hermits offering some strong examples of this.

Furthermore, specific vital needs and urges are structured by binary value modalities from the world of ideas ("ideal value modalities"), most of which operate on a purely subconscious level and occupy the lower tiers in the value pyramid. In the bodily realm of vital properties this would be the universal dichotomous oppositions of useful/harmful, good quality/bad quality, tasty/unsavory, comfortable/uncomfortable, and other similar contrasting opposites. In the emotional realm, the oppositions would be: pleasure/dissatisfaction, entertaining/boring, soothing/irritating, relaxing/energizing, and so on. The stratification of positive modalities in the realm of vital properties is clearly and naturally random, and reversing "extreme points" of values is not necessarily something exclusively negative, while the variation in individual emotional preferences for vital properties is infinite.

If we were to attempt to formulate a universal criteria of positive vital values, we would describe as valuable everything that contributes to a healthy and harmonious reproduction of the person's bodily and emotional ego, as the main foundation for his social and moral ego, with the implication of a moderate and rational attitude to the needs of one's body (one's flesh) and the effort to avoid any destructive passions and emotional states. It is the latter that are primarily responsible for preventing an individual and his personality from moving up the ladder of personal development.

According to one view, personality is the highest level of organization of a human being. It is personality that enables a human being to exercise and preserve his unity, the integrity of his body, and the interaction and integration of two processes that are central to human existence: the mental (intellectual) and vital (life-supporting). It is his personality that enables a person to make contact and interact with his environment. In the process of life, a person constantly engages in exchanges with his environment, taking from it and giving to it. This metabolic process of exchange with the environment continues throughout the person's life. Two factors essential for the harmonious life of a person are connection (compatibility) and coordination, coherence (interaction) of processes ongoing within the person, within his space and those unfolding in the person's environment, physical or social. A human being cannot exist outside of the environment in any way. The environment is essentially changeable by its nature. Every living organism is forced to respond to changes in its environment constantly, recreating time and again the harmony lost after each change. This is what the process of life is essentially all about: the emergence of needs and requirements, which take the body out of its equilibrium, and recovery of the equilibrium lost by satisfying these needs and requirements. We people are creatures of needs, and this is why we are alive. As living creatures, we are subject to biological laws of nature, and life becomes misery without adequately replenishing our life-supporting resources. This is why it is so important to understand and comprehend the significance of a person's ability to support his existence by replenishing his spiritual and material resources.

What are the ways in which these resources are replenished? These ways are quite natural and involve establishing contact by the person with his needs by drawing on his life experience and relying on having an accepting, safe and nurturing environment. The environment can be hospitable or hostile. Specific parameters and properties of the environment can bring either positive or negative unconscious experiences of interacting with the environment. Any experience is a learning experience, but it teaches the people experiencing the environment in different ways. In the development stage when the person is still dependent on his environment, it is especially important to experience a beneficial, nurturing interaction with his environment. This experience enables the person to learn his needs and how to take care of satisfying these needs. This experience is committed to memory as positive. It is then remembered as a state of psychological and physiological conditions of life, to which the person will want to revert for the rest of his life. The skills and knowledge, the experience gained from this event becomes the experience of safely trusting the world and oneself. This is the experience (knowledge and skills) that helps one recognize the conditions that are hospitable and conducive to one's existence. Development under these conditions should eventually result in gaining an extra-intellectual, unconscious, i.e. a purely somatic ("vital") ability for self-regulation, as well as the ability to look for (and find) help when facing challenges of different kinds.

This suitable recognition of, and reaction to, one's needs is what gives a person the resource that enables him to support himself, addressing a variety of (sometimes) complicated and challenging life and existential issues. If the amount of essential resources is inadequate, the person depletes his body and psychology and either becomes ill or has to resort to various short-term "fixes" which may come with longer-term detrimental effects (like doping in sports). The integrative need for vital self-regulation lies at the core of the human being's dual nature as a social creature who needs others for personal development and growth, for development as a well-rounded individual. However, an individual can deal with daily challenges and tasks that are not new. Mechanisms of vital self-regulation and the need for this self-regulation may be conscious, but the processes of their development and operation are largely unconscious, taking place through gaining experience relevant "here and now" at each stage of an individual's personal development. A person cannot develop vital self-regulation without this kind of experience, just as he cannot develop the ability of speech without contact with the social environment.

Vital self-regulation of a human being goes through the initial stages of fusion (as a fetus in the mother's womb) and dependence (as a newborn and young child dependent on his caring parents) in his development, with the parents organizing the nurturing and providing the environment necessary for the young child. Without passing through these initial stages, the human being would not be able to enter the next stage of vital self regulation – the separation stage – in which he separates himself from those nurturing him and caring for him, from his parents and their family before proceeding with an autonomous, independent existence. This is the only natural, benign and desirable way to build the ability to take care of oneself and resort to the help of others when needed. The separation stage involves the actualization of the individual's ability to be his own "parent," without losing his "inner child." To achieve the separation stage, the person has to integrate within himself two opposites of the human condition: the ability to reach out for help (as a way of preserving his inner child, with lively and emotional reactions to the needs of the moment, while retaining the image of a caring parent in his perception), and the ability to form an autonomous, independent existence (by recognizing his own status as a "parent," i.e. someone taking care of himself; as a transition from "vital," i.e. physical and largely unconscious, self-regulation to the "mental" ability to understand and adapt creatively and dynamically to changes in his environment).

We should emphasize that this dual nature, metaphorically speaking, does not catch our fish for us, does not feed us all the time, but rather gives us a fishing rod and teaches us to use it. It may also occasionally provide us with additional sustenance as needed. The fishing rod is the (empirical) experience that cannot be obtained "academically," from the world of ideas (through reading books and listening to oral accounts and explanations – "ideal," rather than material, practical sources of information). Gaining this kind of empirical experience relies on contact, interaction and the example of another real, living, breathing human being in our daily life. The archetype of a caring parent is not so much the figure of a specific parent, but rather a collective image of all parent figures who have offered us their care in our lifetime; and every individual has certainly had such parent figures in his life. Memories of these people are especially significant if help, care and support from them came at the points in the individual's life when the state of his soul and body made vital needs dominant in his life.

One should also not deny oneself the pleasure of distancing oneself from those who have attempted to enslave you or attach you to themselves under the guise of helping you. You will do well to learn to tell the two apart: parental care is essentially selfless, altruistic; your parent is taking care of you, helping you simply because he wants to and can do so. He gives you care. So let his care not create an obligation for you, and let your gratitude not be mandatory. The person, your parent, did something he wanted to and could do – you can accept this gift and get on with your life. Learn to accept gifts and not feel indebted. Vital regulation operates through the person satisfying his vital needs. When several needs arise at the same time, a healthy human organism can differentiate between them (tell them apart, separate one from the others) and rank them in a hierarchy of needs (from more important to less important). Mental regulation operates on the basis of a hierarchy of values, which first satisfies the soul and then the spirit, the pinnacle of our self-awareness. This way, at any given point in time, the individual recognizes one dominant value-centric need that requires satisfaction most acutely, it becomes most salient, as the other values and needs recede into the background (creating the context).

We should also note that complete satisfaction of the more complex needs (including economic needs) is most often impossible or impractical, which is why a person gradually learns from experience to gauge to what extent a need can be satisfied, learns to differentiate between needs on this "metric," and also to defer gratification of some needs and bear with fortitude the delay or impossibility of satisfying a need at a certain point in time or in a certain environment. Harmony in human life is the subjective experience of happiness and well-being, and the ability and desire to restore this state of happiness and well-being if it is lost. Harmony is also the ability to operate independently for the purposes of vital self-regulation and the ability to search for an environment that can help one regain lost comforts or bring a new learning experience. For the purposes of this process, both its aspects – mental and vital – pull together, in concert, to implement the process of passive vital and active mental adaptation. When the individual lives in harmony, he adapts to the environment and exchanges benefits and feedback with it in an artistic, creative and dynamic manner. He can replenish the resources he draws from the environment as he expends them. Vital self-regulation provides the foundation for mental self-regulation, yielding an unlimited source for replenishing one's energy and strength. Two processes – vital and mental – combine to make a person well-rounded and harmonious. For our purposes, this is the most profound issue for the human being, the family, the organization, and, possibly, for the community. Another possible explanation is that today and tomorrow, while the development of human society is still based on scientific and technological progress, rather than scientific and mystic progress, it relegates the development of the human being's creative and spiritual abilities (his subtle worlds of thought and perceptions and thought and serendipitous revelations) to the background. This is why, as we move on to a discussion of classes and types of economics grouped according to types of compatibility, we identify the economics of harmony that can be used to perform an evaluation of the full set of an individual's needs – in other words, the economics of the vital and the mental, which we have considered in this section and which lies at the foundation of the Interactive Economics Model.

List of Sources:

1. Анохов И. В. Игровой аспект экономики. Известия ИГЭА.2013.№2 (88) – Anokhov, I. V. Game aspect of economics. IGEA News. 2013. Issue 2 (88)

2. Балицкий Е. Ментальные контуры, стратификация общества и цивилизационные волны. 19.05.2010.kapital-rus.ru>articles/article/177327 – Balitsky, E. Mental contours, society stratification and civilization waves. 19.05.2010.kapital-rus.ru>articles/article/177327

3. Заманская Е. Витальная саморегуляция- что это такое? 2006. library.by> portalus/modules/psycholgy/redme.php/? – Zamanskaya, E. Vital autoregulation – what is it? 2006. library.by> portalus/modules/psycholgy/redme.php/?

4. Кропоткин П. А. Анархия: Сборник.-М.: Айрис-пресс, 2002 С.47-113 – Kropotkin, P. A. Anarchy: Collected articles. – Moscow: Iris Press, 2002, P. 47 – 113

5. Рахаев Б. Витальные ресурсы, ментальная среда и организационные циклы бизнеса.31.01.2010. finanal.ru>001 – Rakhaev, B. Vital resources, the mental environment and business organization cycles. 31.01.2010. finanal.ru>001

2.2 Values in the Formation of Government Economic Policy

The current classic structure of the state economic policy is based on three components. First, an analysis of the current state of the economy, the starting point for rational state economic policy. This analysis identifies bottlenecks in the economy of a nation, an industry, a region, or some area of human endeavor, evaluating priorities of different tasks with a view to their implementation as well as possible outcomes of resolving various problems and crises and of changing the course of action. Second, this analysis helps to formulate and provide rationale for goals, starting from identifying a "portfolio" of goals and ranking them by the time horizon needed to achieve them (short-term vs. medium term). It also takes into account the scale of impact on the country's economy, measuring any associated costs, and institutional, financial and personnel requirements that implementation of these goals would entail. It helps to identify interdependencies between goals, compatibility of goals and any cross-influences among them. Third is regulation and construction of a tree of goals (a systematic set of goals for socioeconomic development) to build a dynamic system of goals for the country's socioeconomic development, as well as distributing them across a series of timeframes and a hierarchy of levels. The business community must be engaged in developing the state economic policy. It is a fairly common practice today to engage members of the business community in shaping the economic policy. At the same time, attempts to organize an open conversation between the business community and the authorities are often stymied by a lack of legislative support and lack of working mechanisms through which this conversation would be carried out. As a consequence of this, there is no interaction between government offices and agencies and private businesses at the stage of high-level economic planning. Development of political democracy and engaging members of civic society (including business associations and other advocates for the private sector) in formulation of economic policy is currently a necessary condition of further reform of the economy and ensuring continued economic growth for an entire country. However, today's Russia, struggling with foreign and domestic economic crises, shows few signs of this kind of democracy; quite the opposite: the state's hands-on micromanagement and invasive, stifling regulation taking the shape, among other things, of constraining and punitive fiscal actions that discourage entrepreneurs from getting involved in common national programs and projects. Although Russian authorities have seemingly and superficially reduced their pressure on the private business sector, they cannot orchestrate or otherwise achieve a reduction of pressure on the private sector from banks and major corporations, which bribe government officials, creating an environment of corruption in Russia's regions and sectors of the Russian economy.

Building an economic policy that creates organizational mechanisms for engaging the business community (the entrepreneurial community) in formulating economic policy brings the following real benefits:

- making behind-the-scenes negotiations between business leaders and the government authorities more transparent, as well as engaging small and medium-sized businesses in this dialogue, as their strong potential for expansion and development could provide an additional boost to Russian economic growth;

- reducing risks inherent in biased economic decision-making by self-serving local officials as a result of lobbying by their business cronies, which is detrimental to society at large, as it tends to result in suboptimal use of resources controlled by the government and other economic players. Government agencies create or organize intermediaries within their countries and overseas to engage the government, private businesses and other stakeholders in the setting of economic policies, goals and priorities of economic development.

A state's economic policies combine ideological, cultural and scientific concepts followed by the state. Economic policies should serve the purpose of encouraging and promoting the establishment of economic conditions most conducive to implementation of government (state) policies. The state itself regulates the economy through economic policy tools and institutions, the economic policy being defined not only by historical rationales, but also by the state's plans and guidelines, and any current decisions taken in the meantime. These actions can change the government's formal economic policy because it is not carved in stone, not unstable, as it has to provide for the current socioeconomic, military, political and environmental situation. Flexibility and maneuverability of economic policy are generally conducive to the growth of national prosperity, and currently leave much to be desired in Russia. The formulation of a specific type of the state's, the government's economic policy depends on the current phase of national economic development. As a rule, the key indicators those responsible for formulating and constructing the state's economic policy react to are the size and dynamics of the GDP, aggregate demand and supply, aggregate income and consumption, prices, and (un)employment. The economic policy is intimately intertwined with the state's domestic and foreign policies, as well as the state ideology and the state's (the government's) military policy. Economic policy epitomizes the government's political views, the state's political doctrine, and yet, at the same time, it should help to promote the establishment of economic foundations, the economic basis for implementing the desired government policy. This implies that political forces within the country, political parties and movements can exert a perceptible influence on the government's economic course, its current economic policy. Social aspects of economic policy manifest themselves in that the government has to take into account the social reaction of different population groups, especially the dominant groups, in its (the government's) economic decision-making, such as putting together the budget, allocating government funds for spending, etc. Labor strikes and other forms of social protest can sometimes have a decisive influence on specific elements of economic policy planned or executed by the government. Economic policies in the initial planning stages find their most evident manifestation in the structure of the government budget projections, the government's targeted special-purpose programs, laws, parameters of social security, assistance and support for those in need of special terms (lower interest rates) on government loans, special tax rates and other breaks and benefits, government influence on imports and exports, as well as the size of domestic and foreign government debt. Hands-on micromanagement is currently typical for Russia's nationwide economic policy, not only as mandated by government plans and programs, but also as numerous ad-hoc decisions by the Russian president and the government overturning previously approved plans and decisions to meet major short-term exigencies of foreign policy. The explanation lies primarily in socioeconomic, military, political and environmental instability. Frequent revisions of economic policies are possible and happen frequently in Russia, to correct for mistakes in formulating the economic policy, to reflect changes in the government's positions on various issues, or to reflect changes in the government itself.

Implementation of economic policy relies on the use of a combination of measures of direct (administrative) and indirect influence, where the latter include conditions for a quasi-free, guided (or forced) choice by economic players, as well as a set of tools which the government can use to influence the economy. Economic measures and tools include: financial policy, including budgetary, fiscal and monetary policy; economic programming and planning; forecasting. Institutional measures envisage creation, support, and development of certain social institutions. The current tax and budget (fiscal), foreign trade and monetary policies (and more specifically, the policy of regulating revenues through a system of anti-inflationary measures) have no bearing on regulating individuals' and organizations' demand for money; in fact, these policies seem to be decoupled from regulating this demand. The Russian authorities' foreign policies and domestic economic inter-sectoral policies of the past several decades have led the industrial production sector into a dead-end, as trade and services now account for two-thirds of Russia's gross domestic product. The core component of economic policy, social policy, which includes income indexation and setting of minimum wages (as a function of minimal subsistence level estimates), has been hopelessly driven into a corner lately. Social policy targets primarily implementation of specific programs to assist groups of people with low income, and covers such areas as education, healthcare, culture, providing assistance to families with three or more children, and regulating employment and labor relations. However, the primary focus of economic policy and its course have recently tended towards creating a strong sovereign state, in many ways rebuilding a new version of the Soviet Union (the most important thing is to preserve and expand the territory, the area of the country, while the condition of the people living within the country is a distant secondary concern), and there have been few signs recently that this course may be substantially modified or reversed. We propose, for a better, more in-depth understanding of the role of values in formulating economic policy, as an extension of government (state) policy, to look into the connections between morality, politics, and economics, as politics often determines the vector of economic development.

Politics and morality have been in a long heated "argument" essentially since the beginning of history, and this "dialog" between them can be expressed as the following concepts: (1) "parallel, non-overlapping worlds"; (2) a merger of two disparate substances: moral and political; (3) "interactions between two worlds: the moral world and the world of politics." In the first concept, politics is a direct expression of contradictory, primarily economic interests of social groups; it is full of conflicts and heated polemics, and if consensus is ever reached within the context of this concept, it tends to be a consensus that serves the interests of the group(s) consenting to it. Morality is selfless and altruistic, as is their highest manifestation, Christian love. Morality is ever reaching for the sky, for the ideals shared by all humanity that express a human truth of life, a truth consistent with the nature and essence of humanity, rather than some strictly private, corporate self-serving interests. Admission of incompatibility between morality and politics is reflected in two contradictory world-view paradigms: politically motivated moralizing and amoral politicking. The second concept on our list goes as far back as Plato[20] who saw the state as the source of morality and the ideal manifestation of morality, its highest level in our world, as the state is the only thing that establishes justice among people, gives them the concepts of good and evil. This was the underlying reason for creating what was essentially the first model of the totalitarian state in history. Centuries later, German philosopher Hegel also considers the state as a moral entity, a moral concept, the "universal will," the "spirit of the people," the "political virtue," one of the highest stages the Absolute Idea can attain. The state, according to Hegel, is not a means, but rather an end in its own right, the highest of goals, the ultimate goal.[21] If we were to equate politics with morality, politics would become moralizing, and morality would become subservient to politics. Within the context of the third concept above, interaction between morality and politics, just as interaction among systems can take place in two formats: (a) mutual determination (as cause and effect) and (b) mutual infiltration. Mutual determination (Format (a)) of both moral and political consciousness have one thing in common: they both have to do with the spiritual life of society. If the idea of reform matures within society, it will percolate into politics, art, and other formats of public (social) consciousness as well as economics. All the more or less significant events find a reflection in morality. Their social vector is defined through a system of moral, ethical concepts of good and evil, fairness and injustice, responsibility or lack thereof, humanity or

---

[20] Vasilieva, T. V. Athens School of Philosophy. Philosophical Language of Plato and Aristotle. Moscow, 1985, P. 134. (In Russian) / Васильева Т. В. Афинская школа философии. Философский язык Платона и Аристотеля. М., 1985 .C-134

[21] Plotkovskiy, A. A. Hegel's Theory of Law and the State. State Publishing House of Law Literature. Moscow, P. 18. (In Russian) / Плотковский А. А. Учение Гегеля о праве и государстве. Гос-ное изд-во юрид. литературы, М. с. -18

cruelty. Political decisions are "transcribed" into a different frame of reference, which makes it possible to determine their human costs. In turn, politics creates a certain moral and psychological climate in society, which can either strengthen or undermine humanitarian values, hopes, inspire, ingrain and shape fear of organized crime and corruption. Mutual infiltration (Format B) of politics and morality triggers two key processes. The first one has to do with infiltration of moral consciousness by political ideas, whereupon the latter are transformed into moral convictions. A social phenomenon (including a political phenomenon) can become a moral one when it is assimilated into morals and becomes a matter of free choice, a matter of an individual's motivation, a matter of conscience and duty; patriotic sentiments would be an example of this. The second mutual infiltration processes linking morality and politics involves moral values, the concepts of justice, good and evil percolating into the realm of politics, one way or another, causing adjustments to political programs, platforms, strategies and tactics, measuring them against humanistic criteria, moral ideas and constructs, and people's sentiments. This gives politics a moral meaning, bringing it to "the human plane," making it easier for individuals to find affinity for it, understand and appreciate it. While the author of this book supports the latter statement, politicians may have different views on this matter (swayed by their dearly held and espoused convictions), which may explain why Russia's economic outcomes, directly dependent on the above, have been mediocre at best.

The influence of what we could describe as moral politics (as discussed above) on economic policy will primarily affect the successful implementation of general cultural and shared values which any citizen can perceive as changes to his prosperity or the comfort of his environment, a safety net that is there for him – with none of the positives in sight in Russia, and hopes for any of these becoming available in Russia in the foreseeable future remaining rather slim. Speaking of interaction between moral and political consciousness, we note that the latter is manifested mostly through class consciousness, or consciousness determined by political party lines. The situation is similar in the economy and economics: the rich promote the terms most advantageous for their own enrichment which are at odds with the opinions, efforts and best interests of the majority of the general public, forcing them through legislature, executive enactments and financial and economic regulation by lobbying and bribing government officials. We can assume that aspirations of individual social groups find a sufficiently clear expression in the political consciousness. However, different social classes and business groups cannot coexist without making allowances for the essential needs and aspirations of other social strata. If they fail to do this, the result would be an economic war, which may deteriorate into a civil war.

So what is the distinction between moral and political-economic consciousness? Economic and political consciousness serves people's horizontal, lateral aspirations primarily, while moral consciousness serves both horizontal and vertical aspirations (which is the domain of religion, including the Russian Orthodox Christian Church). Actions of various economic and political institutions should be evaluated precisely through the prism of higher moral values (rather than from the perspective of deriving immediate benefits). It is precisely the moral consciousness that sets the guiding lights for political consciousness, and, consequently, for economic consciousness. Concepts of good and evil are central to moral consciousness. In contrast to that, money and power are the cornerstone concepts of political and economic consciousness. The concept of money is frequently associated with power, coercion and restricting an individual's freedom. On the contrary, moral consciousness allows for violence and coercion only as an exception – only if they are needed to rein in the most extreme manifestations of evil. And yet, the two types of consciousness have some things in common and a shared common ground, an area in which they can interact. The state is not an abstract thing. It finds real-world, material actualizations in specific government agencies, offices, and their operation. And the essence of a specific state manifests itself primarily through law and socioeconomic reform. It is no accident that such fundamental principles of life as "Thou shalt not kill" or "Thou shalt not steal" become both moral and legal standards. Both morality and law trace their origins to the church, to religion, which has invariably existed for several millennia in most cultures. However, the church is not a constituent part of the state. Besides, both moral and legal consciousness, both moral and legal approaches to looking at the world, have a common, shared concept of fairness, equitability, equality, which is glaringly absent from economic consciousness. Fairness from the legal perspective means compliance with the laws established by the state. From the moral perspective, fairness means objective evaluation of an individual's actions through the prism of shared human values, higher values. From the economic perspective, values arise from utility, benefits, and the economic *value* of a product, and none of these can boast to possess much spiritual or moral content that would be relevant from a consumer perspective. However, one way or another, operating within the broader context of one society, moral, political and economic interpretation and understanding of values inevitably interact and come into conflict with one another, each putting society into a temporary equilibrium, meeting the material and spiritual needs of an individual.

When we consider the role of the state in the establishment and "operation" of morality, we should note the widely held view that statesmen tend not to be burdened by moral compunctions, or, in the words of Max Weber, "the genius or demon of politics lives in internal tension with the god of love."[22] However, we would have to admit that state as an organizing force has contributed to elevating the power of the human spirit over the elemental forces of nature, by organizing extensive public works, building roads and digging canals, bringing order to society, developing material production and the economy to create the necessary conditions for improving and refining the moral life of society. Moral life needs to have a certain

---

[22] Weber, M. Protestant Ethics and the Spirit of Capitalism. Weber, M. Selected Works. Moscow: Progress, 1990. P. 75. (In Russian) / Вебер М. Протестантская этика и дух капитализма // Вебер М. Избр. произв. М.: Прогресс, 1990. С-75

level of culture as its foundation to be able to develop and improve. For this purpose, the state creates conditions for development of the arts, science, and, more recently [in Russia], for development of religion, manifesting more prominently its role in promoting and implementing moral values. At the same time, the economic interests of the real "powers that be," the "shakers and movers" who are commonly described as oligarchs, or tycoons in contemporary parlance, are present behind the scenes of politics. The current amoral nature of politics is a clear diagnosis of the mismatch between these interests and those of the nation, of Russia, if we were to construe Russia as the majority of Russian citizens, rather than those who have appropriated great wealth, the media and power, and who represent less than 3% of the Russian population. Politics, the economy and morality can come together and find common ground only when and where political and economic interests become the actual interests of the nation, which have room for the individual with his concerns about his daily bread over and above economic gain, expediency and utility. It is very sad and depressing to hear some contemporary [Russian] politicians and oligarchs expound on the fundamental incompatibility of politics and economics with morality. This has to be interpreted as applicable only to the immediate political and economic environment of these characters, rather than the political and economic space of the entire nation. However, the oligarchs' personal environment seems to be expanding and becoming stronger, if standard of living data and expanding oligarch lists are anything to go by. Morality should be foundation of contemporary politics and economics: the institution of ideological and material (economic) power which *defines* social life of a country simply cannot be amoral, let alone subversive to morality. It is common knowledge that Nazism freed the German people and the German army from the "chimera called morality," after which the state, deprived of this phenomenon, could exist for just a little longer than a decade.

Common cultural values, including moral values (such as kindness, beauty, truth, brotherhood, equality, love, creativity, conscience, knowledge, fairness, power as a universal value) for an advanced, developed state, which we are striving to build in Russia, must be employed in evaluating the efficiency of both the overall state policy and economic policy which facilitates implementation of the state policy. It is common knowledge that common cultural values are shaping:

- universal or general cultural standards, which include rules of acting in public places; common rules of civility; civic rights and duties established by law, etc.;

- standards of reciprocity, according to which we expect help from others, as well as standards of social responsibility, which imply that people will help those who depend on them;

- group standards: so-called "nobility codes of honor," rules of business and civic etiquette, regulation forms of address and salutation and so on.

In turn, shared socioeconomic values are mostly focused on prosperity values, as a condition for maintaining people's physical and mental pursuits. These values combine: wellbeing (including health and safety); owning different material goods and services; professional-level skills and mastery of specific activities; good education (knowledge, the ability to acquire and process information, and cultural connections); respect (including status, prestige, renown or fame and reputation).

While political values are centered around civic liberties, the rule of law, upholding the constitution, peace, and so on, vital economic values include life, health, safety and security, wellbeing, and so on. However, society develops and values which are superimposed on one another, become intertwined with one another, creating new value cores connected with both religious aspects of culture and people's growing needs. We have to keep in mind that the 7 billion-strong global community consists of people representing eight current civilizations.

In 1990, the UN Development Program (UNDP) proposed a new metric for evaluating economic and social progress in countries around the world, describing human development as "the process of enlarging people's choices". The definition of human development was expanded in 2010, as defining human development as "enlarging," expanding the range of choice was deemed essentially correct, yet insufficient. Human development implies achieving longer duration of positive overcomes across time and countering processes that lead to hardship for people and increase unfairness. The expanded definition had a bearing on such principles as social fairness, sustainability and respect for human rights. The new definition incorporated experience and research into human development issues: "Human development is a process of expanding people's freedom to lead long, healthy lives of creativity, as well as their freedom to achieve other goals, which in their opinion are worthwhile; actively participating in achieving and securing fairness and sustainable development on the planet."[23]

According to the latest Human Development Index data, released in December 2015, Norway was recognized as the most developed country in the world. Russia's current HDI is 0.798, at the top of high human development countries, where it shares the 50th place with Belarus. Russia has the following key indicators: life expectancy at birth of 70.1 years; average education period of 14.7 years; and per-capita gross national income of

---

[23] Human Development Index. Online Humanities Encyclopedia // Center for Humanities Technologies. – 10.10.2009 (last edited on 16.12.2015). Retrieved from: http://gtmarket.ru/ratings/human-development-index/human-development-index-info (In Russian) / Индекс развития человеческого потенциала. Гуманитарная энциклопедия [Электронный ресурс] // Центр гуманитарных технологий. — 10.10.2009 (последняя редакция: 15.12.2015).
URL: http://gtmarket.ru/ratings/human-development-index/human-development-index-info

US$ 22,352.[24] Core HDI indicators in Russia are depressed by socioeconomic inequality among the people, environmental conditions, relatively low life expectancy, especially for men, more typical for countries with low human development. However, we should not forget that the latest data represents the last prosperous years of 2013-14, while new significant economic problems were added to other negative factors in Russia in 2015, problems which have a significant negative impact on development of the state and the well-being of the country's people. As a consequence, most core indicators have come down, pushing Russia back six or seven years, just as was the case after the 2008 economic crisis.

The US-based Heritage Foundation and The Wall Street Journal have released their latest annual Index of Economic Freedom for 2016. The Heritage Foundation defined economic freedom in 1995 as "absence of government intervention or constraint to production, distribution and consumption of goods and services, beyond the extent necessary for the citizens to protect and maintain liberty itself." Overall, index analysts believe that economic freedoms are stagnating in Russia, while long-term prospects of sustained economic growth "remain grim." The Russian economy is overly dependent on natural resource exports, primarily exports of oil and gas, making balanced development and growth substantially more difficult to achieve and drastically reducing its compatibility. Despite relatively strong economic growth in previous years, made possible by hydrocarbon exports, the country has been relatively closed to trade and investment. Experts note the following among other weaknesses of the Russian economy: excessive involvement of the state (and the government) in many industries, offsetting growth in the private sector and increasing the cost of investment in Russia;

---

[24] UNDP: Human Development Index in 2015. [Online publication] // Center for Humanities Technologies. – 16.12.2015. Retrieved from: http://gtmarket.ru/news/2015/12/16/7285 (In Russian) / Программа развития ООН: Индекс человеческого развития в странах мира в 2015 году. [Электронный ресурс] // Центр гуманитарных технологий. — 16.12.2015. URL: http://gtmarket.ru/news/2015/12/16/7285

non-tariff barriers, which increase transaction costs significantly; lack of an effective system of laws that work, bureaucratic barriers and inconsistent regulations and regulatory changes creating hurdles to investment growth; lack of competition leading to constantly increasing prices, including natural monopoly prices and fees; the burden of corruption.

Certainly, economic policy mostly affects vital values; however, it would certainly make sense to add to this list of indices The Happy Planet Index is a complex metric published every two or three years to measure the accomplishments of countries and regions in terms of their ability to ensure a happy life for their residents. Experts compiling this index believe that countries emphasizing the development of manufacturing and associated economic growth do not usually make their people happier, as economic theories espoused and followed by the governments of these countries have little in common with the life of real people (this appears to apply to Russia as well other countries). A recent comparative prosperity study put Russia into 58th place, leaving plenty of room for improvement in the future.[25]

Economic policy is always a consequence of, and the foundation for, development of government (state) policy, which has been characterized in Russia by a gradual and consistent roll-back of liberal values since the year 2000, and now we can reasonably talk about full rejection of liberalism, which has essentially been completely squeezed out of Russian political life. "Restricting democratic freedoms (freedom of speech, freedom of the press, freedom of the media), replacing regional gubernatorial elections with appointment of governors by the Russian president, the transition from mixed to proportional State Duma (national

---

[25] Prosperity Index of the World's Countries. Online Humanities Encyclopedia // Center for Humanities Technologies. – 10.06.2011 (last edited on 03.11.2015. (In Russian) / Рейтинг стран мира по уровню процветания. Гуманитарная энциклопедия [Электронный ресурс] // Центр гуманитарных технологий. — 10.06.2011 (последняя редакция: 03.11.2015).
URL: http://gtmarket.ru/ratings/legatum-prosperity-index/info

legislature) elections, tightening the state's control over major media outlets, one party ("the party of power) effectively monopolizing the political "market," as the use of authoritarian methods to manage and control the nation's economy is becoming more pervasive. All of this has had a negative impact on the practice of government management and control, slowing down its development and driving down the demand for this type of management."[26] The Russian government focused its attention (and, consequently, its political objectives) on bringing back traditional values, the so-called "binding spiritual core" of the nation. There has been a lot of talk recently about "the feelings of religious believers"; in fact, offending their feelings has become a crime under Russian criminal law. A number of NGOs and NPOs (which have never been numerous in Russia in the first place) have been blacklisted as "foreign agents," and so barred from many kinds of activity, and in many instances even from operating in Russia at all. In its current state, the foundation, the base (terms denoting the economy) is largely consistent with free-market principles that imply competition, initiative, and at least some freedoms, despite very tight and restrictive regulatory control. The success of these interactions relies, to some extent, on accepting, adopting, implementing and developing at least some global liberal values. It is hard to build effective free market mechanisms while ostentatiously rejecting and denigrating all the ideological underpinnings and foundations of a free-market economy. However, we can still observe only growing contradictions between ideological foundations and values in different spheres of the social environment of Russian society:

"...for some reason, bold attempts are made constantly in Russia to "invent" new values."[27]

---

[26] Voskanyan, S.S. Practice of Political Management in Russia: Current State, Problems, Development Scenarios // Vlast. 2015, Issue 5. PP. 29-34. (In Russian) / Восканян С.С. Практика политического менеджмента в России: состояние, проблемы, сценарии развития // Власть. 2015. № 5. С. 29-34.

[27] Melkov, S.A. What Values Should Russia Defend? // Vlast. 2015. Issue 2. PP. 94-97. (In Russian) / Мельков С. А. Какие ценности предстоит защищать России // Власть. 2015. № 2. С. 94-97.

Today, living in conditions of onerous and strict international sanctions, Russian citizens are prepared to limit themselves and many of their needs for a long time, as long as their home country is under attack from across the border. The population of Russia sees itself in a passive role, accepting and approving all the initiatives of the authorities. In this particular case, conformism goes hand-in-hand with other fundamental values such as paternalism and collectivism. Certainly, none of these values exists in isolation, but is rather part of the integral spiritual organism of the Russian people. This system of values that complement and reinforce one another, gives authorities unlimited room for maneuver. It would be a mistake to claim today that liberalism has discredited itself in Russia, as the country has never, strictly speaking, experienced liberal values in action (because Russia has been guided by a hybrid mix of traditional and liberal values since the early 1990s). The Russian government is currently using a hands-on approach to manage the country's economy, which only proves that the government has no effective tools to manage the economy and perform normal day-to-day communication, both within the government itself, including government agencies and institutions, and between the government (the authorities) and the people. Today, the authorities need to make concessions to society in certain things, to stimulate independent civic initiative within society. If society can feel that it has become a reasonably active player across the entire social spectrum, and not just in some areas of economic interaction, then both society and the government and its efforts to manage the economy will be protected from negative and dangerous foreign-policy experiments (and, consequently, from economic sanctions) by exercising social control over the government (authorities). Speaking of the current socioeconomic conditions and recent adjustments to the government's economic policy, we can propose a range of different techniques, methods and tools that would enable the government (and the country) to achieve solid performance of complex and composite indicators building on general cultural and shared economic values which comprise a variety of aspects.

At this point in time, the Russian federal government and regional governments are pursuing a policy of spending cuts, slowing down various programs, imposing new restrictions, while continuing to carve up a shrinking overall "pie." Given the current level of external international pressure, Russia's policy should focus on stimulating domestic demand and supply, on providing room for releasing entrepreneurial energies, reducing the costs and burden of regulation as much as possible (these costs have been rising exponentially in Russia), reducing the overwhelming tax burden and various risks specific to Russia. There are plenty of tools for this in the arsenal: taxes and tax stimuli, interest rates, loans, government investment, government property and assets, foreign exchange rate to the extent the government can influence it, regulatory costs and more.

Adjustment of the government's approaches to small and medium-sized businesses is long overdue. In the current environment, SMEs are more than a purely economic factor, they are also a major social factor, as the SME sector provides employment and new job opportunities, as well as generating a substantial share of gross domestic product. Adjustments to industrial policy and industrial capital are only needed because extensive natural resources account for a large share of the Russian economy, and ideally it would provide for high value-added processing, for example, in the chemicals industry.

The Russian authorities (the government, the president and legislature) must in any case define, refine, and modify foreign policy in a way that would give Russia the necessary access to global capital markets. This is an important condition for stopping the economic downturn and bringing about a quick economic recovery. The Russian government's budgetary policy should serve the primary goal of stopping the economic downturn – after all, the government holds the purse strings to the Reserve Fund and, as a last resort, the National Prosperity Fund, Russia's sovereign wealth fund. Both can be used to cover additional budget deficits. If we take a more moderate option, it would make sense at least not to cut costs so rapidly and dramatically or at least not to cut costs at all for some population groups (strata). Opening access to global capital markets for Russia and influencing the downturn by budgetary policy methods are two key tasks for the country and the authorities.

The Russian Ministries of Finance, Economic Development, and the Russian Central Bank pursue the strategy of keeping down inflation (the inflation targeting strategy) at all costs. As one of the costs, the real purchasing power of the people is shrinking. A strategy needs to be developed to increase the people's purchasing power.

Conditions and attitudes are currently in flux in Russia, with a rising need for an entirely new socioeconomic policy. Economic policy must not be focused simply on economic growth that would imply preservation of the current proportions in the economy, but instead on true full-fledged development. Consequently, proportions must be changed. Structural economic policy should primarily deal with development of the real sector, with priority given to cutting-edge sectors of scientific, intellectual and technological progress. As an important condition, the government must continue to fulfill basic social obligations before the citizens. There should be a place in social policy not only for declarations about the importance of human capital, but also for transformation of human capital into the most important component of social and economic policy. All of this implies measures directed at both development of the domestic market and expanding the export potential of Russian manufacturing and the Russian economy as a whole.

All government policies are currently reduced to reacting to the situation as it changes, to problems as they arise. And the government is reacting, at various degrees of effectiveness, to processes outside its control, including some global trends. The government's policies leave no room for a proactive development strategy, focusing on short-term reactive tactics.

The current development model that has been implemented in Russia for the past 25 years has reached a dead end. This model essentially relies on Western investments and technologies for proceeding with modernization of the Russian economy. It has become abundantly clear today that access to Western investments and technologies will be blocked by Western countries for political reasons, whether or not sanctions against Russia will remain in place going forward. Therefore, this model needs to be changed. Middle Eastern, Eastern and domestic investments rather than those coming from the West should become the main source of modernization of the economy. As for technology, Russian science should become the source of technological modernization in the country. And economic policy needs to be modified accordingly. More money coming more directly from the government should be invested in the economy. The most important thing is to avoid channeling this money through the usual channels: from the government to the banks, and then to the forex market, where it would bring down the Russian Ruble, while bringing extraordinary profits to forex market speculators and bringing no benefit to the economy at large. And this model needs to be developed further, using the quantitative easing model successfully applied in the US in recent years, and introduced by the European Commission for the EU in 2015.

As for monetary and lending policy, the central bank should assume greater responsibility for economic growth. The central bank must be placed under the political control of the government. So far, the situation has been changing in the opposite direction over the past two decades, until central banks have come to control governments, and not the other way around. The key problem is to secure governments' independence from central banks, which are usually not accountable to an electorate or any appointing agency. Increasing central banks' responsibility would make it easier to demand that the central bank should contribute to economic growth, as people's prosperity should take precedence over having a strong currency. Integration of the economy with politics, science, culture, social services and administration into a single unified and well-coordinated system is especially important today. Elements of this system would complement and reinforce one another. All of these areas of life and operation of society are based on, built upon, and rely upon the values that determine the directions and stages of society's integrative development.

2.3 Sectors of the Economy and a Model of Their Interaction

The modern rapidly changing social and political environment sees interaction between social, societal and economic agents: government agencies, public associations, political and religious groups active within the country; businesses and other market players in different regions and sectors, scientific, research and cultural organizations. Russia, with its diversity of plentiful resources and vast undeveloped areas can adjust its course to use of domestic products, liberating itself from the influence of (periodic sanctions imposed by) countries providing a large share of Russian imports of mass consumer goods and food. This could also become an opportunity for Russia finally to create a domestic agricultural, industrial and innovative, cross-sector market, significantly reducing its dependence on imports and noticeably decreasing the effects of corruption on centralized flows of goods, which should help to improve cooperation between regional industrial complexes. The current situation could change the economics of resource extraction industries. The contemporary Russian economy should be defined by strong industrial complexes spanning multiple industries. At present, such complexes exist mostly in the oil and gas and defense manufacturing industries. These get the most attention and the greatest preferences from the government, and they are very prominent in government policy. This makes the situation difficult for other sectors, especially those geared towards consumers, which fulfill citizens' social needs. In Russia's case, ways to increase government revenues would be linked primarily to finding a solution to the problem of natural resource rent. This problem arises from the high importance of natural resources in the Russian economy and the vast scale of differences between the country's regions, which are the root causes that make natural resource rent a core factor of economic relations. Natural resource rent, i.e. the excessive profits from the operation of the most lucrative natural resource deposits, for now stays in the pockets of producers (the resource owners and operators), although it must belong to the whole society. The oligarchs successfully lobbied for the introduction of a mineral resource tax, which is effectively included in the price consumers pay for their products. Expropriating the rent to state revenue (following Norway's example) would make it possible not only to level the playing field for different industries, but also to reduce the tax burden significantly for most of the players in the overall economy. The dominance of resource sectors creates a downward pressure on the overall growth rate of the national economy. The dominance of the energy sector especially is a major hurdle to development of R&D-intensive sectors. Conditions need to be created that would enable different sectors to compete on an equal footing and to interact effectively with agencies and offices of the federal and regional governments.

Infrastructure is gaining increasing importance; it is playing an extraordinary role not only in ensuring that manufacturing processes are efficient and supported by efficient logistics, but also in developing social services and the living conditions of the general population, and helping to make the economy more diverse and evenly balanced, and to develop new territories. Strengthening the (tax) revenue base is particularly important for (Russia's) regions. Several ratios are used to describe the degree of specialization of economic regions: the regional localization ratio (the weight of a specific industry in a given region divided by its weight in the economy of the entire country), the regional per capita production ratio (the weight of a specific region in the national production of a given sector divided by the weight of that region in the country's population), and the regional exports ratio (the quantity of a given product carried from the region divided by the total amount of the product manufactured/produced in the region), but these cover only inadequately the essential aspects of regional specialization. The experience of countries with a well-developed free-market economy shows that structural reorganization of the economy (a structural "perestroika") should be tackled in several stages, and should be started at the so-called "focal points of growth" – industries which can provide a solid foundation for overall growth and development today and tomorrow, not in some distant future. Since the market cannot perform a rapid structural reorganization of the economy on its own, this function has to be fulfilled by the state, the government, which implies that the structure of the economy is subject to government regulation. Reorganization includes the following stages: development and implementation of industrial policy; cutting and eliminating the obsolete and development of advanced industrial companies, industries and segments and types of agriculture, while ensuring faster development of the more efficient sectors. While choosing the location for manufacturing and other industrial facilities, it is essential to take the ecology, or environmental factors, into consideration. This environmental factor is the key factor of interaction among all levels of the national economy, the factor that defines the overall long-term targets for each sector in the economy.

Five commonly known types of economic system are: the traditionalist system, pure capitalism, a centrally planned command economy, a mixed system and a synthetic system. At this point in time, as the majority of the Russian population is dropping below the poverty line, the country has a need for an active social policy, for distribution of subsidies from the government's social support funds and for provision of government services to Russian citizens, as a way to guarantee full employment with a focus on self-realization – as both full utilization of the people's potential and public recognition for their work (in line with the Swedish model). We can also talk about other models, including the Japanese model, which adopted the Russian/Soviet experience with central planning and use of "inter-sector balance" where the key strategy of economic growth focuses on development of R&D and science-intensive production (while borrowing inventions and technology from other countries);

this system also holds university education in high regard and relies on close interaction between the government and the private sector (including a tough stance on corruption); we will cover this interaction in greater detail below.

Let us discuss the synthetic economic system built around a "green economy" with a focus on social (spiritual and material) issues, as the most promising for both Russia and many other countries. This should enable us to get a clear look at interaction between economies. The need for such a synthetic system arises from the fact that the desire to get rich quickly, the unrestrained craving for money and power, envy and aggression, the determination to dominate others, have resulted in predatory exploitation and wanton overuse of the treasures of our planet, the progressive depletion and deterioration of these treasures and destruction of natural habitats. Our planet today is "sick with humans," so we must talk about finding a cure for this human-centric disease, the unhealthy tendency to put man at the center of everything. In this context, we need to find a way to re-orient humanity's way of thinking, humanity's attitudes towards itself and the world around it, in order to save the overall biological environment, the biosphere. As a reminder, the features of this type of economy include a transition to a completely different economic basis of production; making environmental concerns a core consideration of economic development, inaugurating a new era in operation of economies and human economic existence, for Russia as well as other countries (a necessity as a factor of the overall condition of the global ecology); satisfying a sharp increase in demand for organic food, ecofriendly housing and voluntary downward reassessment (and voluntary self-restriction) of human needs; re-distribution of public resources to favor education, culture, healthcare, and to transform the material foundations and assets of these sectors (achieving humanization of the economy); the strong role of social and cultural factors, and the high percentage of affluent, well-educated, entrepreneurial people in the population. This, as we can see, requires achieving a compatibility of the requirements of the body with the values of the spirit in harmony with the existing bio-system of Planet Earth.

By way of reminder, interaction is understood, for the purposes of this book, as an objective and universal form of motion, a form of development that characterizes the existence and structural organization of any material system.[28] The Dictionary of Economics defines interaction as comprising direct and reciprocal influences, impacts of things upon one another, exchanges of matter, energy and information between different objects, between living organisms and the environment, formats of cooperation between people in various collaborative contexts. Interaction comprises direct and indirect (mediated) relations between objects and systems. Possible interaction types include: complementary/collaborative (in which partners approach and view each other's positions rationally and objectively), contrarian/antagonistic (unwilling to understand and accept the positions and opinions of other partners, while displaying and forcefully advocating their own intentions), hidden/secretive (where the partners' positions are not explained or fully disclosed to the other parties). Interaction styles and types include: cooperation (where motives are collaboration or competition), counteraction/resistance (with individualism as the key motive), compromise and willingness to accommodate the other party (to achieve a meaningful common goal) and avoidance. In our view, examples of positive interaction would include:[29] productive dialogue, cooperation (cultural, technological or related to trade) and partnership. Negative examples would include: opposition, stand-off, antagonism, a clash (socioeconomic, organizational, political and so on).

The positive interactions listed above represent concert, cohesion, lack of contradiction in the condition of inter-relations between objects, persons or systems, in the results of their operation, making their development and collective movement or progress

---

[28] Словарь логики/Dictionary of Logic. Logic/Sovmestimost-348.html

[29] Морозов В. А. Совместимость социально-экономических систем. М., Экономика, 2013.

compatible. Compatibility is the denominator of interaction. The depth of compatibility can be evaluated through interconnections, mutual influences and interaction, with the latter defining the quality of compatibility.

Technological compatibility is regulated by international standards, whereas in social psychology compatibility is defined and categorized as group compatibility or interpersonal compatibility. Compatibility in a broader sense is best explored through the way the individual relates to his environment, and primarily to specific organizations and institutions within society. In this case, we need to look at a broader context to evaluate compatibility. One has to look at several compatibility levels: the level of physical product and physical, material assets, the social level, the political, religious, cultural and world-outlook, scientific (intellectual) and spiritual levels. The order of compatibility levels shown above is of absolute importance in this case. The order is based on A. Maslow's famous hierarchy (pyramid) of needs.[30]

The first compatibility level is the level of physical, material products and physical assets, serving as an indicator of the next level up, the level of economic condition (stabilization and stability, growth, or weakening). The state of the first and second levels is the necessary condition for successful realization of social mechanisms responsible for providing social and financial security to people of different social strata, groups and organizations. Essentially, this is a necessary condition for people's prosperity, giving them the opportunity to realize their potential at higher categories (higher levels of compatibility). As social groups and regions consolidate and become dominant, the political platform for their centralization and regulation begins to take shape. The results of state ideology and material prosperity define the operating vector of the theological level. The cultural code, the common historic values of different religions that define both the diversity and unity of people, define the

---

[30] Maslow, A. Motivation and personality. 3rd Russian Ed. St. Petersburg: Piter, 2003
Мотивация и личность. 3-е изд. Спб.: Питер, 2003.

degree of cohesion in society. The state of globalization of society focuses its capabilities for accelerating the discovery of the intricacies of the environment and using it intellectually for human development and growth. At the same time, each of the levels relies on its own unique set of tools implemented by special organization and institutions of society (see Table 3, a modified version of the table used in Section 2).

Table 3. Levels of compatibility with the environment and methods for achieving these levels

Compatibility Level	Methods for achieving the compatibility level	Examples of key organizations and institutions
Cognitive (scientific) - spiritual (7)	Cognitive, Spiritual	Research and scientific research organizations, theology
Cultural and related to world outlook (6)	Mental, Cultural	Cultural and artistic organizations, educational institutions
Religious and theological (5)	Theological, Spiritual	Institutions affiliated with the world's main religions, interdenominational organizations, sects, religious brotherhoods, religious orders, other religious worship organizations
Political (4)	Historical, Patriotic	Political organizations, Political parties, Government agencies and Government offices
Social (3)	Institutional	Social groups, Social strata, Castes, Classes

Economic (2)	Incentives, Disincentives	Banks, Exchanges, Investment firms, Asset managers, Funds
Level of Products and Physical Assets (1)	Organizational, using technology and physical assets	Companies engaging in manufacturing, trade and those operating in the service industry

The key types of organizations listed in Table 3 for each level create their combined product. The product can be considered to be of an adequate quality and fully usable if all those involved in the processes leading up to its creation work in concert. Lack of contradiction, unconstructive conflict and stagnation makes it possible to join forces to create a product together at each level, defining the operation of self-organization patterns and mechanisms, resulting in interaction of participants involved in a process. We note that, when physical conditions are ripe (at the lower levels of compatibility), the probability is high for rapid mental progress (a favorable condition of the mind – i.e. the next higher levels) for adequate understanding of spiritual values.

At the same time, at levels 3-2, social institutions are striving to achieve stability and full performance of the financial and economic sector (level), and support its smooth development, to ensure their own stable and sustainable existence. The state exerts its power, mostly through political institutions (Levels 4-3), to preserve mutual respect and coordination among social groups and organizations (Level 5) by bringing to bear the mechanisms of pressure and indirect trust available. The theological and religious system (Levels 5-4) uses the historical culture, traditions and patterns of moral and spiritual behavior as a foundation to claim and defend its positions in areas spanning multiple countries that are home to nations, ethnic groups and peoples that gave rise to a specific religion or denomation, bringing together and solidifying these political forces into a cohesive community. In the contemporary world, globalization of human values (Levels 6-5), which is only just starting to make itself felt, aims to help the preservation and further evolution of the entire diversity of cultures, the experience of which it can use to formulate the concept of a humanist development of society as an integrated entity.

Because our main focus is on interactions between economies and interactions as such in economics, let us project on the proposed model the economic components of these levels, the aspects and spheres of life of society and associated organizations and institutions which comprise the levels of compatibility (correspondence), levels that offer us differentiated insights into interactions between these components. In other words, let us mark all the key varieties of economics and key types of economies in this model and attempt to take a look at their position vis-à-vis one another in the overall structure (Fig.1). The vertical "axis" shows types of economies and varieties of economics crossing the boundaries between levels, economies with multiple functions (institutional, underlying systemic, information, evolutionary, green economies, the economy of health, micro-, meso-, macro-, mega- and nanoeconomics; free market, state-run, traditional or mixed economies).

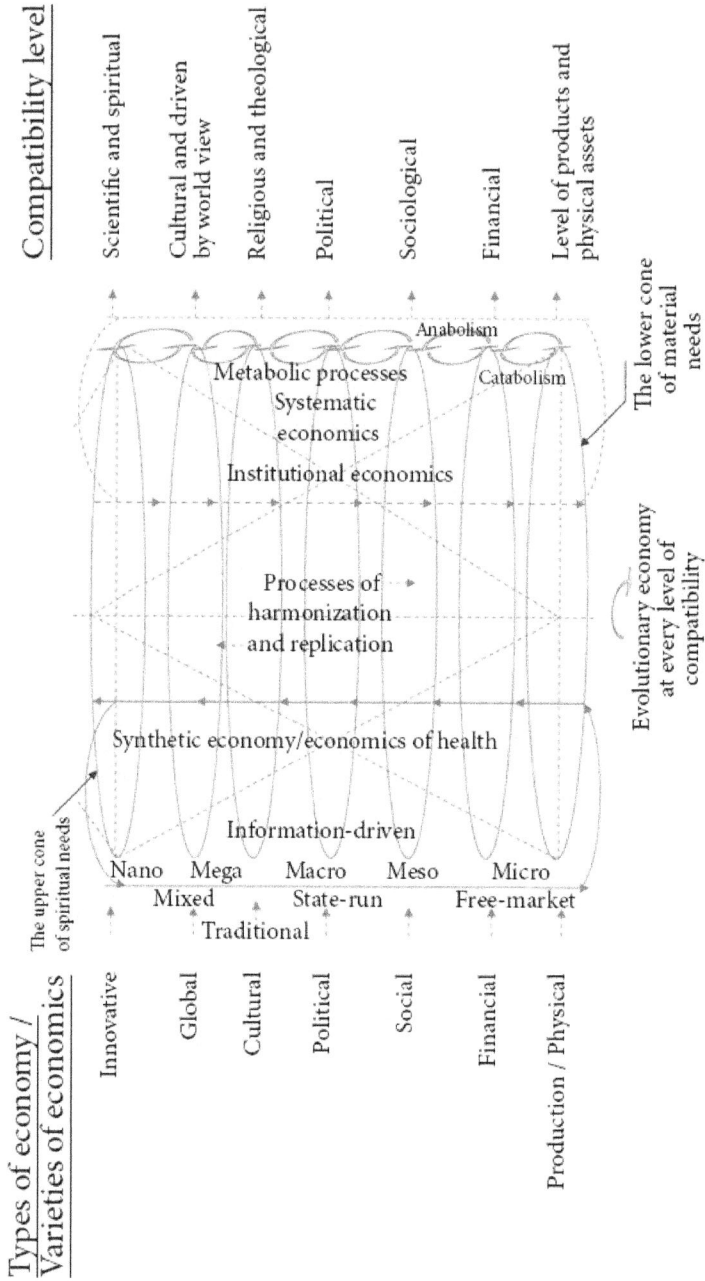

Fig. 3. The economy of interaction: a structural mode

Let us recall the main purpose of levels within this structure:

- (7) – Putting together integrative knowledge;

- (6) – Globalization (and analysis) of universally shared human values;

- (5) – Combination of values of religious institutions and organizations;

- (4) – Combining different ideological behavior patterns and formats;

- (3) – Development of social institutions;

- (2) – Development of financial and economic institutions;

- (1) – Using products delivered by manufacturing companies and material assets.

The relative placement of different economies could raise some questions, but on the whole it is in line with the unified field philosophy[31] [2] and cyclical development (progress) from material needs (the lower cone) to renewable cognitive and spiritual values (the superimposed upper cone), after which the cycle repeats. It is important that in the new cycle the base of the lower cone would match the base of the upper one, signifying a match between the cause and the effect. Action is the starting point of interaction among players ("subjects") within a system. Only their shared common interests and regulation of their interaction can ensure increased efficiency of the system's operation. This objective is achieved as the ultimate goal of the system based on aggregate evaluative metrics

---

[31] Bondarenko, O. (A series of books) Philosophy of Unity. Bishkek, 2000. (in Russian) / Бондаренко О. (серия книг) Философия единства, Бишкек, 2000

used to measure the performance of interacting economies. At the same time, a categorization of interactions is needed that uses process parameters for the economies and economic players involved, with each of these parameters serving its purpose.

This leads to the creation of separate chains of interaction within a system of different economies provided that: all the participants in the interactions share common goals; have structural cohesion; and coordinate and mutually adjust their interests (both shared and private) in the interaction process.

The effect of these relationships can be described by the degree or reasonable uniformity (repeatability of actions), reflecting the order in the system within which interactions are taking place. Factors such as the degree of coordination, flexibility and stability, heterogeneity and maneuverability, the ability to innovate and changeability determine the efficiency of the process of interaction between different economies within the country's national economy.

The national economy is a complex socioeconomic system that comprises many components and has a unique complex structure. Production of material, physical goods is the core, the foundation of the integrated national economy; the physical production sector provides employment to more than 68% of the total Russian gainfully employed workforce. The following types of structural components of the national economy can be identified: 1) the household; 2) a complex social entity, sectors of which interact organically; 3) a sector of the economy; 4) a territorial entity; 5) infrastructure of the national economy based on the nature and type of interactions between different areas of the economy; 6) foreign trade and entities and structures engaging in it. We can match sectors of the economy with compatibility (correspondence) levels in the following way:

- the economy of physical production (*Compatibility Level One*): sectors producing material (physical) goods, including manufacturing, agriculture, construction; sectors that serve to deliver material goods to consumers (transportation, postal service and telecommunications serving businesses); trade sectors connected with the production process (retail, food service industry, purchasing, distribution and logistics, production of semi-finished goods.

- the non-production economy comprises the following sectors:

Compatibility Level Two: credit, finance and insurance sectors;

Compatibility Level Three: the service sectors, including public utilities and housing, consumer services, consumer transportation, postal services and telecommunications;

Compatibility Level Four: federal and regional government and defense;

Compatibility Levels Three, Six, and Seven: social services, including public healthcare (Level 3), culture and art (Level 6), education, science and scientific support (Level 7).

Interaction enables the national economy as a whole to regulate itself and to generate organic interaction between its components.

There are two types of entities (substructures) constituting the structure of the national economy: economic entities (substructures) responsible for operation of all the economic units (players) in the national economy and non-economic entities (substructures) which define the operation of non-economic players such as culture, art, education, and so on. Analyzing the latter is widely believed to be of interest in the context of economics only so far as these players (units) or their interactions and interconnections affect the operation of the national economy. In my view, the time has come to move on to interaction between structures (substructures and entities) in the same plane of time and content. Then, according to the compatibility theory [4], non-economic agents and substructures (of the second type) will begin to exert a constant influence on the economic entities and substructures (of the first type). This will be possible if the consumer value of a product is defined by the product's quality (values, the things the product stands for), i.e. with a synthetic economy, and if the economic environment created will encourage producers to produce new environmentally friendly products (and technologies) voluntarily.

Swedish scientists proposed the interaction marketing concept in the late 1980s. We set out the core idea of interaction marketing above (the idea that marketing management should focus not on finding a comprehensive marketing solution so much as on building a relationship with the customer and other parties involved in the sales process). In this context, relationships become the most important resource a business organization can have along with its material and financial assets, human and other resources. Relationships as a result of effective interaction in this case become a product integrating intellectual and information resources – the main factors that ensure continuity of free market interactions. This is what gives such a great importance to economic relationships (universal and closely intertwined targets for each level) between components of the national economy, their hierarchy and priority of higher compatibility (correspondence) levels over lower levels when dealing with the questions "what, where and when" shown in the structural model in Fig. 1.

Let us write down the full spectrum of the economy of interaction as a combination, as a sum of seven levels of the economy:

$$E = (E_1, E_2, E_3, E_4, E_5, E_6, E_7),$$

where E_1 is the production economy, E_2 the financial economy, E_3 is the social economy, E_4 is the political economy E_5 is the cultural economy, E_6 is the global economy, and E_7 is the innovation economy. The full spectrum of the economy comprises and unites all seven levels of the economy, and all processes that affect the various levels and the overall economy as a whole.

For each level, we can introduce a numeric parameter for the aggregate size of an economy of specific type, $E_i = 1, ..., 7$:

$E\_i = V\_i \cdot Pi(price/quality)$,

where V_i stands for the gross product produced by the specific economy, and $Pi(price/quality)$ represents the value of the product it generates. We note that this calculation of the overall size of an economy is comprehensive, taking into account both specific products (goods) produced by the economy and their value. For example, the Soviet Union produced certain material goods, such as flannel shirts, but their value was lower than that of imported denim pants.

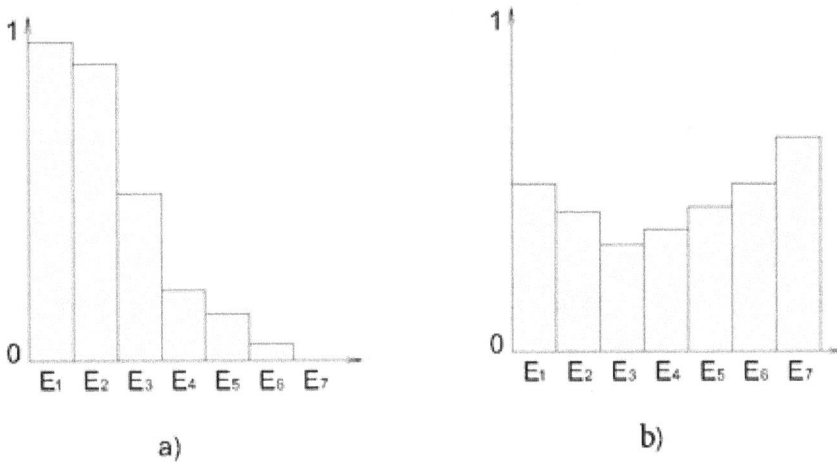

Fig. 4.

Figure 4 shows the various possible states of the economy. We range all economies from 1st to 7th as a horizontal bar chart, with the height of each bar representing the cumulative size of $E_i, i = 1, ..., 7$, normalized, i.e. proportionately adjusted so that the largest possible value is 1. So, Figure 1a represents an undeveloped manufacturing economy. For example, Economies E_1 (the economy based around manufacturing) and (the fi E_2 nancial services economy) generate a large aggregate product, i.e. these two sectors of the economy produce a large amount of added value, whereas economies E_5 (the cultural economy), E_6 (the global economy, including exports that cross sectoral boundaries) and E_7(the innovative economy) are still in an embryonic state.

Figure 4b represents an economy in an unstable state. In this state, resources that previously went into production of value added at levels E_1 , E_2 and E_3 were redirected into development of levels E_5 , E_6 and E_7 . This has resulted in growth of these levels, however, it did not provide adequate amounts of manufacturing product to these levels of the economy. To ensure stability in this situation, the aggregate volme of E_1 (Level One of the Economy) would have to be increased. One of the ways to achieve this would be by increasing the value of goods produced V_1 . And V_1 can be increased through innovations that a developed innovative economy E_7 can provide.

Let us take a closer look at processes through which economies $E_1, ..., E_7$ interact. Let the aggregate compatibility economy be in the initial state of

$E^{initial} = \left(E_1^{initial}, E_2^{initial}, ..., E_7^{initial} \right)$. In this case, the ending state

$E^{ending} = \left(E_1^{ending}, E_2^{ending}, ..., E_7^{ending} \right)$ for any level $E_1 = 1, ..., 7$ can be described as:

$$E_i^{ending} = E_i^{initial} - K(E_{i-1}, E_i, E_{i-1}) + Green\left(E_1, ..., E_j | j \leq i\right)$$
$$\cdot [A(E_{i-1}, E_i, E_{i-1}) -$$

$$K(E_{i-1}, E_i, E_{i-1}) +$$
$$S(Information(E_1, ..., E_7), Institution\left(E_j | j \geq i, ..., E_i\right))]$$

where $A(E_{i-1}, E_i, E_{i+1})$, are anabolistic (i.e. constructively metabolistic) processes that are defined by level E_i itself and its nearest neighbors E_{i-1}, E_{i+1}. These processes are either beneficial and constructive, or at least non-destructive (producing a zero effect). With a zero outcome of anabolistic processes, the economy begins to stagnate. So, global economy E_6 relies on constant growth of production economy E_1 , which has to be supported by growth of innovation economy E_7. If the growth is driven solely by expansion of production capacity rather than increases in quality, the overall economy becomes unstable, which may result in its inability to meet the exponentially growing needs of E_6 at the next stage of development 32[5].

Processes $K(E_{i-1}, E_i, E_{i+1})$ are catabolic, relying on level E_i itself and its immediate neighbors E_{i-1}, E_{i+1} to take place. The efficiency of catabolic processes depends to a great extent on the level of innovation available in each economy. For example, if waste recycling is done using methods that pollute the environment, catabolic processes are destructive. And conversely, if, for example, precious metals are extracted from discarded obsolete electronics, catabolic processes are constructive and positive.

$Green(E_1, ..., E_j | j \leq i)$ are bottom-up processes of the green economy. The product they generate is carried upward, therefore level i green economy relies on all the levels of the green economy below $E_1, ..., E_j | j \leq i$;

$S(Information(E_1, ..., E_7), Institution(E_j | j \geq i, ..., E_i))$ are processes that go with a systematic economy that depend on data-driven, green, and institutional economies:

---

[32] Morozov, V.A. Compatibility of socioeconomic systems – Moscow, Ekonomika, 2013 (in Russian) / Совместимость социально-экономических систем. М., Экономика, 2013

Information$(E_1, ..., E_7)$ are the processes taking place within the data-driven economy which rely on all levels of the economy $E_i, i = 1, ...,7;$

Institution$(E_j | j \geq i, ..., E_i)$ are top-down processes of the institutional economy. The higher levels set the rules by which the lower levels operate, and therefore the institutional economy at Level i depends on all the economies above it $E_j | j \geq i, ... E_i.$

We can see that in this model, all the processes in the overall economy rely on the green economy to take place Green$(E_1, ..., E_j | j \leq i)$. This means that no processes, whether anabolistic or catabolic, can take place and produce results effectively and efficiently, unless they have a well-developed green economy to draw upon.

Poor degree of development and lack of coordination between processes in the innovative economy E_7 and the political E_4 and production (manufacturing) E_1 economies can cause destructive processes at all levels of the overall economy. For example, development of the space program is a priority for humanity. However, there are many different technologies that can take humanity into space. Purely in energy terms, nucear technology would be among the most efficient ways to send vehicles into space. However, overemphasizing research in this field would result in a growing number of potentially hazardous nuclear power plants and other nuclear facilities (Germany, for example, has completely relinquished nuclear energy), increasing interest in nuclear power, and more countries starting their own nuclear programs, destabilizing the global political environment. This is why relatively green technologies were chosen for space exploration, technologies that can support the growth of the following economies: industrial E_1, financial E_2, social E_3, cultural E_5 (let us recall how many art projects are created to promote the green economy, ranging from the

Avatar blockbuster movie to the ubiquitous fascination with the "vintage" style which serves to give a new life to objects past the end of their "normal" useful life), and the innovation economy E_7.

For the same reasons, the processes underlying the institutional

$Institution(E_j | j \geq i, ..., E_i)$ and data-driven economy $Information(E_1, ..., E_7)$ come to depend on how well developed the green economy is. When drafting new legislative bills, rules and regulations, we must consider not only their possible effects on the economy on which they have a direct bearing, but also the fact that any law, any economic term or regulation creates repercussions at all levels of the contemporary economy. The success and effectiveness of processes that implement rules imposed by the higher levels of the economy on the lower levels depends to a great degree on how green these processes are.

We need to mention that these processes are all integral parts of the overall system. We know that systematic economics considers changes in economic parameters in four dimensions (in which economic organizations operate) that include the environment, processes, projects and actors. At the same time, the study of economics is also concerned with parameters of micro-, meso- and megaeconomies. The economy is a complex system that has multiple levels. Although all of these levels are inter-related and interdependent, the operating principles of households, business organizations and sectors are different from the principles guiding the development of the economy as a whole. And economic theory explores the issues of efficient use of resources at different levels. For example, microeconomics considers the interests of economic agents (players): entrepreneurs, business owners and businesspeople, hired employees, their needs and motives, market demand and consumer behavior, as well as other similar aspects. In other words, microeconomics deals with the patterns and "natural laws" of operation of individual economic agents (players) in a market economy, looks at prices and production volumes in specific markets, demand and supply factors for specific goods, the particulars of behavior of business organizations in different types of economic environments and conditions. Macroeconomics explores the system of trade and economic operation in the country's economy as a whole, looking at the aggregate income and employment data, at aggregated price movements, defining the government's economic policies and policy focus areas. It deals with concepts such as aggregate supply and demand, the domestic product, the country's financial system, inflation, the federal budget, macroeconomic weights and proportions, and regulation. Mesoeconomics, or medium-level economics (the terms "mesoeconomics" and "mesoeconomy" came into use relatively recently) studies the patterns of operation and interaction of specific sub-systems within a country's economy along geographic lines (considering regions, prefectures, cities, municipalities, etc.) or along sector lines (looking at manufacturing, agriculture, defense manufacturing, etc.) This book has a section below on geographic parameters of the economy. Megaeconomics (global economics) explores the key formats of international economic relations (such as international manufacturing and international cooperation, workforce and capital migration, international foreign exchange and international trade).

Both positivist and prescriptive analyses are used to explore economic phenomena and processes. These analyses are the purview of positivist and prescriptive economics, respectively. While positivist economics considers phenomena and processes the way they *are* (the actual state of things, the reality), prescriptive ("normative") economics tends to be concerned mostly with judgment about the way things *should* be. An example of a positivist (factual, experience-based) statement would be: "If the national currency depreciates, this is going to encourage an increase in exports." A prescriptive (judgmental) statement would be:

"Undergraduate students' stipend allowance should ensure a reasonable standard of living[33]."

As we summarize our discussion above, we can draw some conclusions:

1) We have provided definitions of interaction as it contributes to and detracts from socioeconomic and social and legal relations in society.

2) Based on the postulates of "compatible development of the society," we proposed a multilevel structural model describing the interactions economy that comprises the key types of economy (22 types altogether).

3) We consider mutual influences and preeminence of certain types of economy within the structural model in the study of a simulated economic system that includes the green economy as a key development vector. We identified the priorities of different types of economy within this system.

4) To achieve an effective and efficient itneraction between different types of economy, it is important to follow a consistent policy targeting a non-contradictory set of targets and performance indicators (as well as the conditions necessary for achieving those targets) across all levels of the economy in all federal and regional development programs, plans and incentives.

5) Interaction between the elements of the national economy must not be a one-off incident, but must rather be continuous, recurrent and constant; it must not be the result of forced action, but rather a self-organizing operating principle. The key condition here is to shape development plans and development programs for the national economy starting from the upper levels of economy, rather than

---

[33] Макконнелл К., Брю С. Экономикс: принципы, проблемы и политика. – М., 1993. – С. 23 / McConnel, K., Bru, C. Economics: Principles, Issues and Policies. – Moscow, 1993. P. 23 (in Russian)

allocating uncertain leftover resouces for them (while reducing the effects of personal idiosyncracies and self-serving motives of government officials and agencies).

6) And finally, but crucially, it is important to use a systematic approach to long-term planning and forecasting and strategic aministration. This is the basis for economic ideology – the vital and mental economics *(economics of the future)* that defines the forward path for all types of economy, adjusting development vectors for each of them in the process of meeting long-term targets and desired sociopolitic and cultural outcomes (including those that have to do with world outlook and the fundamental philosophical paradigm).

This section enables us to provide a preliminary definition of the interactions economy as a combination of production-based, non-production based and inter-functional economies. In other words, the interactions economy implies compatible interconnections, mutual influences and partnership between mineral resource and processing sectors, the service sector and multifunctional economy that define the material and consumer level of the life and operation of society, which result from its spiritual orientation and scientific and moral development.

List of Sources:

1. Словарь логики. Logic/Sovmestimost-348.html. / Dictionary of Logic. Compatibility (in Russian)

2. Бондаренко О.(серия книг) Философия единства,Бишкек,2000 / Bondarenko, O. (a series of books) Philosophy of Unity. - Bishkek, 2000 (in Russian)

3. Маслоу А. Мотивация и личность.   3-е изд. Спб.: Питер, 2003. / Maslow, A. Motivation and Personality. 3rd Ed. - St. Petersburg: Piter, 2003 (in Russian)

4. Макконнелл К., Брю С. Экономикс: принципы, проблемы и политика. – М., 1993. – С. 23. / McConnell, K., Bru, C. Economics: Principles, Issues and Policy. – Moscow, 1993. – P. 23 (in Russian)

5. Морозов В.А. Совместимость социально-экономических систем. М., Экономика, 2013. / Morozov, V.A. Compatibility of Socioeconomic Systems. – Moscow, Economics, 2013 (in Russian)

6. Панов П.В. Институты, идентичности, практики: теоретическая модель политического порядка. М.: РОССПЭН, 2011. / Panov, P.V. Institutions, Identities, Practices: A Theoretical Model of Political Order. - Moscow, ROSSPEN, 2011 (in Russian).

7. Структура национальной экономики.Реформы в экономике России.qrandars.ru>struktura-nacionalnoy-ekonomiki.html / Structure of the national economy. Reform of the Russian Economy. qrandars.ru>struktura-nacionalnoy-ekonomiki.html (in Russian)

8. С.Фишер,Р.Дорнбуш, Р.Шмалензи.Экономика.М.Дело.2001. / Fischer S., Dornbusch R., Schmalensee, R. Economics. Moscow, Delo, 2001 (in Russian).

9. Ханингтон С. Столкновения цивилизаций. М. 1998. / Huntington, S. Clash of Civilizations. Moscow, 1998 (in Russian).

2.4 Interaction between Commercial and Government Structures

Concerted actions, well-coordinated intentions and steps taken by all economic players based on a consensus of economic interests that do not go against socio-ecological, administrative and legal and regional and cultural policies and interests of the government and the people, forming the foundation for interaction, multilateral links and relations and multidirectional influences within the economy.

Developing the interaction mechanism, interaction format and interaction method constitute the content of the interaction process. The key goal of the government in interactions is to expand the benefits that private enterprise can bring society. The government can achieve this goal either by creating effective incentives for entrepreneurs and for the private sector in general to provide these benefits, or by setting up regulation in a way that would make it mandatory for the private sector to produce and deliver these benefits to society. On the one hand, this helps to achieve a certain level of economic freedom for business owners, entrepreneurs and the private sector in general. On the other hand, self-regulation forces come into play, further fine-tuned through careful regulatory action by government agencies, legislatures, and other regulators.

Here are the main principles and typical features of interaction:

- parties involved in interactions must be in compliance with applicable laws and regulations, must be authorized to do what they are doing, and should not engage in anything illegal;

- preserving consensus and keeping peace among the participants in the process of economic interaction;

- the players assume mutual liability (legal, economic, financial) and responsibility (social and moral) for one another;

- there is a mechanism in place that provides bilateral motivation for the parties to interact in ways that promote development of socioeconomic processes while making sure the country's resources are used efficiently.

Interaction between organizations is possible in the following contexts:

- practical implementation of government policy in manufacturing, finance and foreign trade;

- government system (federal and regional) for purchasing goods and services from the private sector of the national economy;

- organization of private-public partnerships to run commercial projects;

- use (or lease) of municipal and federal (government) property;

- allocating foreign trade quotas to business organizations;

- overcoming barriers to starting and operating one's own business and barriers to more people doing so;

- creating a natural competitive free-market environment for all businesses and commercial organizations that takes into account the specifics of the regional infrastructures, and especially a rational social infrastructure conducive to doing business more efficiently. Some of the things already being done in this area include support for the creation and development of social partnership (as adjusted for national and historic specifics) and a system for the training of professional entrepreneurs. Creating the right environment is an essential and crucial task of government agencies and offices, especially the right environment for innovation, supporting not only the supply, but also the demand for improved, new products.

When taken together, the principles, formats and ways of organization mentioned above represent the mechanism of interaction between private businesses and government and municipal agencies and organizations; this mechanism is the key driving force for development of the nations' overall economy. The operation of this mechanism is most evident in the military industrial complex, where government bureaucracy and business owners support and reinforce each other, using their joint efforts to define the need for different types of armaments. This is probably the appropriate place to describe a typical marketing relationship, which provides the following benefits:

- achieving lower costs, especially customer acquisition costs;

- a business organization enjoys a growing number and value of sales, because regular customers, the organization's patrons, are increasing their spending at an accelerated rate, and the net profit exceeds discounts offered to this customer category. Losing this customer segment would mean forgoing higher profits available to the business organization;

- the business organization gains a key group of customers that offers it a convenient market for testing and introducing new products or new offers, while incurring a lower risk, which reduces uncertainty for the firm as a whole;

- the business organization benefits from building a barrier to competitors' entry to the market by maintaining a steady customer base; additionally, having a base of satisfied customers is key to employee retention.

Relationship marketing can bring the following benefits for the consumer:

- close interaction of customers with the company, which can bring psychological benefits (customers get to interact with the same employees; they do not have to get used to or adjust to new people every time they contact the company);

- social benefits (establishing rapport, friendly rotations with employees);

- interaction with the business firm, which brings economic benefits among others (including discounts and so on);

- the service provider adapting the service to each customer based on a long history of cooperation (doing business) with the customer.

As a reminder, relationship marketing is based on the following key principles:

- a focus on a long-term relationship rather than one-off transactions, and consequently, an emphasis on customer retention rather than customer acquisition;

- finding an economic rationale for customer retention; this would include targeting the higher-margin customers (customer segments);

- a stronger focus on quality than in conventional marketing;

- using a broader marketing toolset in relationship marketing, because the conventional marketing toolset (the four P's: price, product, promotion, and place) is not adequate for building a long-term relationship with the customer;

- internal marketing (aspects of marketing directed at the company's own employees) as an important component of relationship marketing.

For many industries, relationship marketing is a defining factor in strategic financial and economic partnerships.

We identify the following parties (participants) in interactions, from largest to smallest:

- associations and unions of companies and businesspeople grouped together along geographic and sector lines, as well as political and/or ethnic lines, as a result of lobbying efforts or for lobbying purposes;

- large corporate centers, corporate groups and business organizations serving multiple companies;

- separate smaller business organizations.

Representatives that result from such processes of association (chambers of commerce, unions, associations, councils) serve to express the coordinated interests of business owners and entrepreneurs of all types and size. This works in a different way in every country; however, it is the authorities, the government, the political regime currently in power that determine whether these representatives are viable and effective and how effective they are. Being viable and effective can be defined as having the social, political, financial and economic power to effect (to implement) the social development of the country's economy and the economy of the community present in that country. This power enables the representatives to prepare and develop the key decisions and recommendations for specific sectors of the economy; to help their constituent members (business organizations, corporations) to promote their product and bring them to the market, to protect their interests in their interactions with the government, government agencies, regional and municipal authorities, trade unions or other parts of society. Companies that benefit from this promotion and help with bringing their products to the market can be engaged in industry, agriculture, trade and the service sector. As a general rule, the government and the private sector (private businesses and entrepreneurs) always have both mutually conducive and contrary functions, and their work tends to be both complementary and conflicting.

Interaction between private business organizations and government agencies has been poorly developed: it was underdeveloped in the period of transition [from command to market economy] and is underdeveloped still for a number of reasons, which are, to some extent, the result of a worsening crisis of foreign policy, and include:

- an inflexible and consequently ineffective tax policy;

- business regulations now in effect are ineffective or counter-productive, as they were approved as a result of lobbying by business tycoons (the oligarchs) pursuing their narrow interests (one of the problems is that regulations often fail to consider social aspects of economic activities);

- inflexible and prohibitive interest rates on available bank loans;

- many business organizations do not have sufficient capital (much of their plant and equipment are obsolete and heavily depreciated); working capital is also a problem;

- customers' and business partners' limited ability to pay for a business organization's products and services (and unfavorable terms of trade offered by large businesses);

- lack of markets or government/municipal orders for the broader business community (all available government orders are already spoken for because of corruption and nepotism);

- high transportation costs;

- nepotism and corruption run rampant at government and municipal agencies, with many businesses in Russia's regions falling under the control of criminals, with the connivance and outright support of various law enforcers;

- no duly constituted and legally operating businesses are allowed to engage in constructive dialogue with the authorities (government agencies, municipalities, etc.);

- a growing number and rising activity of natural monopolies trying to set higher prices on their products and services;

- the government is doing all manner of things in the sphere of innovation, including creating a supply of innovation, except for playing its key role of creating demand for innovation (through demand for new, advanced, high-tech products).

If the government, the authorities were to narrow the necessary breadth of interaction, they would be essentially shooting themselves in the foot, undermining their own prospects for success and prosperity.

Forums, conventions and meetings of various business alliances, as well as meetings of their governing bodies (committees) play an important role in consolidating the efforts of business owners and their interaction; the meetings should include banks focusing on specific industries as well as those serving a range of industries. Unfortunately, various expert boards and advisory councils are often put together in the "old way," usually with committee members drawn from different sectoral government ministries and agencies without any involvement of executives or owners of major business corporations. The current effective disenfranchisement of business associations has its roots in the transition period, when newly private companies were established from the ground up (and were small) or were spun off Soviet-era government-owned giants, making many industries highly fragmented. The richest business elite, the owners and executives of large consolidated corporations, actually does not need any corporate associations, nor are they interested in creating a political party to promote and defend their interests, because they already have informal direct access to the Russian government and Russian leadership, which also have no need for establishing any business associations. And only those businesspeople and business organizations that have no informal access to senior government officials need to organize, to form associations and unions which would:

- protect the rights and interests of association members at government agencies and legislatures;

- regulate and support interaction between private businesses and government agencies and legislative bodies;

- help member companies to diversify and coordinate their activities, including their operations on foreign markets;

- consolidate legal protection and create a regularly updated body of essential business and legal information for member companies and organizations.

Russia is still lacking an effective working system that would enable interaction between the state, the government, and private business, because existing business associations and unions are too fragmented, too competitive, too localized and too intent on vying for supremacy in representing the country's businesspeople and in having direct access to government officials and legislators, causing these associations to be entangled in political strife. Government officials find this situation highly satisfactory, and do what they can to maintain this fragmentation to be able to impose their will on relatively small business associations. Real democratic changes in Russia would result not so much in financial stability imposed from above as in an ability to offer Russia and its whole nationwide community a development model that would integrate, in a cohesive social and economic environment, regions that have economies of different sizes and compositions and offer wide social and cultural diversity. Russian regions must be allowed, like the constituent regions (states, prefectures) of other countries, to pursue their regional needs and interests before they have to concern themselves with national economic interests. To achieve this, they would have to engage in "lateral" cooperation with other regions as their equals, augmented by "vertical" cooperation from the federal government. At this time, the federal government does not have enough resources to finance all the federal programs in all the regions as mandated by the federal government and national legislature. Actual allocation of funds for development programs is done without a transparent public discussion and outside the legislative guidelines (boundaries), and is guided by different criteria from those mentioned above. To enable this horizontal interaction between regions, some of the available financial resources will need to be channeled into improving the tax base of Russia's regions so they would reduce their dependence on financial aid coming from the central (federal) government.

This section provides a brief look at the elements of interaction between businesses (their owners, entrepreneurs) and the government, as well as discussing interactions between the federal government (and other federal branches of power) and regional authorities and regional government agencies. We also consider the role of interactions between business markets and the non-productive, social economy, for society as a whole. The latest theories of economic science and contemporary economic practice focus on the social contract between business and society, the social partnership. To improve the quality of interaction in a way that can benefit both parties involved in the interaction, they turn to social cooperation. A. Mueller-Armack, one of the authors of the social market economy concept, says that a social market economy can be defined as an idea of introducing political order for the purpose of uniting a society that is based on competition, private enterprise and private initiative with social progress that depends on the productivity of the market economy (through creation of a comprehensive and multi-aspect system of social security)[34].

List of Sources:

1. Жильцов Е.Н., Егоров Е.В. Экономика и управление социальной сферой. –М: Издательско- торговая корпорация «Дашков и К», 2015 / Zhiltsov E.N., Egorov E.V. Economics and Managing the Social Services. – Moscow: Dashkov and Co. Publishing and Trading Company, 2015

---

[34] Muller – Armack, A. Soziale Marktwirtschaft// Handwoerterbuch der Sozialwissenschaften. Bd.9. Stuttgart, u.a., 1965.

2. Козлов А.А. Организация эффективного взаимодействия государственных органов и предпринимательских структур. Docme.ru>doc/235124/organizaciya.. gosudarstvennyh… / Kozlov, A.A. Organization of Effective and Efficient Interaction Between Government Agencies and Private Businesses. Docme.ru>doc/235124/organizaciya.. gosudarstvennyh… (in Russian)

3. С.Фишер,Р.Дорнбуш, Р.Шмалензи.Экономика.М.Дело.2001. / Fischer S., Dornbusch R., Schmalensee, R. Economics. Moscow, Delo, 2001 (in Russian).

4. Широкова Г.В. Управление изменениями. Хрестоматия. - С-Пб: Издательство «Высшая школа менеджмента», 2010 / Shirokova, G.V. Managing Change. A Reader. – St. Petersburg, Higher School of Management, 2010 (in Russian)

5. Muller – Armack, A. Soziale Marktwirtschaft// Handwoerterbuchder Sozialwissenschaften. Bd. 9. Stuttgart u.a., 1965.

CHAPTER 3

CREATING AND MONITORING A COMPATIBLE ENVIRONMENT: MECHANISMS AND INDICATORS

3.1 Values-Based Government Administration

Since the 1990s Russian has experienced pluralism; equal rights for alternative forms of ownership of the means of production; freedom for entrepreneurs; the free movement of goods, services and financial resources; new opportunities for cross-border trade and investment; and the privatization of much of the state sector. This led to the emergence and dynamic growth of a private sector economy, a vigorous flow of goods, the appearance of competition and more complex economic infrastructure, free market pricing, and the digitalization of much economic activity. Changes in the system of ownership lead in turn to changes in structure of government administration. The state has had to gradually move from direct management of the economy to the regulation of economic processes.

In a competitive economy, there are fewer constraints on the market than in a planned system. The exchange of goods and services is no longer governed by an individual's personal status, while production responds to consumer demand as measured by citizens' ability to pay for goods with money, which serves as an impersonal intermediary in any transaction. When economic activity takes place under conditions of market competition, an enormous number of buyers and sellers are involved. In a sophisticated mixed economy, however, there is still a place for the state sector, which plays no small role in allowing it to function. As long as there is government property, there must also exist a corresponding system of government organs that branches out to manage it, taking on both executive and allocative functions. Here the state applies both economic and non-economic (administrative) methods in exercising to the full its rights as owner. Within this sector, a distinction is made between state enterprises – which are not subject to privatization and act as monopoly suppliers whose principal client is the state itself – and others. Such enterprises are directly subordinated to the corresponding ministries or other executive organs of the central government. Their role is to provide basic infrastructure of significance to the country as a whole and they operate primarily under a regime of fixed prices; the defense industry and some other enterprises also fall into this category. These enterprises are not commercial entities, but they have great social significance. Government bodies must therefore constantly monitor their activities. Other state-owned enterprises may be classified as commercial, as they are required to finance themselves in a competitive market environment. The government provides these enterprises with the right to make free use of its property. The state's property fund thus only manages a portion of its holdings, as it has no right to interfere in the operations of such enterprises.

With respect to other sectors of the economy, the state – that is, its organs and officials – acts as a regulator. This does not mean that the state has lost its authority. Government regulation serves to protect citizens from the possible harmful consequences of economic activity, to safeguard the rights of consumers in the face of illegitimate actions taken by commercial structures, to stabilize macroeconomic processes, and to establish official reserves.

Article 2 of the Constitution of the Russian Federation proclaims that the highest value is the human being and obligates the state to protect the rights and interests of its people. At this stage and for the foreseeable future, goal formation in government administration should take place with reference to quality of life: strengthening the rule of law and public order, satisfying citizens' fundamental material and intangible needs, and upholding the right of the population to a dignified human existence. During every period of the past two centuries, the state's goals have remained essentially the same. For the most part, government authorities have never seen the population as a motivating force in goal formation; as a rule, it has been assigned an instrumental role in the process of achieving subjectivist goals, with indeed little attention paid to the *cost* of those resources. In Russian history, the mechanism that determines domestic and international economic policy has always operated far from public view.

State bodies are known to have three types of goals: task goals, orientation goals and goals related to self-preservation. Orientation goals should be consistent with the overall interests of the members of the collective that has been made responsible for reaching the assigned task goals. Defining the content of goals of this type can be very complex, as the motivations of individual actors within the administration can be quite diverse and difficult to identify. If state authority is viewed as a collection of tightly intersecting and interacting organizations, we may say that orientation goals should be aligned with social (task) goals, regardless of the sphere of management authority. This amounts to correctly answering the question: what are the ultimate consequences of the functioning of this organization (collective), of the actions taken by each official and employee? A profound value socialization of orientation goals requires the establishment of a direct dependence between the material, formal, political and moral status of a government employee or entire collective on the one hand, and the ultimate outcome of their activity, as tested by time, on the other. The strategic goals of government administration can be harmonized with values in the course of discussions organized by an official body. It is important to resolve any contradictions between the views of the participants, a process facilitated by the classification and systematization of values.

The process of forming social, value-based orientation goals in a collective can on occasion run into certain difficulties. Problems with overcoming narrow departmental or local interest become apparent precisely when orientation goals are not aligned with the social nature of the task goals, which are displaced and supplanted. Under these circumstances, administration becomes an end in itself, and the actual purpose for which the administrative body was established takes on simulated forms that serve to cover the pursuit of far removed or secondary questions. It is important not to lose sight of the overarching purpose of government administration in the mass of individual, regional or local sub-goals – something that we have seen from time to time in the implementation of various economic policies. The concept of public value in government administration first emerged a quarter century ago. Its creator, Mark Moore, an American professor from Harvard University, detailed his vision in the work "On Creating Public Value: Strategic Management in Government". This was devoted to a single fundamental thesis: that organizations in both the government and business sectors share a common reason for existence, namely, that they both constitute and create a certain value for all citizens.[35] The word "value" is known to take on two different meanings in academic literature. In the wider sense, as applied to administration of a country, region or local government, it refers to the importance of some object, one whose significance is determined by the people who live in the given territory, or by those who make use of that object because its characteristics are consistent with the personal priorities that shape their behavior, goals and constraints, as well as the motives behind their decisions.[36]

Let us examine the case of "public values" in the administration of territory under a developed democracy, where users lack the right to refuse to pay for the production of public-sector goods and services, but do have the right not to make use of them. Defining the value of the work performed by a government body is not easy. Nevertheless, a choice is made about the goods required by society, although under current circumstances in Russia that choice may be coerced. Even so, it provides a basis for conclusions about the value of a government structure's function. The choice of good and the value of its producer are shaped by the means used to take a collective decision. Such decisions are taken in accordance with the views of the majority; other citizens may be opposed, but are still required to pay for plans that have been approved. For all who participate in the process of carrying out those plans and decisions – including the employees of government organs and their subdivisions, agencies and institutions – it is essential that the outcomes of their work conform in fact to the list of tasks drawn up and approved by the majority. Moreover, those outcomes make it possible to demonstrate to dissatisfied citizens not only the value created in the form of public goods and services, but also the value of

---

[35] Mark Moore, Sanjeev Khagram. On Creating Public Value: What Business Might Learn from Government about Strategic Management. Corporate Social Responsibility Initiative working paper, No. 3. March 2004, 224–225.

[36] V.P. Kaisarov. "Ценностно-ориентированный подход в стратегическом управлении крупным городом" ["A Values-Based Approach to Strategic Management of a Major City"], Vestnik S.-Peterburgskogo universiteta Series 5: Economics, no. 4 (2008): 129

government activity. In consequence, the outcomes of planned future administration, whether at the national level or for part of the country's territory, will be valued more highly than they were at the stage when a collective decision was taken, since it is now far easier to justify the costs. General outlays on government administration are, of course, covered out of taxes, which are involuntary, and also at the expense of the public's rights and freedoms. Citizens are not in a position to refuse payment of taxes even if they make no use of public goods. Conclusions can now be drawn about the creation of a genuine public value, if citizens are confident that the outcome – the value of the activities of government bodies – outweighs the value of their tax obligations and limitations on their rights and freedoms. In such cases, the implementation of a national strategy or policy at the federal, regional or municipal level is productive. Schematically, this can be illustrated as an alignment between the actions of government employees, politicians' preferences and citizens' preferences, which yields a set of perceptions about the value of the work done by government employees, the value of public goods, and the outcomes of social choice (Fig. 9). In speaking of compatibility between values and goals in government administration, we can say that if the former constitute an infinite imagined future, the latter cover a finite and planned future. Progress towards goals can be measured with the help of specified indicators, whereas a value must be assessed in comparison with others (for example, other countries or territories). A value, then, should apparently be seen as a standard for measuring the impact of regulating influences in national and regional policy. In the previous section, where we described the role of values in economic policy, composite indicators were sufficient to provide a grasp of how Russia performs relative to other countries on the resolution of complex issues related to the quality of life and meeting public needs.

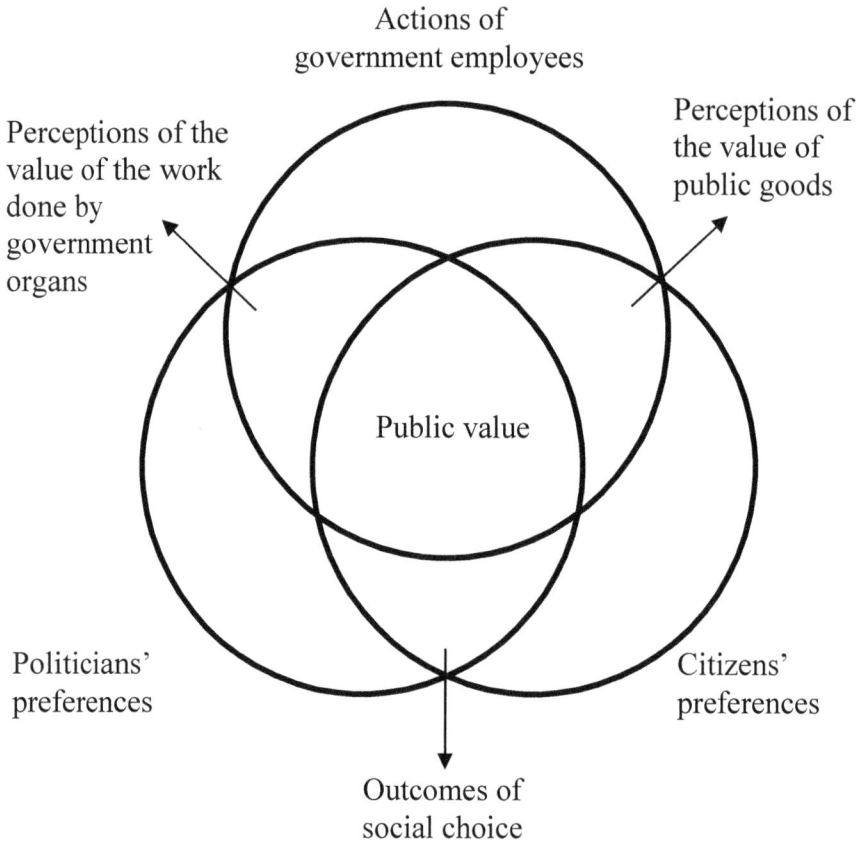

Fig. 5. The creation of public value

In Russia's case, it has been proposed that this echelon of composite indicators needs to be probed more deeply and made more concrete where they emerge directly from the results of government management of the economy. Among the basic indicators today the reasons for Russia's sharp setbacks can be seen in low life expectancy and per capita income. Russia ranks close to last among Eurasian countries in terms of life expectancy (due to increased alcoholism and stress). The country has close to a million abandoned children, many of whom stand in need of adoption and a proper upbringing. When it comes to the nation's health, the overall sense of crisis is at least as great as in politics and economics: the birth rate is low by European standards but accompanied by an "African" death rate caused by illness and external factors (accidents, murders, alcoholism, etc.). Corruption and extortion lead to violence in society and a whole range of crimes, notably theft and robbery. As some of these issues have already been discussed above, here we will examine environmental performance: the country's ecological condition and management of natural resources are measured on the basis of 22 indicators in ten categories. These reflect various aspects of the environment and the resilience of its ecosystems; the preservation of biological diversity; measures to combat climate change; public health; economic activity and its impact on the environment; and the effectiveness of government environmental policy. In 2016, these indicators were compiled for 180 countries, which were assigned rankings. Finland had the top-ranked environmental performance. Russia ranked 32nd out of a total of 180, between Azerbaijan and Bulgaria, a 24% improvement over the preceding two years[37]. There was, however, no noticeable decline in the number of accidents in the oil and gas industry across our vast country, or in fires and pollution from waste products. If the preceding indicator is responsible for close to half of health impacts, the next to be considered – food security – is responsible for more than 30%. It is also considered a major indicator of a country's socio-economic development. International experts define food security as a state in which all people at all times are physically, socially and economically able to access food in amounts that meet their needs and are sufficient for them to carry on an active and healthy lifestyle. Analysis of food security was carried out for 109 countries in 2016. The United States topped the rankings at the start of the year.

---

[37] "Рейтинг стран мира по уровню экологической эффективности в 2016 году." ["Countries of the world ranked by environmental performance in 2016."] http://gtmarket.ru/news/2016/01/29/7292. Centre for Human Technologies, 29.01.2016.

Russia ranked 43rd out of 109[38], between China and Belarus, down three places over the past two years. According to expert assessments, today roughly 5% of the Russian population does not receive a sufficient volume of wholesome food to carry on an active and healthy lifestyle.

The process of combating corruption in a country starts with government administration. In reviewing the Corruption Perceptions Index, it should be noted that this is a composite measure incorporating statistical data and information provided by international organizations. All of these sources measure the general incidence of corruption (frequency and/or size of bribes) in the state and business sectors and cover a large number of countries. The 2015 index was compiled for 168 countries and is based on data received from sources in the previous two years. Countries and territories are ranked on a scale of 0 (highest level of corruption) to 100 (lowest level of corruption) based on perceived corruption in the state sector. According to the data for 2015, the least corrupt country in the world is Denmark, which scored 91 out of 100. That year saw Russia improve its ranking to 119th with a score of 29[39], on a par with Azerbaijan, Guyana and Sierra Leone. Compared to previous years, Russia's score has improved by just two points and its significantly higher ranking reflects changes in other countries' performance. Among the countries that rank below Russia are Kazakhstan (123rd), Ukraine (130th), Tajikistan (136th), Uzbekistan (153rd) and Turkmenistan (154th). Lower-ranked countries, besides suffering from conflict, are also characterized by dishonest leadership, unreliable government structures (such as police and courts) and insufficiently independent media.

---

[38] "Economist Intelligence Unit: Рейтинг стран мира по уровню продовольственной безопасности в 2016 году." ["Countries of the world ranked by food security in 2016."] http://gtmarket.ru/news/2016/01/29/7291. Centre for Human Technologies, 29.01.2016.

[39] "Transparency International: Индекс восприятия коррупции 2015 года." ["Corruption Perceptions Index, 2015."] http://gtmarket.ru/news/2016/01/27/7287. Centre for Human Technologies, 27.01.2016.

Democratic countries, where respect for laws and regulations is profound, typically measure themselves on the Global Competitiveness Index. This index, together with the accompanying ratings, is based on the most extensive research available in the area of economic competitiveness. Information is aggregated into 12 pillars that shape national competitiveness: institutions, infrastructure, macroeconomic stability, health and primary education, higher education and training, goods and services market efficiency, labor market efficiency, financial market development, technological readiness, domestic market size, company competitiveness, and innovation potential. No one factor on its own can ensure a competitive economy. The impact of increased expenditures on education, for example, might be offset by an inefficient labor market or other institutional weaknesses that prevent graduates from finding work in their fields. The impact of each factor on a country's competitiveness depends on its starting conditions, on the institutional and structural factors that position it relative to other countries in terms of development. Russia today ranks 45th on this measure[40].

Today – as ever – the most immediate tasks in state building and public administration include setting the government's priorities in the development of intellectual, ethical, legal and managerial culture, as well as legislative and informational support for the development of cultural studies as a science and academic discipline via a major expansion of training (retraining) for government administrators in order to provide them with critical cultural understanding and prepare them for the challenges of globalization and formulating issues relevant to the culture of work and the parallel construction of an industrial society in Russia. This discipline is the chief source of innovations in cultural understanding, which provide the indispensable intellectual capital for competitive national development. Cultural studies create concepts, methods and research

---

[40] "Индекс глобальной конкурентоспособности." ["Global Competitiveness Index."] http://gtmarket.ru/ratings/global-competitiveness-index/info. Centre for Human Technologies, 09.09.2010 (most recent update 30.09.2015).

techniques; analyze the accumulated experience of national development and state-building practices; and generate conclusions and new strategies based on values, as well as forecasts that optimize the human being while ensuring a competitive, contemporary approach to social development.

For the purposes of state building and government administration, cultural studies cover the following areas and opportunities:

- profound and substantive goal formation, identification of strategic areas and the selection of timely priorities for national development, based on the history, theory and practice of national and global culture in various civilizations;

- formulation of invariant models, strategies for management and innovative approaches to life and public administration that can ensure positive trends in national development, labor force quality (with a role for anti-monopoly policy) and national competitiveness in the global economy;

- development of multi-functional programs to draw on the creative output of the country's academics and professionals, as well as national and international scientific achievements, in the process of state building and government administration;

- effective training and nurturing of administrators who have the broad base of cultural knowledge essential for taking decisions on government policy;

- development of scientifically sound forecasts of the country's future development, taking into consideration national value needs and interests, on the basis of a systematic cultural analysis of the distinguishing features, achievements, laws and trends of global development;

- constructive dialogue between cultures and civilizations in order to avert terrorism and conflict, facilitate international cooperation and promote interactions between cultures as a source of well-being for all.

A number of theoretical and methodological approaches to defining the effectiveness of government administration currently stand out. These include approaches based on: the concept of leadership; an extension of Weberian rational bureaucracy theory; the application of life cycle theory to performance effectiveness; a direct relationship between effectiveness and the professionalism of government organs; economic analysis that links improved effectiveness in government administration to the presence of a mechanism for inter–departmental competition, a system for applying innovation, and the socio-political accountability of government organs, above all to taxpayers; ecological models emphasizing that the outcomes of bureaucratic activity depend on the nature of the external environment (organizational ecology) and the ability of government organs to manage changes and innovation in order to adapt to those changes; and the concept of management quality (where within government organs a system is put in place to promote continuous improvement in processes and public-sector services).

The choice of what mix of approaches to use in defining the effectiveness of government administration in Russia in various time periods is affected by the country's enormous size: of its 85 constituent territories, more than half are comparable to mid-sized European countries. This forces us to pay particular attention to the methodology for territorial/regional administration, given the diversity of options that define an overall scheme for interregional interactions at various stages of the country's development. In our case, the choice should fall on a value-oriented approach to strategic management of a territory/region. The value-oriented approach to strategic management of a territory/region is based on the concept of public value, an idea that can be traced to "managerial" techniques. These have been widely popularized in practice in other countries, where there has been a trend away from administration and bureaucratic compulsion toward "cooperation and understanding"[41], both in business and in government, incorporating changes in management paradigms that date from the end of the 20th century. The diagram below illustrates the economic, social and systemic aspects of management that together form a values concept in the theory of enterprise management.

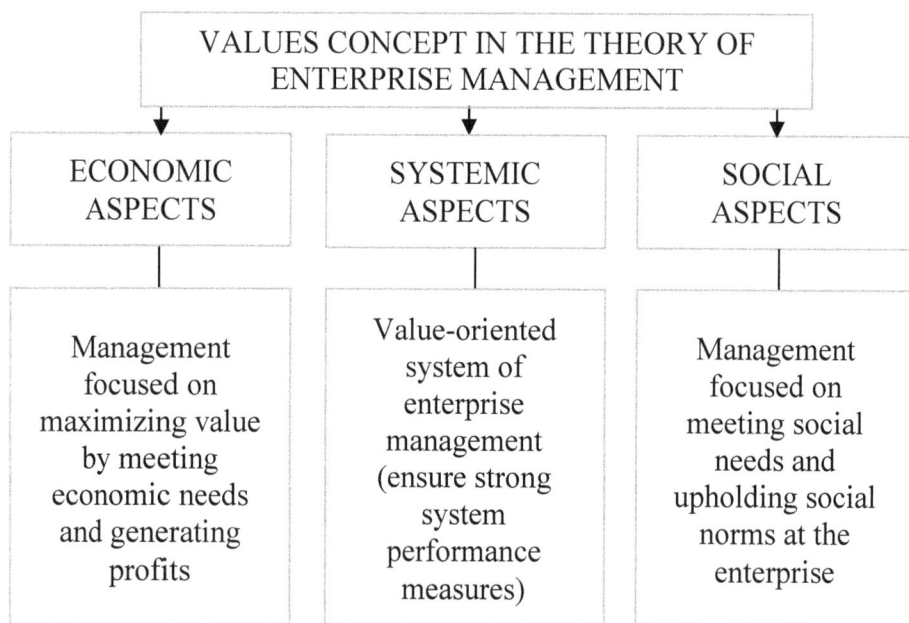

```
┌─────────────────────────────────────────────────────────┐
│         VALUES CONCEPT IN THE THEORY OF                  │
│            ENTERPRISE MANAGEMENT                          │
└─────────────────────────────────────────────────────────┘
```

ECONOMIC ASPECTS	SYSTEMIC ASPECTS	SOCIAL ASPECTS
Management focused on maximizing value by meeting economic needs and generating profits	Value-oriented system of enterprise management (ensure strong system performance measures)	Management focused on meeting social needs and upholding social norms at the enterprise

Fig. 6. Multiple aspects of management in a values-oriented enterprise

Three criteria distinguish the value-oriented approach from the traditional approach:

---

[41] Роберт С. Каплан, Дейвид П. Нортон, Организация, ориентированная на стратегию [Robert S. Kaplan, David P. Norton, The Strategy-Focused Organization] (Moscow: Olympus Business, 2004), 143–145.

- administrative activities are evaluated on the basis of outcomes that constitute a value for the population, rather than by the volume of resources developed or the number of tasks performed;

- feedback takes the form of dialogue or consensus, and is more than a formality;

- management actions are shaped by informal contacts and networks, in the absence of which they would be one-sided and unidirectional.

Values" in the territorial system aimed at, regional strategy (Public Values – standards and requirements formulated by society) include: basic social norms and standards; public participation in the process of collective choice and action; reference points in the strategic regional development model; a focus on outcomes ("developing the mix of goods") that benefit each resident, rather than a generic mix of static public goods and services; and a detailed presentation and disaggregation of strategic regional development goals.

In formulating a regional policy, issues related to goal-setting and their ties to the value-oriented approach are of special significance, since the goal concept and the interrelated notions of practicability, purpose and value provide the foundation for developing any territory system. In order to reach the intended goals, financial and non-financial indicators are developed for each one, together with a series of steps to be taken, including deadlines, budgets and assignments of responsibility. In the case of municipalities and rural settlements, four main components (outlooks) come into play: budget, population, internal processes and potential[42]. A sequence of actions with their associated deadlines is tied to the goals, as are a budget and specific accountabilities. In a system with balanced specifications, strategic goals feed into one

---

[42] Horváth & Partners, Внедрение сбалансированной системы показателей [Introducing a Balanced Scorecard] translated from German, 2nd ed. (Moscow: Alpina Business Books, 2006), 19.

another, as shown on cause-and-effect strategy maps. For some reason the term "strategy map" has come into Russian as "road map" – a somewhat different concept. Once a strategy map has been prepared, two or three specifications/indicators should be selected for use planning and tracking progress towards the strategic goals. A full description of the regional strategy requires that individual strategic goals be linked to another.

Introducing a balanced scorecard (BSC, a technique widely used by state planners in the USSR, although with a rather different focus) and applying modern technology together allow us to construct various possible development schemata. This strategy is incorporated into the regional socio-economic development program. Where the concept of public value is applied, it is essential to identify conflicts with the existing system of administration. These conflicts can be resolved through restructuring, for example, laws and regulations. Particularly important here is the choice of method for evaluating outcomes (possibly a BSC). A flexible basic set of balanced scorecard outlooks for the long- and medium-term administration of territories (regions) involves the interaction of four components, each of which is made up of strategic goals, indicators, target values and strategic actions. Those components are:

- a "Population" outlook, which details goals pertaining to the structure and needs of the population, set for the purpose of achieving general well being;

- a "Budget" outlook, which details goals that should be set so as to make effective use of budgetary funds;

- a "Processes" outlook, which details goals that support the achievement of goals in the "Population" and "Budget" outlooks;

- a "Potential" outlook, which details goals for developing that potential in accordance with the needs of a particular time period.

To implement a value-oriented approach, using the example of a territorial (regional) socio-economic development program, four elements (criteria) may be required:

- a flow chart whose content is shaped by the mix of strategic initiatives;

- a target section that includes a strategy map for the municipality (rural location) used to trace cause-and-effect relationships;
- a forecast and analysis section that includes separate development analysis and forecasts for various sectors of the economy and for each goal, broken down further by target indicators;

- an organizational section, detailing the sequence of actions to be taken, drawn up separately for each strategic goal, identifying the responsible parties and the system that will be used to evaluate their performance. Furthermore, various links to stakeholders in the region/territory should be active, rather than formalities, as in the traditional approach.

Such measures are useful, since in the process of applying the value concept authority becomes decentralized and monitoring can weaken, possibly with a negative effect on the quality of outcomes, since in this country activity revolves around an individual rather than an institution. For the purposes of value-based goal setting, the task today is to identify Russia-specific optimal ranges for choosing priorities. The goal set must consist of an optimal mix of measures for implementing value principles, including those related to autarky (self-sufficiency) and statism, corporatism and ideological considerations.

At this time, states operate on national models and the key question is how successfully those models perform in practice. Polemics about the choice of "correct" model for the state sector have ceased: even in Russia the issue has become a practical matter of trial and error. Nevertheless, certain general principles and structures of the national model remain in place. The fundamental principle is that no government can accept a large but inefficient and financially-burdensome state sector. If it is inefficient, it must be cut down in size to minimize the financial burden; if it is highly-efficient, it can play a very significant role in the national economy. Today there are three models for the state sector: the western European model (as in Portugal, France and a number of other countries); the North American model (US and Canada); and the Asian model (Japan and South Korea). The first is characterized by a large, highly-efficient and generously-financed state sector that covers a diverse range of industries. In the second model, the state sector is typically underdeveloped and inefficient, focusing on purely governmental functions such as defense and social infrastructure, with tight restrictions on financing. In both models there is a clear boundary between private-sector business and the state. In the third model, that boundary is blurred and the interests of the state and business are interwoven thanks to the exchange of representatives between government and corporate structures. Formally, the state sector in this model is of modest size, with the national government providing a noticeable degree of financial and organizational support. Each of the three models has its own distinguishing features shaped by history and geography.[43]

In concluding this section, it should be noted that the neo-institutional school of economics, which emphasizes limits to rationality in human behavior (North's "rules of the game"[44]), has made it essential to analyze both formal and informal institutional structures, leading to a new perception of government and territorial administration. Academics turned their attention to the human factor,

---

[43] Национальная промышленная политика конкурентоспособности: опыт Запада – в интересах России [National Industrial Competitiveness Policy: Applying Western Experience to Russia's Interests] (Moscow: Russian Academy of Sciences Institute of World Economy and International Relations, 2002), 278 pages.

[44] Douglass C. North, Institutions, Institutional Change and Economic Performance (Cambridge: Cambridge University Press, 1990), Russian translation by A.N. Nesterenko (Moscow, 1997), electronic publication: http://gtmarket.ru/laboratory/basis/6310, Centre for Human Technologies, 07.09.2013.

seen from a psychological point of view. This led to the examination of human beings (citizens, consumers, clients, voters and investors) as the focal center of new theories that have been applied, among other areas, to issues in federal and regional administration. Research confirms that individual priorities, internal convictions and various personal values have come to play a leading role in the study of management. As a result, over the past twenty years the concept of public values has gradually been incorporated into the strategic management of states and territories, in response to the actual values of the population. This helps government organs to become yet another institution that reflects popular preferences in the area of public goods and services. At the same time, government officials and employees (and their analogues in other public-sector bodies) must themselves respond to inner values: by doing so they reinforce the government's authority and increase the attractiveness of employment in the public sector.

3.2 Compatible Indicators and Interaction Factors

Different systems of metrics are available today to measure the performance of companies. One of the most up-to-date measurement systems, providing a broad range of metrics for comprehensive analysis and opportunities for further improvement is Balanced Scorecard (BSC). BSC is very popular around the world as a conceptual framework for management of strategy implementation, introduced by Drs. Robert Kaplan (of the Harvard Business School) and David Norton.[45] The essence of BSC (also known as SIM – a system of interconnected metrics) can be reduced to: (1) evaluation and assessment of financial and "soft," non-financial aspects of

---

[45] Роберт С. КАПЛАН, Дейвид П. НОРТОН. Сбалансированная система показателей. От стратегии к действию. М.: ЗАО «Олимп-Бизнес». 2003.

economic activity (the latter include human, organizational, information aspects and are described as "key efficiency indicators of business activity"); (2) formulating strategy from several different perspectives, setting strategic objectives and measuring the fulfillment of these objectives by metrics.[46] The main distinguishing feature of a balanced scorecard is its close connection with the business processes aiming to satisfy customers' needs, the processes in which all of the company's employees are involved. BSC (or SIM) guides management towards focus on rational and adequate strategic development and growth, in contrast to traditional management, which generally tends to overemphasize financial performance.

At the same time, balanced scorecard and similar evaluation systems were always developed with single companies in mind and included metrics designed to measure the business processes of one business organization (at the microeconomic level), only rarely rising above this level to address issues facing small clusters of business organizations. Now, at a time when integrative processes are becoming stronger, work is under way to develop metrics that would measure the performance of larger-scale entities, including municipalities, districts (counties) or regions (territories). Balanced budgets are prepared not only for the whole country, but also, very meticulously, for federal districts, regions, and "mega poles" (mega hubs), while there are no metrics to describe interactions of these systems. Therefore, these entities and their areas of operation, which belong in the socioeconomic, sociopolitical, religious, theological, cultural, philosophical outlook-related, scientific, educational, applied scientific (including innovation and implementation of new technologies) and educational spheres of societal progress, are largely left without a comprehensive and interconnected set of characteristics and metrics that would be collectively logical and interdependent, providing a reasonably complete picture of an entity's development over time and a sound evaluation of its

---

[46] Роберт С. КАПЛАН, Дейвид П. НОРТОН. Стратегические карты. Трансформация нематериальных активов в материальные результаты. М.: ЗАО «Олимп-Бизнес». 2004.

performance and efficiency. Their collective influences upon one another, their interactions would be a definitive "auditor" of how well these entities live up to their mission and how effective their strategies are, thereby providing an assessment of the progress of society as a whole.

We propose, taking into account our research presented in Exploring Compatibility,[47] to help in making a list of core and ancillary metrics, including subsystems making up an organization[48] and the social environment (without losing sight of the main player in all of this – the human being) to evaluate the performance of larger entities and groups: entire manufacturing and non-manufacturing sectors of economies, economic mega hubs and regions; national and international economies. A review of literature on the subject indicates that the balanced scorecard methodology (or the largely similar system of interconnected metrics) is not used at higher (macro) levels of economics, nor is it used in combined-factor models of macroeconomic analysis. In this connection, we believe it is advisable to use the proposed approach based on compatible interaction metrics (CIM) for developing a system that would be helpful in evaluating the socioeconomic, cultural and educational, scientific, research, and applied research and other aspects of operating efficiency of different entities and areas and spheres of society. This proposed evaluation system addresses not only the aspects and matters measured by BSC or SIM, but also the matters and aspects arising from interactions between the individual and society.

For this purpose, we have used the compatible model of interaction economy (figure in Section 2.2) we proposed above to identify and describe the key types of economics both corresponding to specific compatibility levels and "straddling," or integrating, different compatibility levels to match various kinds of relationships and interactions within society. We propose identifying metrics that

---

[47] Морозов В.А. Совместимость социально-экономических систем (основы теории совместимости). М, Экономика.2013.
[48] Клейнер Г.Б. Стратегия предприятия. М., Дело, 2008.

correspond to specific compatibility levels and that connect different levels as primary and secondary, or complementary, metrics. Primary metrics are defining for the entire period during which a specific goal is reached, whereas complementary metrics apply only for the duration of achieving (smaller) targets, which serve as milestones or components on the way towards reaching the overall goal.

In the comprehensive economics of interaction described above as a combination of seven economic levels:

$$E = (E_1, E_2, E_3, E_4, E_5, E_6, E_7),$$

[economic] efficiency is used to measure interconnections, reciprocal influence and interactions of the levels. Economic efficiency is treated both as the overall operating efficiency of a system and as the efficiency of its elements and factors affecting the overall system. We are going to provide two indicative examples of paradigms of interactive metrics (CIM) from business administration and social services. As we consider the efficiency of (and the efficiency of control over) an economic entity or system, the efficiency of its elements and relevant factors can be measured at different compatibility levels and also in areas crossing two or more levels. If we were to attempt to describe the efficiency (quality of compatibility) of the seven levels of interaction from a functional perspective, we could use evaluation of a developing (improving) organization management structure as an example (evaluation of this kind can be used for any micro- or meso- organization, i.e. a stand-alone organization or a group of organizations, a regional industrial hub or an industry within one region). The following function can be used to evaluate the compatibility (Sm) as a measure of efficiency of a new organization structure:

$$S_m = F(V_p; F_p; S_t; N_f; E_n; i_k; R_p)$$

Where we have used the primary metrics only, leaving all secondary metrics outs of the equation, to provide a "cleaner" example:

V_p for lost volumes of output;

F_p for lost revenue;

S_t for changes in employee compensation/payroll;

N_f for moneys lost to actions by fiscal authorities;

E_n for changes in ethnic composition of the workforce;

I_k for lost human capital;

R_p for product sales lost to innovation (both through competition and necessary upgrades).

The efficiency (effective compatibility) of an organization's management structure (Syc) can be recorded as an equation combining the organic component (k) and the mechanical component (Mk) as follows:

Syc = Ok / Mk= (flexibility + organicity)/(precision + technological efficiency) = 1;

$$S_m = e^{Vp} \times e^{Fp} \times e^{St} \times e^{Nf} \times e^{En} \times e^{Ik} \times e^{Rp}$$

S_m : Efficiency = 0 – incompatibility;

Efficiency = 1 – compatibility;

S_m values between $1 < S_m < 2$ represent evolutionary development;

S_m values of $2 < S_m < \infty$ reflect revolutionary development.

We will discuss, in greater detail, another example pertaining to non-productive (i.e. "social") economy – *the* compatibility of factors affecting the health of the public. As discussed above, compatibility is a type of a relationship between concepts on the one hand and statements and judgments on the other. Two concepts can be properly described as compatible if they have overlapping (partially matching) or identical (perfectly matching) semantic scope; in other words, compatible concepts have at least one component in common. At the same time, they can also be overlapping, subordinate or governing in respect of each other. Besides, two statements which can both be true (i.e. the fact that one of them is true does not preclude the other one from also being true[49]) are sometimes described as compatible.

The health of the public depends on many factors in our life, which may be compatible or contradictory (incompatible), slowing down our internal and external development both as individuals and as a society in which we live. These factors lie in different planes, different aspects of the personality of an individual (and society) and are determined by the current focus of the individual's (or society's) efforts, be it labor or recreation, studying or raising children, spiritual or physical growth and advancement.

Russian nationwide statistics over the past several years have consistently pointed to an unsatisfactory overall state of health of the Russian population. And yet, experts have only done pinpoint analysis of cause-and-effect relations, revealing the mechanisms underlying the perceptible deterioration of the health of the public.

Scientific and technological progress in the current state of technology is pushing society in a direction that is incompatible with supporting good human health and a healthy state of the environment. As we talk of environmental health, we often imply the

---

[49] Dictionary of Logic. Dictionary of Definitions by Efremova (in Russian) / Словарь логики. «Толковый словарь Ефремовой». enc-dic.comSovmestimost-348

state of the ecology, the environmental, natural conditions and factors, including the climate, the weather, the landscape, flora and fauna, and more recently also environmental pollution, and, more rarely, what we all need to do about it. However, more recently, the idea of a "green economy" has been gaining wider recognition. At the same time, the health of the public also depends on the sociopolitical environment, the laws and regulations supporting and governing its operation, and effective hierarchy and lateral structure of power, administrative coordination of different regions, and, finally, the ideological environment of interactions and interrelationships within society that determine the health of the people, or, in other words, a compatible condition of society.

During the Perestroika of the mid-to-late 1980s, as the old laws and regulations were going by the board, and new laws to replace them had yet to be enacted, the government apparatus was removed from control, coordination and regulation of economic processes. Vertical (hierarchical) lines of command and power have fallen apart, creating the impression of permissiveness, a pervasive feeling that local politicians could get away with anything, inciting separatism along ethnic and regional divides. Lifting the government monopoly on distillation and sale of liquor and production of essential medical drugs undermined social balance and, as a consequence, led to a deterioration in the health of the people. Investment funds for the general public turned out to be a sham, while the real value of privatization vouchers distributed to the people was negligible when people attempted to sell them to intermediaries; this combined with a confiscatory monetary reform depriving the people of their savings. The privatization undermined the trust of the general public in the government, its agencies and administrative offices. All these factors are exacerbated by organizational, legal and socioeconomic factors that include:

- Collapse of the USSR economy, 50% decline in industrial output;

- Transfer of industrial fixed assets into private hands;

- Galloping inflation and emergence of intermediaries (resellers) in great numbers on the market;

- Hypertrophy of the banking system and banks' involvement in various financial pyramid schemes and facilitation of capital flight from Russia (up to USD 1 trillion);

- Dramatic reduction of government revenues and expansion of the shadow economy;

- Significant reduction in spending on defense, security and law enforcement, healthcare, education and culture;

- Widespread and persistent delays in wage payments to private and public-sector employees;

- Gradual elimination of various social organizations that had been financed by state-owned industrial companies (athletic facilities, healthcare, culture);

- Migration of large numbers of people, which also tends to have an adverse effect on the overall quality of life, because Russian-speaking migrants do not receive adequate financial support due to the government's lack of financial resources.

- Commercialization of many healthcare and medical services, with all pharmacies becoming privately owned and drug prices on the rise, bringing a lack of motivation for medical doctors to provide quality healthcare, and practical elimination of disease prevention services.

The then-existing state-managed system was destroyed, with its set of spiritual and ideological values, on which three generations of Soviet and Russian citizens were raised, leaving them in an ideological vacuum. This was combined with impoverishment of a substantial part of the country's population, increased uncertainty about the future for all strata of society, wide-spread dissatisfaction with a deteriorating social security net, declining personal and public safety, propaganda of violence, self-indulgence and lax mores in the mass media, especially on television, exacerbated by depressing sentiments over the "lost" Cold War that saw a sharp decline in Russia's international prestige and ability to project power. A combination of all of these factors resulted in the destruction of Russia's national moral stereotype, the moral core of the nation and constant stress for the people of Russia. The stress manifested itself through higher incidence of alcoholism, and unprecedented growth in illegal drug and substance abuse, including abuse by underage children; rampant economic and violent crime, murders, including unmotivated murders by violent teenagers. Criminal gangs became much more common, their activity far more pervasive, while corruption at all levels of government started spreading and still persists to this day. Aggression is becoming the dominant format of human behavior.

One significant socioeconomic factor determining the state of health of the public is level of education, a complex metric that usually includes (or determines) one's occupational profile, income, overall and hygienic culture, ability to understand and follow recommendations for one's way of living, one's lifestyle and the necessary healthcare one should seek. The concept of the "way of life" has existed for years, reflecting the most significant traits of socioeconomic and political systems. We can describe the way of life as a specific historically determined mode of operation in material and non-material (spiritual) areas of life; not so much of operation as any specific type of activity, but rather a combination of essential features of human activity and culture of a specific group of people.

In this case, we are using the broadest possible understanding of culture (culture as such), including the healthcare culture as a component of the overall culture of humanity. In more specific terms, the impact of culture upon health is such that the lower the culture level, the greater the likelihood of developing diseased conditions, and the lower the quality of other aspects of health. The following elements of culture have an immediate, direct and the greatest overall significance for the state of health: the culture of eating (eating healthy), the culture of living (i.e. the culture of keeping one's abode in a proper condition conducive to one's good health), the culture of organizing one's rest and recreation (including entertainment), and the culture of hygiene (the culture of healthcare). When one follows the best practices of all these cultural aspects, one can reasonably expect to have better health.

The overall broad spectrum of sociocultural factors that need to be addressed in a sociopsychological analysis of the health of a society can be subdivided, for the purposes of such analysis, into macrosocial (societal) and more narrowly defined cultural factors. For example, many generations preceding the contemporary civilization in China were looking for increasingly more effective ways to preserve health and achieve longevity, constantly accumulating experience and knowledge, which became the foundation for the rich yang sheng culture (yang sheng means roughly "the nourishing of life"), the culture of nourishing and promoting health and longevity. The methods of this culture can take many different shapes and are implemented through psychological regulation of one's mood and outlook on (attitude towards) the world surrounding the individual.

Economic liberalization and liberal market reform in Russia went hand-in-hand with active spiritual processes of replacing the fundamental ideological perspectives, changing the criteria for good and evil, with the introduction of new social goals and values. The new features were alien to the Soviet and Russian culture, and are still widely seen as signs of spiritual decay. This caused very powerful stress for many people. This stress makes the Russia of the 1990s different from the US of the 1930s, the Great Depression era, in that the US overcame the socioeconomic crisis without having to change its moral foundations. And the main reason for any stress and suffering comes from an interaction between external forces and one's internal response to their influence.

Spirituality is always present in any society, but it can be either positive or negative. Its nature is shaped by internal and external conditions. The life expectancy of adults is determined mostly by their spiritual state, which is "measured" by how happy a person is, by his "quality of life." Quality of life includes such parameters as health, the ability to have children and procreate, obtain satisfaction from one's life (to enjoy one's life) and by moral anomalies (murders, robberies, divorce, child abandonment).

When we evaluate the quality of daily life from a contemporary perspective, we must first look at the fact that an adult spends a third of his time working, i.e. engaging in some kind of gainful labor activity. So it is essential to prevent labor from causing deterioration to the individual's health condition. The main detrimental factors in the workplace are excessive content of gas or dust in the breathing air, vibration, monotony, neurological and psychological stress, and an uncomfortable working position. Failure to address these factors can result in higher probability of developing a diseased condition, developing an occupational disease, becoming injured, disabled or killed in the workplace (or outside the workplace).

At the same time, daily living conditions are also an important factor affecting the health of the population. A working-age individual spends the majority (2/3) of his time outside the workplace, going about his daily life, at home and outside, in the environment available to him. This makes the comfort and amenities of one's home essential for restoring one's ability to work after a day

129

of labor, to maintain one's health at an adequate level, to improve one's cultural and educational level, and so forth.

An individual certainly needs rest to maintain and strengthen his health. Rest is the state of repose, relaxation, or an activity that helps to relieve fatigue and restore one's capacity for work. The main condition for obtaining good rest and recreation is having access to facilities that include adequate (or better) living conditions, growing numbers of theaters, museums, art galleries amd exhibition halls, development of TV and radio broadcasting, expanding systems of libraries, arts centers, parks, resorts and health farms and tourist organizations, and so forth. Physical exercise (the so-called "physical culture" is now playing an increasing role in human life. Lack of exercise (poor physical culture associated with physical inactivity, a sedentary lifestyle) is the other side of technological progress, typical of our time. Insufficient exercise is common for industrial and even agricultural workers, exacerbated by the modern amenities of our daily life. Modern science has demonstrated that longevity and a large capacity for labor are impossible without a regimen of physical activity. The effects of physical exercise are manifold, affecting the function of practically all the organs and systems in the human body, but they are especially important for the cardiovascular system.

The cultural approach under consideration here is based on describing social structures, processes and institutions in the broadest possible categories. And there are several key ways in which culture can influence health.

Specific conditions of life – conditions of labor, daily routines, eating habits, conditions of one's home, rest, education, upbringing, cultural needs and political and ideological environment – essentially, everything that used to be described as the overall conditions of collective living in texts on social hygiene – are the terms and factors influencing one's health. At the same time, we need to identify the decisive conditions and factors to construct a compatible cause-and-effect model explaining the effects of various factors on health.

Different combinations of sociopolitical, cultural and economic factors serve to identify risk groups, usually groups of people more predisposed than others to develop certain medical conditions. These risk groups include children, the elderly, pregnant women, migrants, singles, the long-term unemployed or the sporadically employed, the homeless, people with deviant behaviors and lifestyle choices (sex workers, drunks, drug addicts, psychopaths and so on), as well as people in hazardous workplace environments, etc.

For a better understanding of such fundamental concepts as "way of life" and "living conditions", we need to bear in mind that the concept of the way of life addresses the question *how* an individual is thinking, behaving and acting, whereas living conditions pertain to things and people surrounding the individual, the conditions (demographic, material, socioeconomic, political, moral and ethical, healthcare-related and others) in which he is living, working, going about his daily routines, the things and people that *shape* his "way of life." Therefore, the living conditions are all the material and non-material, intangible factors determining, mediating and facilitating the individual's way of life.

Readers are invited to superimpose, visually, using the provided diagram, and conceptually, the contemplatory wisdom of the East with the pragmatism of the West as a way to achieve harmony in all spheres and aspects of life. Let us consider a compatibility diagram for five crucial aspects (areas) of our life, common for the whole of humanity.

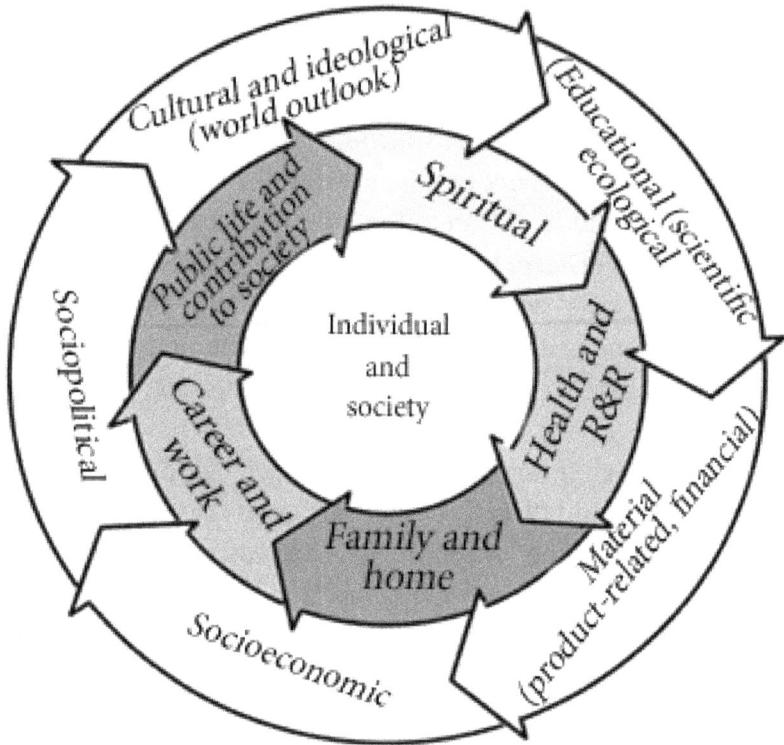

Fig. 7. Compatibility of five areas of human life in the environment of societal development

These elements combine into a portrait of life, where balanced compatibility of the five spheres enables people of the West *and* East to enjoy a happy and harmonious life every single day.[50] Unfortunately, these areas appear to be out of equilibrium today. The author of this textbook has polled approximately 80 people of working age for the following average breakdown of these areas:

---

[50] Дель Пи. От успеха к удовлетворению. Феникс, Ростов-на-Дону.2005.

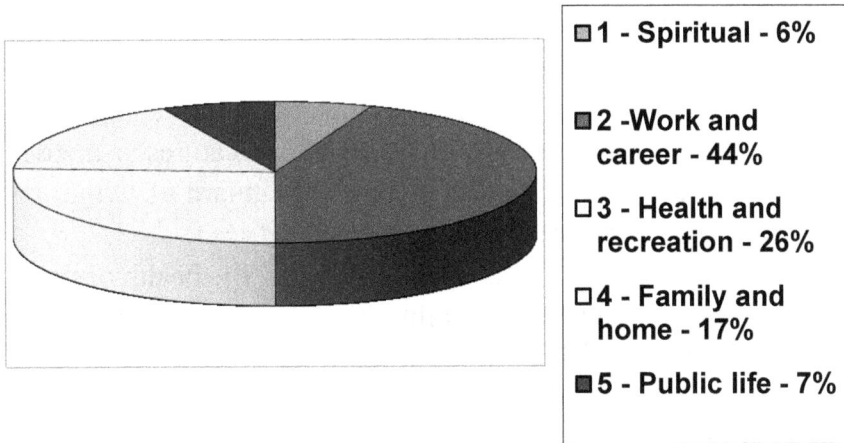

Fig. 8. Average distribution of time for five areas of life

The way of life is often associated with the notions of "living arrangements", "standard of living", "quality of life" and "lifestyle". Essentially, this is a broad area of metrics reflecting consumption of material and spiritual values, which is amenable to quantitative measurement.

In this day and age, the annual statistical reports Healthcare in Russia and Demographic Yearbook of Russia alone report approximately 1,200 metrics directly or indirectly reflecting the public state of health of the people of Russia. In order to construct, as described above, a compatible cause-and-effect model of determining factors of health, one would need to divide and group the factors by compatibility levels. Using the basics of the Compatibility Theory[51], we identify seven key levels, in ascending order from an individual's needs to his values, from the standard of living (the lower three compatibility levels) to quality of life (Compatibility Levels 4-7): the product – property level (1); the financial and economic level (2); the social level (3); the political level (4); the level of religion and

---

[51] «Exploring Compatibility \ foundations of a theory» (Quickstone Publishing UK, England) - 2014.

theology (5); the level of culture and ideology/world outlook (6); the level of science and spirituality (the learning level) (7). It is noteworthy that the relative importance of metrics, their subordination to or control over one another spans all the Levels from 1 through 7. Level Seven is definitive for compatibility of metrics. Let us pick three key characteristics (features or metrics) for each of the levels to "paint" a picture of standard of living through quality of life of the people through these metrics.

Here is a description of factors affecting the health of the public (grouped according to compatibility levels), reflecting the standard of living and quality of life:

$$1 \begin{cases} v_1 - Living\ conditions and\ consumption\ of\ key\ foods \\ v_2 - natural\ population\ growth \\ v_3 - life\ expectancy\ at\ birth \end{cases}$$

$$2 \begin{cases} d_1 - economically\ active\ and\ economically\ inactive \\ \qquad population\ by\ age \\ d_2 - the\ population`s\ monetary\ incomes\ and\ expenses \\ d_3 - size\ of\ minimum\ living\ wage \end{cases}$$

$$3 \begin{cases} c_1 - number\ of\ (un)employed, level\ of\ economic\ activity \\ c_2 - number\ of\ people\ employed\ in\ healthcare \\ c_3 - number\ of\ hospitals\ (hospital\ beds), health\ resorts\ and \\ \qquad rehab\ facilities, walk-in\ clinics, orphanages \end{cases}$$

$$4 \begin{cases} k_1 - spending\ on\ environmental\ protection \\ k_2 - incidence\ of\ infectious disease\ and\ malignant\ tumors \\ \qquad in\ the\ population \\ k_3 - child\ mortality, aged\ 0-14 \end{cases}$$

$$5 \begin{cases} m_1 - number\ of\ robberies\ and\ murders \\ m_2 - marriages\ and\ divorces, aborted\ pregnancies\ (abortions) \\ m_3 - incidence\ of\ alcoholism\ and\ drug\ addiction \end{cases}$$

$$6 \begin{cases} t_1 - incidence\ of\ psychoses\ in\ the\ population, including \\ \quad psychological\ disorders\ in\ adolescence \\ t_2 - number\ of\ recreation\ facilities, wilderness\ resorts, \\ \quad camping\ grounds, children's\ health\ facilities, sports \\ \quad facilities \\ t_3 - adult\ literacy, number\ of\ school\ admissions, at\ all\ levels \end{cases}$$

$$7 \begin{cases} i_1 - number\ of\ people\ engaged\ in\ science, research\ and \\ \quad development \\ i_2 - number\ of\ post-graduate/post-doc\ school \\ \quad admissions/\ graduations \\ i_3 - number\ of different\ innovative\ products/goods, \\ \quad including\ as\ a\ percentage\ of\ all\ goods\ shipped \end{cases}$$

Attempting to record formally the different groups of features at a functional level, we offer our own version of the compatibility function of people's health factors with more generalized (aggregate) metrics corresponding to compatibility levels listed above:

The compatibility of people's health factors

$$S_{zn} = F(V_p; D_{min}; C_m; K_3; M_{id}; T_D; I_m)$$

Where V_p are levels of natural consumption needed to ensure the average lifespan

D_{min} is the economic and financial resources needed to provide a minimal living income

C_m stands for provision of jobs to the workforce and of socioeconomic infrastructure to children and retirees

K_3 represents institutional, legal and financial support by the government for underprivileged parts of society while upholding public security and safety for all citizens

M_{id} represents the moral and spiritual efforts of religious and cultural organizations to help people overcome or get rid of their moral anomalies (propensity to commit murders, robberies, divorce partners, abandon children, proceed with abortions)

T_D is a mass cultural movement to promote and study integration and globalization of international quality-of-life values

I_m stands for clean-up and improvement of the environment and the individual by implementing new scientific discoveries and increasing the range and share of innovative products available

We can take this further by attempting to describe the compatibility of factors affecting the health of the public (S_{zn}):

The compatibility of the population's social health compatibility (S_{zn}) factors is shown as a conditional formalization through a ratio of social and spiritual descriptors (F_{QL}) reflecting the quality of life (QL) and socioeconomic parameters (F_{SL}) reflecting the standard of living (SL):

$$S_{zn} = \frac{F_{QL}}{F_{SL}};$$

where F_{SL} and F_{QL} can be expressed mathematically as:

$$F_{SL} = \sqrt{\begin{aligned}&(C_V V_p(V_1, V_2, V_3, \dots))^2 + (C_D D_{min}(d_1, d_2, d_3, \dots))^2 + \\ &+(C_c C_m(c_1, c_2, c_3, \dots))^2 + \\ &+(\tfrac{1}{2} C_K k_3(k_1, k_2, k_3, \dots))^2;\end{aligned}}$$

$$F_{QL} = \sqrt{\begin{aligned}&(\tfrac{1}{2} C_K k_3(k_1, k_2, k_3, \dots))^2 + (C_M M_{id}(m_1, m_2, m_3, \dots))^2 + \\ &+(C_T T_D(t_1, t_2, t_3, \dots))^2 + (C_I I_m(i_1, i_2, i_3, \dots))^2;\end{aligned}}$$

where $C_I, C_T, C_M, C_K, C_C, C_D, C_V$ are the weights of different population health factors;

$C_I < C_T < C_M < C_K < C_C < C_D < C_V$ is the condition for existence of a spiritually democratic society

$S_{zm} = 1$ represents perfectly balanced compatibility

$S_{zm} < 1$ represents incompatibility, intellectual and spiritual degradation of society

$S_{zm} > \infty$ represents compatibility of development in the context of spiritual and educational development of society

Spiritual and bodily health, as we see it, is an absolute, eternal life value occupying the top spot in the hierarchy (pyramid) of needs. The need for health is universal, valued by both individuals and society as a whole, because health has a tremendous impact on the quality of labor as a resource, on productivity, and, as a consequence, on the country's Gross National Product.

To do this, we need to develop and improve the type of economy and format of government; modernize the nature of the political regime and look out for manifestations of unique sociocultural policy; observing the principles of friendly inter-ethnic relations, and monitoring the dynamics in the harmony of unity.

The proposed methodology enables us to evaluate from different perspectives, comprehensively and efficiently the development of the individual and society in the process of this development, evaluating the development compatibility (efficiency) of different subjects of study ranging in size and complexity from a single organization to a community, based on accounting for and making day-by-day adjustments to reflect the subject's development, changing the sequence of economic, social, political, cultural and innovation mechanisms (economies).

It may appear that we are using too many parameters, but, for analysis of closer interactions between economies associated with specific compatibility levels and to identify economies spanning several levels, one can put together more compact groups comprising primary (target) and auxiliary (substantially relevant, material) parameters, namely:

Group 1 – financial and economic indicators which have a strong influence on social development (Levels 1 and 2);

Group 2 – socioeconomic indicators that determine the prospects and strategy of social development (social groups, peoples, ethnic groups of all sizes) (Levels 2 and 3);

Group 3 – sociopolitical indicators, bringing together and mobilizing social communities (measuring motivation and inducement) (Levels 3-4);

Group 4 – cultural and social indicators, identifying the desirable traditions, moral codes and ethical scenarios for development of society (Levels 5-6);

Group 5 – indicators reflecting innovation and production, showing the progress of products for consumption to new levels of quality (Level 7 in Cycle One and Level 1 in Cycle Two).

This introduction must include a mention of synergies, also known in economics as the cooperative effect. This effect is achieved through concerted action (operation) of a group of factors, helping the overall effect to exceed significantly the mere summary effect (a synthesis) of constituent factors. The synergistic (cooperative) effect is sometimes recorded as "1+1=3." In other words, the right combination of all seven compatibility levels enables them to produce additional quality, because communication channels at one level reinforce the effect of others. Essentially, we are using a serial/parallel model to achieve our ultimate goals and address the intermediate objectives on the way there, by including different economic mechanisms (different types of economy) to ensure continuous development and transformation of the economy (or a sector, region or company) in the desired directions and at the desired stages. We all realize that it is easier to change the world by concerted effort, and if a model includes spiritual as well as material components, this would make it easier to understand and more appealing, more motivating for all participants in integration processes.

List of References and Further Reading:

1. Danilin, O. Principles for development of Key Efficiency Indicators (KEI) for industrial companies and using them in practice. // Company Management. 2003, Issue 2 (21). (In Russian) / Данилин О. Принципы разработки ключевых показателей эффективности (КПЭ) для промышленных предприятий и практика их применения // Управление Компанией. 2003. №2(21).

2. Dell, P. From success to satisfaction. Fenix, Rostov-na-Donu, 2005. (In Russian) / Дель Пи. От успеха к удовлетворению.Феникс,Ростов-на-Дону.2005.

3. Egorov E.V. Politics of healthcare development in contemporary Russia // News of the Moscow State University. Sereis 6: Economics, 2009, Issue 6. (In Russian) / Егоров Е.В. Политика развития здравоохранения в современной России // Вестник Московского университета. Серия 6: Экономика, 2009. № 6.

4. Kaplan, Robert S., Norton, David P. The Balanced Scorecard: Translating Strategy Into Action. Moscow: ZAO Olymp-Business. 2003. (In Russian) / Роберт С.КАПЛАН, Дейвид П.НОРТОН. Сбалансированная система показателей. От стратегии к действию. М. ЗАО «Олимп-Бизнес». 2003.

5. Kaplan, Robert S., Norton, David P. Strategy Maps: Converting Intangible Assets Into Tangible Outcomes. Moscow: ZAO Olymp-Business. 2004. (In Russian) / Роберт С.КАПЛАН, Дейвид П.НОРТОН. Стратегические карты. Трансформациянематериальных активов в материальные результаты. М.: ЗАО «Олимп-Бизнес». 2004.

6. Kleiner, G.B. Company Strategy. Moscow: Delo, 2008. (In Russian) / Клейнер Г.Б. Стратегия предприятия. М.,: Дело, 2008.

7. Malinova, O.Yu. Citizenship and Politization of Cultural Differences. // Political Studies. 2004. Issue 5, P. 7 (In Russian) / Малинова О.Ю. Гражданство и политизация культурных различий // Политические исследования. 2004. № 5. С. 7.

8. Morozov, V.A. Exploring Compatibility. Foundations of a Theory. Moscow: Economika. 2013. (In Russian) / Морозов В.А. Совместимость социально-экономических систем (основы теории совместимости).М,Экономика.2013.

9. Preisner, A. The Balanced Scorecared In Marketing and Sales. Moscow. 2009. (In Russian) / Прайснер А. Сбалансированная система показателей в маркетинге и сбыте. М. 2009.

10. Rampersaud, H. Universal Scorecard: How to Achieve Results While Keeping Integrity. Moscow: Alpina Business Books. 200X. (In Russian) / Рамперсанд Х. Универсальная система показателей: Как достигать результатов, сохраняя целостность. М.: АльпинаБизнесБукс. 200

11. Dictionary of Logic. Efremova's Dictionary of Definitions. enc-dic.com/Sovmestimost-348 (In Russian) / Словарь логики. «Толковый словарь Ефремовой». enc-dic.com/Sovmestimost-348

12. Sokolov, A.B. The Impact of Political and Socio-Economic

Factors on Health of the Public in Post-Soviet Rusia. Russian Academy of Law. S-K Branch. 2001. (In Russian) / Соколов А.Б. Влияние политических и социально-экономических факторов на здоровье населения в постсоветской России «Российская академия правосудия. С-К филиал. 2001.

3.3 Efficiency (Compatibility) of Operation in a Region as a Socioeconomic Entity

The culture of entire countries and ethnicities, people's ethics and moral values, and the individual's spiritual world today are made completely subservient to the individual's material standard of living. Values have lost their true meaning and have taken on shades of material objectives. The spiritual, intellectual potential of society which is preserved in a concentrated format in religions, public institutions, and in science, the arts, literature, in the cultural traditions of specific ethnicities cannot exact any kid of a perceptible influence on laws and priorities in the life of society. In the general situation of irrepressible growth in influence of criminal and corrupt systems, these are becoming increasingly connected from the inside with government systems.

To ensure smooth and effective transition to new development principles, Russia will need to focus on its own resources in all aspects of the life of society. This means not only developing the national economy with a strong focus on support for domestic manufacturers and providers of all types of products and services, but also creating a contemporary national security system specific to Russia, including a new law enforcement system. The most important components of this new necessary focus on domestic resources and opportunities are:

- helping the recovery, restoration and development of Russia's own national fundamental science, with adequate research and development and technology development facilities and assets;

- preservation and development of the national culture and art, careful preservation of and bold support for the national traditions of all ethnic groups living in Russia;

- building and developing, in connection with the above, new systems for education and upbringing, the provision of healthcare of all kinds, as well as systems of facilities for rest and recreation (including tasteful entertainment) for the people.

On the most fundamental level, a society has to be based on the ideological concept defining the place of the individual and society in the context of their attempts to understand the world around them, and also in the context of inter-connections, interdependence and interactions between an individual and society as a whole. This place, this position is the starting point for building and shaping the ethic and moral life criteria for every individual, the principles for his interactions with nature, shaping his inner, spiritual world, that which defines the unique life and existence of the individual. It is up to the government and religion to confirm and support all the eternal values in the life of contemporary society.

As for the key metrics and evaluation criteria of a community's social development, we note that the outcomes of social policy for regional development are evaluated by changes in the standard of living and quality of life. The standard of living is defined by the degree to which people's needs are satisfied. Four key components are commonly identified in the standard of living:

1) immediate conditions for living and procreation (daily necessities and basic services, housing, food);

2) working conditions (workplace safety, injuries and occupational disease, sanitary conditions and hygiene);

3) conditions for human development (human rights, income level and structure, the development of available social services, rest and recreation, birth rate, etc.);

4) environmental security (the state of the environment and environmental spending).

The degree to which people's needs are satisfied should be measured not only in comparison with the level at previous points in time, or in other countries, but also against scientifically motivated benchmarks that take into account the law of rising needs [1]. The UN-recommended system of metrics for measuring (evaluating) the standard of living includes metrics for measuring and/or evaluating: a) the demographic situation in the country (birth rate, death rate and other parameters); b) living conditions in terms of sanitation and hygiene; c) consumption of consumer goods; d) housing conditions; e) education and culture; f) employment, terms of employment and workplace conditions; g) people's incomes and spending; h) cost of living and consumer prices; i) availability of transportation; k) state of rest and recreation opportunities and facilities; l) social security; m) human rights [2]. GDP per capita (alternatively average/median household income) has been one of the most common metrics for the standard of living in recent years.

In the past, an individual was driven by values and even conceived his needs on the basis of values acquired from a young age through education and upbringing. These values used to determine his quality of life. Essentially, quality of life is an integrative evaluative metric, comprising narrower metrics reflecting both the material/physical and social/cultural well-being of an individual. The following are indicators of such well-being: (1) workplace conditions and workplace safety; (2) availability of spare time and the individual's ability to use it; (3) environmental conditions; (4) people's health and physical condition, etc. Factors affecting the efficacy of social policy include: (1) the state of the national economy; (2) the political situation; (3) climate and nature, geography; (4) traditions, culture and similar.

To get a real picture of the standard of living, one needs a certain benchmark index. A consumer basket – a scientifically motivated balanced set of goods and services that satisfy specific functional needs of a human being over a specific period of time, given the specific conditions in the country and real economic opportunities – represents just such an index. Compatibility of values and needs is decisive for an individual, a family and society as a whole. According to the unified field philosophy and the compatibility theory (as it applies to compatibility of needs and values) [5], there are seven compatibility levels, including: the level of products and assets (1), the financial and economic level (2), the social level (3), the political level (4), the level of religion and theology (5), level of culture and ideology (world view) (6), level of innovation and advanced products (7). A specific type of economy pertains to each of the respective levels: production economy (1), financial economy (2), non-production / social economy (3), political economy (4), traditional (5), global (6), and innovative (7) economies. Consequently, other types of economy: information, systematic, institutional, and evolutionary in-between "connector" economies spanning several different levels. A harmonizing economy uniting the individual, society and nature is the "green economy," or, more properly, the "economy of health of the human being, society and the environment," which determines the sustainability of the overall development and becomes the economy of interaction for the corresponding levels with their associated types of economy. However, let us go back to the available system of evaluative metrics, for the time being.

There are a number of global rating lists focusing on integrated metrics of societal development that are widely used to compare various aspects of the international development of different countries. Let us take one of the rating lists, which comprises ten sections of metrics, and focus on the sections immediately relevant for the purposes of this book. The first and most important of these is the UN Human Development Index (HDI), calculated from data that describe the essential aspects of human well-being: health, education and prosperity. HDI includes other metrics, such as life expectancy; elementary school coverage (gross elementary school admissions ratio); access to clean drinking water, GNP per capita, etc. The underlying idea for HDI is based on all-important paradigms of developing human potential such as productivity (efficiency); equality (equal opportunity to realize one's ability); sustainability (access to the benefits of the contemporary civilization); expanding opportunities. Taken together, they reflect three essential properties: healthy life, level of skills (education/knowledge) and an adequate standard of living.

The second rating list is the Wealth of Nations Triangle Index. This index is based on the assumption that the prosperity of a certain country is based on sustainable economic and social development and on an adequate information infrastructure. As many as 21 variables are considered when measuring a country's performance in each of these three categories.

The third rating list is the KOF Index of Globalization. It is calculated by breaking down the globalization process into such components as integration of information and economic integration. The index measurements look at frequency of international contacts between people. The fourth rating measures competitiveness by comparing progress in some areas in a certain country with the best achievements in the same area. The fifth rating is an index of economic freedom measuring the degree of the government's non-involvement in production, distribution and consumption of goods and services while providing an adequate level of security and freedom to the country's citizens. For the Russian economy, given its ongoing market monopolization processes, it could make sense to introduce a rating for the level of corruption. However, such a metric can only be "measured" by subjective expert assessments better suited to evaluation of qualitative parameters, making it hard to evaluate the situation objectively.

And possibly the last rating list relevant for our purposes is the City Quality of Life Index, which compares prices for more than 200 goods and services, including real estate, food, clothing, home appliances, cost of transportation and entertainment. Out of a multitude of similar rating lists and their sections, we propose focusing on the current method used for evaluation of development in the Russian regions, which was introduced in 2013 by Russian Government Order No. 1142, dated 3 November 2012, to support implementation of Russian Presidential Decree No. 1199, dated 21 August 2012, regarding efficiency evaluation of Russian regional governments [3].

The government order formally sets the rules for providng grants (development money transfers from the federal government to regional governments to support and/or reward the achievement of the best possible scores by a Russian region in an efficiency evaluation of the regional government of that region. The rules come with an efficiency evaluation methodology for Russian regional governments and a list of criteria on which regional executive power (regional governments or administrations) are evaluated for efficiency. Efficiency evaluations are carried out by regional offices of the federal government in the regions being evaluated. The Russian Ministry for Regional Development submits to the Russian government an annual draft presentation for the President of Russia, evaluating the efficiency of the regional and local governments of the Russian regions for the previous year. The methodology of evaluation of local and regional governments' efficiency is based on the following two lists of metrics:

- a list of 12 metrics for evaluating the efficiency of executive power in Russia's regions;

- a list of individual 36 metrics for evaluating the efficiency of executive power in Russia's regions.

Individual metrics are assigned to different sections in the following way: economy - 3; people's incomes – 6; labor and employment – 3; demographics and healthcare – 4; education – 5; providing housing to citizens – 5; housing stock and utilities – 5; creating a comfortable, secure and safe living environment – 5.

The other list of 12 overview-type parameters used for evaluation of efficiency, also applies to the sections listed above. The algorithm for evaluating the efficiency of regional executive bodies (governments) of Russian regions includes a "comprehensive evaluation" of operating efficiency calculated as a linear equation that puts all variables in equally dependent positions, and leaving only one metric – that for criticizing the (regional) leadership at a relative advantage, as a comparison benchmark. A composite index of leadership efficiency is determined primarily by the average growth in the overall efficiency of the region or territory under their control and the average efficiency level over the same time frame. The sections of different metrics are placed in identical conditions, with no metrics or groups of metrics getting any priority or special treatment. Certainly, every region and territory faces its own unique set of challenges, and this kind of a one-size-fits-all approach may dilute the assessment of a great effort or elevate an inferior one. Quite possibly, to identify common goals and objectives for the country as a whole and for its regions and municipalities, metrics and groups of metrics would have to be ranked by their priority and significance (this may already be the case in some undisclosed documents, but there is no mention of this in the published methodology). The list of additional metrics for the efficiency evaluation of local (municipal) administrations of city districts and municipalities approved by Russian Government Order No. 1317 [4], dated 17 December 2012, is quite similar in this respect. It comprises 40 metrics matching the sections listed above, with some additional ones. The federal list is missing the Culture Section, which is included at the municipal level and contains three metrics, including two metrics reflecting economic (property and construction-related) purposes. The sole metric in the Sports and Physical Exercise Section is repeated at both federal (nationwide) and municipal levels. Healthcare matters are shown in the tables above, but are covered by only one metric. As for additions to the approved (36+12), we believe it would be advisable also to introduce explanatory metrics (used by the Russian Statistics Committee) reflecting (providing possible explanations for) the spiritual or mental state of the people. These would include the incidence of alcoholism, drug addiction, psychiatric disorders; the number of marriages, divorces, abortions (adding to the metrics also the death rate and causes of death, including death rate and causes for children under 14); the number of undergraduate and graduate admissions; changes in the number of retreats, camping grounds, healthcare and rehab institutions, and sports facilities. Certainly, it would be impossible to cover absolutely everything, but, as the saying goes, if you want to reap a good harvest, you have to dig deeper for some manifestations of the fundamental truth about the life of the people of our country.

Let us go back to compatibility theory (theory of interaction), for which we have identified seven levels of interaction of material needs and spiritual values. We should always superimpose on our system of values the hierarchy of needs (the best-known of them is the A. Maslow pyramid), taking into account the law of rising needs and the age-old picture of values which should define the priorities for the set of metrics that would be responsibe for preserving these values in society for subsequent regulation of material needs. If we attempt, very approximately, to distribute all the metrics (36 and 12) across seven levels of compatible (efficient) development, the distribution will look similar to that shown in Table 4:

Table 4. Approximate distribution of efficiency metrics by compatibility levels

Individual Metrics	Compatibility Levels						
	1	2	3	4	5	6	7
Vector (units)	3	2	8	8	1	3	3
Fanning out (units)			2				
				1			
				1		1	
			1		2		
Efficiency Metrics	Compatibility Levels						
	1	2	3	4	5	6	7
Vector (units)	1	1	2	3			
Fanning out (units)				1	1	1	
				1	1		
Total by Level	4	3	10	17	6	10	11

Indeed, all the metrics are valid and robust, closely interconnected and interdependent. A great majority of metrics cover a broad range of socioeconomic factors from different angles. However, this methodology essentially does not assign any priority of importance to any groups of metrics or metrics within groups or across the board. The hierarchy of compatibility levels resolves this issue automatically.

We have mentioned above the harmonizing economy – the economy of interaction, driven by harmony between individual/society and the environment (nature). This type of economy used to be described as "green" in the past, but we call it "the economy of health"; however, some economists use the term to cover only human health, still including nature under the "green economy" heading. Based on the interaction of economies model [6], we intend to base evaluation of regions' sustainable development on somewhat different principles. We propose exploring these principles with a fascinating example describing the health of the public. What can be more important to a federal government or a region than strengthening and improving the (material and spiritual) health of the public?

Our task is to evaluate the efficiency (in other words, development compatibility) of a specific sociopolitical entity, for example, a region within the Russian Federation. Compatibility of development is a crucial metric describing both the current state across all seven development levels and the possibility of future development, of moving products from one level to the next, and ultimately the possibility of sustainable development.

We can pick some of the metrics reported in the Russian federal government's statistics as the key factors describing the communal health of a sociopolitical entity (e.g. a region). Depending on the depth and precision needed for the purposes of the analysis, we could choose two or more factors for each of the compatibility levels. We should approach the choice of factors with a degree of caution. First of all, these factors should describe the incredibly complex and varied range of processes in society from a comprehensive array of perspectives. To achieve this, factors must be selected with consideration given to interconnections between them and their mutual determination, and it is better to choose one broader, more general factor instead of several similar ones [7]. For example, we can replace the metrics for sales of tobacco products and alcoholic beverages, for the number of laws regulating consumption of tobacco and alcohol, including their consumption in the public space, for the number of deaths caused by drunkenness, and for the legalization of light drugs, by a single metric for the incidence of alcoholism and drug addiction as one that most comprehensively reflects this aspect of social processes.

We mentioned in the preceding Section three factors for each of the seven compatibility levels:

v1 – life expectancy at birth

v2 – natural population growth

v3 – housing conditions and consumption of key types of food

d1 – economically active and non-active population, breakdown by age

d2 – cash income and expenses of the population

d3 – minimum living wage

c1 – number of employed and unemployed, index of economic activity of the population

c2 – number of healthcare employees

c3 – number of hospitals (hospital beds), health resorts, pharmacies, walk-in-clinics and orphanages

k1 – spending on environmental protection

k2 – incidence of infectious disease and malignant tumors in the population

k3 – child death rate, age 0-14

m1 – number of robberies and murders

m2 – number of marriages and divorces, aborted pregnancies (abortions)

m3 – incidence of alcoholism and drug addiction

t1 – incidence of psychiatric disorders in the popualtion, including aberrant behavior in teenagers

t2 – level of literacy in the population, number of school admissions at all levels

t3 – number of rest and recreation facilities, retreats, camping sites, children's health resorts, sports facilities

i1 – number/volume of various innovative products, including their weight share in total volume of goods shipped

i2 – number of employees in science, research and development

i3 – numbers of gradulate school and post-doctorate program enrollment/graduation

We note that all factors [8] should be calculated as per capita indexes. Most parameters need to be divided by the population of the entity (country or region) that is the subject of analysis. However, some factors, such as v1, do require this step.

To evaluate compatibility in several regions, we need to pick a benchmark ("etalon") region, the compatibility value for which is known, for example, from existing research. This can be either one of the regions we are attempting to analyze or a distant region, different in its sociopolitical metrics, such as Moscow versus other regions in Russia, or a Swiss canton, as well-research sociopolitical entities (regions).

Let us introduce relative factors (metrics) for the health of the public (social health) of the region we are analyzing versus a benchmark region. For example, The first factor v2 will have its correspondence in the relative factor v2:

$$v2 = \frac{v2_{local}/N_{local}}{v2_{etalon}/N_{etalon}}$$

where $v2_{local}$ is the natural population growth in the region at the center of our analysis, N_{local} is the overall population in the region, $v2_{etalon}$ is the natural population growth in the benchmark ("etalon") region, and N_{etalon} is the total population of the benchmark region.

We have to review separately the negative health factors (metrics), such as m2, the incidence of alcoholism and drug addiction. In this case, the relative factor has to be calculated as follows:

$$m2 = \frac{1 - m2_{local}/N_{local}}{1 - m2_{etalon}/N_{etalon}}$$

where $m2_{local}$ is the number of alcoholics and drug addicts in the region under our review, N_{local} is the total population of that region, $m2_{etalon}$ is the number of alcoholics and drug addicts in the benchmark region, and N_{local} is the total population of the benchmark region.

This way, instead of absolute health factors, we are using relative health factors calculated from the available data for a benchmark region.

We can calculate the efficiency (developmental compatibility) using the following formula:

$$S_{local} = \frac{1}{\sqrt{7}} \sqrt{\begin{array}{l} z1(c_{v1}v1 + c_{v2}v2 + c_{v3}v3)^2 + \\ +z2(c_{d1}d1 + c_{d2}d2 + c_{d3}d3)^2 + \\ +z3(c_{c1}c1 + c_{c2}c2 + c_{c3}c3)^2 + \\ +z4(c_{k1}k1 + c_{k2}k2 + c_{k3}k3)^2 + \\ +z5(c_{k1}k1 + c_{k2}k2 + c_{k3}k3)^2 + \\ +z6(c_{m1}m1 + c_{m2}m2 + c_{m3}m3)^2 + \\ +z7(c_{i1}i1 + c_{i2}i2 + c_{i3}i3)^2 \end{array}} \cdot S_{etalon}$$

This formula enables us to calculate the efficiency (developmental compatibility) for region S_{local} by comparison to health and compatibility factors of benchmark region Setalon. Coefficients $c_{v1}, c_{v2}, c_{v3}, c_{d1}$ are weights that need to be calculated precisely. They are subject to some specific limitations:

The sum of weights within one compatibility level must equal 1, e.g.: $c_{v1} + c_{v2} + c_{v3} = 1$, $c_{d2} + c_{d2} + c_{d3} = 1$, $c_{c1} + c_{c2} + c_{c3} = 1$ and so on. This requirement reflects the fact that all of the compatibility levels make the same contribution to the overall compatibility of the system (region in our case). For example, a system with compatible development compatibility cannot be created only with some of the compatibility levels (e.g. the first four: the level of products and assets, the financial level, the social and political levels, leaving the other three levels to stagnate with zero development).

The weights determine the contribution of a certain factor of health of the public to compatibility of the whole system (the region). Each weight can be within certain limits, and the specific value for a calculation must be determined by the terms of analysis for each specific region. For example, $c_{m1} = 0.4 \div 0.5$, $c_{m2} = 0.3 \div 0.4$ $c_{m3} = 0.1 \div 0.3$, which indicates that factors cm1 and c_{m2} have a greater significance.

Weight values are taken from social and statistical studies about the influence of certain factors of the health of the public on societal development. These weight factors then need to be verified and fine-tuned by expert assessment.

Weights $z1, ..., z6$ reflect the mainstream significance of a level and are needed to account for specifics of the region we are analyzing, be they historical or natural. In most cases, each of these weights equals 1.

As we have discussed in previous books and articles [6, 7, 8], numeric values of S_{local} correspond to the following states:

$S_{local} = 1$ – balanced compatibility;

$S_{local} < 1$ – incompatibility, intellectual and spiritual degradation of society;

$S_{local} > 1$ – forward-looking compatibility for development, spiritual and learning development of society.

Thus, we have proposed a convenient and efficient way to evaluate the compatibility of a system's (or an entity's) development based on a benchmark region. After carefully studying the region, which is the subject of our analysis, after identifying and measuring all of its health factors and refining the weights we can calculate the developmental compatibility for the region we are analyzing. Furthermore, a more meticulous and detailed analysis of society health factors and subsequent study of the influence of society health factors $v1, v2, v3, d1, ..., i2, i3$ on developmental compatibility, can enable us to measure the necessary and sufficient values for them, at which $S = 1$ compatibility can be ensured. Therefore, we would no longer have to consider the benchmark region, and can estimate the developmental compatibility of a sociopolitical entity (a region), without the need to consider any other regions or use any other existing research for benchmark comparison.

List of References and Further Reading:

1. The Great Soviet Encyclopedia. Moscow: Soviet Encyclopedia, 1969-1978. (In Russian) / Большая Советская Энциклопедия М.: «Советская энциклопедия», 1969-1978

2. Zherebin, V. M. Standard of Living of the Population – The Way It Is Understood Today Zherebin, V. M., Ermakova N.A. // Issues in Statistics. 2008. Issue 8. PP. 3-11. (In Russian) / Жеребин В. М. Уровень жизни населения – как он понимается сегодня/ В. М. Жеребин, Н. А. Ермакова // Вопросы статистики. 2008. № 8. С.3-11.

3. Russian Government Order No. 1142 dated 3 November 2012 to support implementation of Russian Presidential Decree No. 1199 dated 21 August 2012 regarding efficiency evaluation of Russian regional governments Garant.ru>Products Prime>Documents Newsfeeds Prime >70154132 (In Russian) / Постановление Правительства РФ от 3 ноября 2012 г. № 1142 «О мерах по реализации Указа Президента Российской Федерации от 21 августа 2012 г. № 1199 "Об оценке эффективности деятельности органов исполнительной власти субъектов Российской Федерации". Garant.ru>Продукты Прайм>Документы ленты прайм >70154132

4. Russian Government Order No. 1317 dated 17 December 2012 (In Russian) referent.ru>1/ 207820 (In Russian) / Постановление Правительства РФ от 17 декабря 2012 г. № 1317.referent.ru>1/ 207820

5. Morozov, V. A. Exploring Compatibility. Foundations of a Theory. Moscow: Economika. 2013. (In Russian) / Морозов В. А.

Совместимость социально-экономических систем (основы теории совместимости).М,Экономика.2013.

6. Morozov, V. A. Economics of Interaction (Introduction) and Compatibility Theory. // Creative Economics. 2014. Issue 8 (92). (In Russian) / Морозов В. А. Экономика взаимодействия (введение) и теория совместимости// Креативная экономика. -2014.-№8(92)

7. Morozov, V. A. Economics of Interaction Mechanisms. // Creative Economics. 2014. Issue 9 (93). (In Russian) / Морозов В. А. Механизмы экономики взаимодействия// Креативная экономика. -2014.-№9(93)

8. Morozov, V. A. Compatible Metrics in Economics of Interaction. // Creative Economics. 2014. Issue 10 (94). (In Russian) / Морозов В. А. Совместимые показатели экономики взаимодействия// Креативная экономика. -2014.-№10(94)

3.4 Expanding Mechanisms and Modes of Interaction in the Social Sphere

Interactions are based on a "menu" of needs and values of the interacting parties. In order to understand interaction, one must first find out the properties of the parties to interaction, and understand the foundations and rationales for these properties. The underlying reasons, the content of interaction determines the quality and quantity of such interaction.

In many countries around the world, the social environment, or the so-called "third sector" of the economy to a large extent consists of and is shaped by organizations, usually privately controlled, which are established and operated to produce public benefits, rather than generate profits. In Russia, this sector first emerged in the last decade of the 20th century, when laws were passed regulating this sector, the first professionals were trained to work in it and the first umbrella organizations appeared to coordinate its operations. The financial meltdown of the late 1990s caused operations in many areas of the third sector to grind to a halt, including rehabilitation centers, shelters, orphanages and hospices. Many business owners set up non-profit organizations (NPOs) in the early 2000s, mostly for business and tax reasons, to reduce a tax burden that could be quite substantial in the for-profit sector. A majority of these organizations had insufficient staff, mostly of inadequate quality, and often had few assets, if any. In fact, only a fifth of all registered volunteer organizations after the financial meltdown of 1998 and the subsequent stagnation were actually operating for their stated purpose.

NPOs essentially have three ways to survive and continue operations in the current tough economic environment:

1. Developing close connections with the regional, local or municipal government (administration) to ensure a constant inflow of finance enabling the NGO to hire more people and experience no problems with raising finance;

2. If money does not come in from the government, it has to be raised from the for-profit sector (by approaching specific companies or individuals for donations); this requires a lot of ingenuity and widely advertising one's socially important operations;

3. One-off method: receiving a large lump-sum donation from a sponsor, which could attract scrutiny (tough questions and possibly a tax audit) from the tax authorities.

At this point in time, the first approach is mainly used in Russia. Regional administrators and governments mostly work with the people they know and trust – usually the administrators' and government members' business partners, friends, family members and such like – essentially engaging in nepotism and/or cronyism. Narrow selfish interests and corruption replace the democracy of a free market driven by supply and demand wherever we have cartels and clans "calling the shots." It follows from the above that the main necessary condition for the existence and operation of non-profit organizations across Russia is a constant independent inflow of financing from the government and government organizations and agencies. However, today we witness precarious and intermittent cash inflows into the non-profit sector, with unbalanced and unfair competition among NPOs for donations. In France and Germany, government is the primary source of finance for NGOs, however, the system does not operate this way in Russia for several reasons: insufficient financial resources and lack of efficient ways to channel money to NGOs; lack of free competitive tenders; lack of "social patriotism;" lack of financial reporting transparency of NGOs; and low public awareness of the "economy's third sector." There are examples of successful, effective interaction between NGOs and federal or regional government agencies or municipal organizations in Russia that operate mostly for the following purposes (and under the following conditions):

- to develop and implement programs for which competitive bids (proposed projects) are invited from independent organizations;

- to create and develop programs that involve mixed working groups, helping to achieve cross-pollination of contemporary ideas and relevant proposals to address pressing social problems;

- when bids are accepted for providing social services to the general population.

These formats are becoming less and less productive today as the tax policy that applies to NPOs becomes more restricting and tax breaks and other benefits previously available to NPOs are gradually phased out. That said, new restrictions and taxes do not yet apply to NPOs in some areas including education, culture and support for people with disabilities. At the opposite end of the spectrum, life is hardest for environmental or human rights non-profit groups, especially when they have to turn to government officials for assistance to resolve any issues, because their core activities overlap with the responsibilities of government agencies regulating the environment and enforcing the rule of law, which may appear to be encroaching to respective government officials. The hierarchy of key current problems, hurdles to an effective dialogue between the government (authorities) and NPOs can be ranked by their weight in overall adverse influence on interactions between the government and NPOs:

- government officials fail to realize that dialogue is important and are unwilling to work together with NPOs;

- government officials often lack professionalism;

- authorities are generally suspicious of non-profit organizations;

- authorities are striving to manipulate NPOs;

- centralization of power (the antithesis of democracy), corruption, formal interaction lacking any real substance ("purely for reporting purposes") are some of the other significant factors.

Other relevant factors include: low professionalism of NPOs, low consolidation levels within the "third sector" (the realm of social services); passive attitudes of NPOs and the general public, NPOs' lack of respect for authorities; the "third sector's" poor public image and lack of convincing authority.

Taking into consideration the features and causes listed above that are hurdles to effective interaction between the authorities and NPOs, the often-stated objectives to develop dialogue and interaction may seem illogical and even strange. Quite possibly, according to some available studies, organized and conducted as part of the Program, these objectives should be interpreted as follows.

1) A toolset for interaction has been developed: interaction formats and mechanisms have been defined and established based on actual experience. Further refinements to this toolset will depend on improvements to legal foundations, as the authorities can only do what the current laws require them to. In this context, refining legislation and legal fundamentals takes center stage, while the need for extensive development of formats and mechanisms recedes.

2) Non-profit leaders realize that the weakness of civil society stems from insufficient initiative and an insufficiently proactive stance from NPOs, the general public's passive attitudes, lack of support for NPOs from society at large and low consolidation levels of the "third sector" itself. However, these are very complex problems that can be solved only in the long term, and understanding this can be an additional discouraging factor, resulting in a certain apathy. A possible solution that appears both realistic and achievable in the short term is to raise the professionalism levels of both government officials and NPOs, as well as ensuring openness, transparency and fairness, and monitoring execution to make sure commitments are followed through. This should help to expand the ranks of those who will put into practice the ideas of public involvement in policy development and implementation at both nationwide and regional levels.

Economic sanctions imposed on Russia by the EU and the US have made the situation extremely difficult for NPOs which have come to rely on financial contributions from private businesses and individual sponsors who now have to think about their own survival and many of whom have begun to "tighten their belts," cutting all non-essential costs. Federal financing of all types has also been drying up. After years of readily available financial injections, NPO employees are unable to procure funds for NPO operations on their own or to achieve sustainable operating independence using proceeds from the sale of goods and services that would be strictly aligned with the NPO's stated purpose. At the same time, the nature of interaction between government agencies and NPOs has already started shifting to administrative pressure on NPOs because the available financial resources are declining, and because the government too often chooses to push for meeting the Russian Statistics Agency's target social indicators, which serve as an important sociopolitical barometer. We must not forget that this pressure is brought to bear by providing or withholding various breaks and special arrangements for providing services essential for NPO operations (office space or other premises, equipment, communication devices and so on).

The number of legal entities registered as non-profit organizations in Russia was 678,521 in 2014, or approximately 14% of all Russia-registered businesses and organizations [4]. As for non-profits focusing specifically on social issues, 113,237 NPOs in this category were in the registry of organizations as of January 1, 2014, which is just 16.7% of all non-profits registered as legal entities [8]. The body of NPOs established to serve a social purpose can be divided into the following categories by type of activity:

- prevention of child abandonment and promotion of good parenting; support of mothers and children; improving the quality of life for older people; social adaptation for people with disabilities and their families and other account for 26%;

- charity and promotion of charity, volunteer activities – 16%;

- protection: against disasters, legal, environmental – 8%;

- activity in the fields of education, training, science and culture, promoting patriotic, spiritual and moral education – 30%;

- healthcare, disease prevention and promotion of people's health, promotion of active healthy living, exercise, assisting inter-ethnic and anti-corruption activities – 20% [5].

The composition of the Russian NPO sector shows a prevalence of organizations engaged in education, culture, and promotion of patriotic, moral and spiritual education of the young, promoting improvements in the moral and psychological condition of the general public and the spiritual development of the individual. The current breakdown of NPOs by sphere of operation is largely positive, although the results of their operation – the quality of education and instruction, the incidence of psychiatric disorders given the current suicide statistics and drug addiction levels are still far from encouraging. This may also have something to do with the fact that a large majority – over 80% – of all non-profit organizations have a staff of only four people or fewer. This means that few NPOs have people with appropriate qualifications and skills on staff. Most non-profits have to engage unskilled people without relevant work experience. The small amount of funds allocated to finance non-profits could also play a role in this: 70% of NPOs serving social purposes have received no more than 300,000 Rubles per annum apiece in recent years.

Table 5 shows the distribution of NPOs focused on social goals by sources of finance and in-kind asset contributions in Russia for 2013:

As you can see from Table 5, government contributions to social NPOs account for a little less than 20% of the total, while private businesses and individuals contribute approximately 15%. The largest source of finance is NPOs' proceeds from the sale of goods and services. Contributions from overseas account for only 3% of the total. Notably, NPOs that own or rent office space and/or other premises tend to make a greater impact and generally have more success in achieving their goals. NPOs that do not have premises at all constitute 35% of the total number of non-profit organizations in Russia. Meanwhile, 24.2% rent their office space or other premises (including 10.4% which rent space from the government or municipality) and 30.2% have been granted their premises for use for the purposes of operating the NPO without charge (including 18.2% that use premises that are kept on the balance sheets of the government or government and municipal agencies).

Statistics show that reliable large-scale, repeatable mechanisms were required to ensure the fulfillment of the people's social needs through the third-sector economy over the past 10 years. Therefore, it would make sense to use private businesses and free-market institutions to achieve the broader use of such mechanisms, especially since this area includes more than 25 directions of socioeconomic activity in the Russian Statistics Agency's official reports alone.

Table 5. Distribution of NPOs by source of financing and asset contributions

Sources of finance and in-kind asset contributions received by NPOs	As % of total contributions
Total amount received	100
including:	
funds and contributions received from the Federal Government	10.5

Sources of finance and in-kind asset contributions received by NPOs	As % of total contributions
grants received from non-profit non-governmental organizations developing civil society institutions (provided as subsidies from the Federal government)	0.2
contributions coming from the budgets of Russian regions	4.2
contributions from local (municipal) governments	2.3
contributions from government-controlled extra-budgetary funds	0.6
contributions (including donations) and grants from Russian individuals excluding cash and other assets received (inherited) under wills and testaments of deceased donors	12.9
cash and other assets received (inherited) under wills and testaments of deceased donors	1.2
contributions (including donations) and grants from Russian non-profit organizations excluding grants provided by non-profit non-governmental organizations developing civil society institutions	5.4
contributions (including donations) from Russian business (for-profit) organizations except for interest and returns on endowment capital	13.8
contributions received from foreign governments, government agencies, international and foreign organizations	2.9
contributions received from foreign nationals and individuals without citizenship	0.0
interest and other returns on endowment capital	0.7
proceeds (revenue) from the sale of goods, services, property titles (excluding returns on endowment capital)	37.4

Sources of finance and in-kind asset contributions received by NPOs	As % of total contributions
non-sales revenues and proceeds (excluding returns on endowment capital)	2.3
cash and other assets received as donations from business organizations established by the NPO, except for cash, real estate or securities received as contributions to the NPO's endowment capital	0.3
Other contributions received	5.3

Many NPOs today have no way of measuring their social effectiveness even though they may meticulously prepare and file their legally required reporting and other documentation. They receive most of their financing in the form of donations, which deprives them of the incentive to be inventive and innovate to generate revenue on their own. Lack of incentives for NPO operation results in a crisis of confidence with the general public (two-thirds of poll respondents do not believe that social entrepreneurship can be effective at all, and think that socially focused NPOs' objectives are best accomplished by the government alone). Competitive tenders organized to distribute grants to NPOs to achieve specific results are often plagued by subjective biases in terms of organization, technology and financial aspects, which makes it hard to pick an NPO that would be a good match for a specific grant and undermines monitoring of the efficiency of project implementation. Therefore, currently existing NPOs and foundations that distribute special-purpose grants to NPOs should in the near future learn to act as transparent associations of social entrepreneurship organizations, directing funds received from the government to social entrepreneurs provided that their operations are effective and efficient. This new type of relationship should help to transform the operation of sociocultural entrepreneurship institutions within society by receiving wide media coverage, improving the general public's confidence in social entrepreneurship and help to engage more people (as private individuals) in financing various projects through other interaction formats. Project tenders over the past five years have shown an increase in participation by sole proprietors (with a median age of 45), which is indicative of the need for changes in taxation in this area, as the tax burden on sole proprietors is significantly lighter than that for for-profit (business) organizations owned by multiple investors.

As we turn to the current situation with NPOs in Europe and Asia, we should note that different players exist in the field of social entrepreneurship. They have different organization formats and pursue different purposes. Companies, foundations and associations exist in France and Spain, in Egypt and in the Czech Republic, in the US and India, which engage in social business operations. They operate in a very diverse range of sectors, including the manufacture of goods, provision of services to the general public, training and education, micro loan online portals, organizations that help to preserve and pass on folk crafts and to increase employment. We note that the biggest difference between commercial and social entrepreneurship lies in the definition and application of core values. In a way, social entrepreneurship is the middle ground between conventional (for-profit) entrepreneurship and charity. The biggest distinction between for-profit and social entrepreneurship lies in the definition of core values. The core target values for a social entrepreneur are broad, general positive changes in society; social entrepreneurs often focus on helping underprivileged and oppressed parts of society. However, this cannot imply that social entrepreneurs consciously avoid making a profit from the values they create, as they need to live a full life and continue their operations. No comprehensive approach to defining "social entrepreneurship" has been developed to date. The point of social entrepreneurship (SE) is to address, alleviate and resolve social problems; actions to achieve this goal can involve social influence, innovation, financial self-sufficiency (breakeven), financial stability and sustainability, territorial reach and repeatability. The essence of operating as a social entrepreneur(ship) is to reinvest all profits from operations into the continued development of this social entrepreneurship or the local community, as a matter of principle, rather than maximizing the returns for the sole entrepreneur or multiple owners of this organization. In this case, a social enterprise is a model for a private business organization aiming to achieve a specific result in the life of the general public and the local economy, maintaining a healthy environment for the society to live in, or smoothing over local ethnic pecularities. These formats of social business can help to achieve massive positive change in the social life of any district or city. Overseas social companies may have different organization formats: a social interest company, a limited liability company, a trust company or a cooperative. Deep engagement in the life of the general public relies on close cooperation with local communities and partner agencies.

Europe has agencies that help social companies and are financed by regional governments or municipalities; similar agencies exist in Russia; for example, in the operation of local public utilities and housing management (however, reporting and competitive tenders in these areas in Russia are significantly different from those used overseas). For the purposes of interaction between social companies and government agencies, ministries and institutions, NPOs are a very useful integrator/semiconductor. We call it a semiconductor, because this intermediary has operating and management costs that are an additional burden for the general public. The people of Russia have to feed, sometimes without any good reason or justification, this intermediary layer of NPOs in several areas of social services. And possibly, creating a broad network of financially self-sufficient and self-supporting social companies with transparent reporting would help to reduce the price of social services and deploy the money allocated by the government for the social sector more efficiently. An example here is the way this is done overseas in some cities where social problems associated with poverty, unemployment or housing and public utilities are still very acute, where social entrepreneurs deal with these problems directly without the involvement of NPOs, reducing the cost of such services to the public. This approach is beginning to gain acceptance in Russia in providing employment opportunities for mothers, who are increasingly working from home as seamstresses, travel agents, hair stylists on call, private tutors, live-in tutors for rich children and caregivers for people with severe disabilities, or in similar occupations. This category can also include some healthcare (e.g. pediatric dentistry) units, laundry service outlets, repair shops for home appliances, barber shops and similar service organizations employing people with disabilities.

Russian federal lawmakers and the Federal government have not yet created a foundation of laws and regulations that would promote the establishment of a network of social companies for a broad spectrum of public services. Laws must be in place regulating business infrastructure with special benefits and breaks for social entrepreneurs and social companies, in addition to some benefits already in place to stimulate operations targeting social purposes. At the same time, the mass media will have to join the effort to promote social enterprise in all Russian regions (only about half of Russian regions are currently covered by social businesses). International experience suggests that one way to encourage the active participation of the public in the development of Russian regions and regional groups could be crowd sourcing, a method of aggregating resources and funds through the use of information technology to address issues and solve problems facing the government, the private sector and society at large (including ways to organize people to work towards resolving these problems). The crowd sourcing formula can be recorded as Project = satisfaction * time. Another format of interaction, a way of raising finance for a specific project, is crowd funding. This is a method of raising finance from large groups of individuals for the purposes of developing and making a certain product, implementing a certain project, helping people in need, or organizing events, supporting business organizations, etc. The following crowd funding models are used, among others: donations (without expectation of any kind of a return); donations in exchange for non-financial benefits; investment with a financial return (a.k.a. crowd investing, including the royalty model, people's lending and shareholder crowd funding). The advantage of crowd funding is that it offers a way to raise finance without the involvement of banks, venture capital funds or stock exchanges within a short period of time by organizing effective media coverage. It needs to be used actively for the treatment of people suffering from disease, to support people with disabilities, and to address local (regional) environmental issues. At the same time, to address issues that arise in social services, science, education and culture, NPOs could use more effective methods such as project finance (for specific projects) and operating fund-raising (to cover utilities and materials costs). This is a creative activity to raise funds (by convincing prospective donors) to implement projects of social importance that address issues associated with supporting education, or society's spiritual and cultural environment. Educational, healthcare and cultural organizations engage in fund-raising, bypassing NPOs and formal projects. Fund-raising assumes a greater role as the non-governmental sector becomes more important for addressing problems experienced by the public. Investment can come from an organization for which this investment is part of its PR strategy. As a result, a social project would be presented to the public, rather than "sold." In this case, investors reap benefits in terms of respect from potential customers, improving their public image and indirectly earning additional profits because of this.

Another interaction format is endowment. Although endowments offer some tax benefits for endowment funds, they are generally limited to a highly private, closed "retail" mode of operation, as they are not required to file public reports or disclose information on asset value. Endowment as a financing tool is unavailable to smaller organizations whose services are in relatively lower demand (for example, for humanitarian, educational and some other organizations), and endowment fund management can result in conflicts of interest. Tax and other benefits for donors and contributors to endowment funds in Russia are rather inadequate. This tool is not widely used in Russia at this time, although it provides development finance for education, science, culture and healthcare. Typical recipients of endowment funds are universities, museums, theaters, libraries and some other organizations.

The United States introduced another format for using private investment to finance social development based on Development Impact Bonds (DIB), a type of Social Impact Bonds (SIB).

If a project achieves a positive outcome, the government compensates the private investor's capital expenditure through tax revenue. However, if a project fails to produce a positive outcome, the investor will not receive any compensation, which implies a risky long-term term investment in USD. However, financial compensation to investors can be tied to the level of success accomplished. This way of attracting investors can be appealing to individuals as a comparatively efficient way to invest. Many websites that offer buying and selling bonds (short and long-term debt securities, including Treasury bills, or T-bills) over the Internet, tend to target institutional investors and professional brokers. These websites either limit access to professional research and recommendations, information or other essential tools, offering them only to licensed market professionals, or offer these tools for a fee that is too high for "small-time" individual ("retail") investors to afford.

In addition to actively implementing and using the formats and instruments listed above and described in Table 6, Russia would do well to focus on social entrepreneurship. Social entrepreneurship and other interaction formats can be supported by:

- strengthening the role of social companies in providing social services by enacting new laws (social services could include assistance to socially vulnerable people, including children, expanding the coverage of healthcare services and environmental protection);

- conducting tenders, grant allocation contests and placing government orders for social and environmental initiatives with these social companies;

- creating a community of social entrepreneurs and regional markets for social services capable of producing locally innovative solutions matching the needs of socioeconomic development in an urban environment;

- municipalities could provide financial support for social entrepreneurship development programs and to encourage and promote other legal, organizational, financial and economic formats of socially beneficial activity.

Only about 1% of all companies are engaged in social entrepreneurship in some form at this time in Russia. To improve this, the percentage of such companies will have to be increased at least to 10% as quickly as possible. We must create institutional opportunities and the right conditions on the ground for developing Russian domestic entrepreneurship using examples of businesses' social orientation, the values and culture of ethnic groups living in Russia, and a broad base of socioeconomic education starting from middle or high school. Entrepreneurship implies change and renewal, so encouraging its development should help to generate new ideas, technologies and jobs, and the quality of service should improve.

Table 6. Categorization of capital raising methods and instruments to finance operations of organizations focused on social purposes

Financing instruments and methods	Functions, specific features and risks	Method and speed of information transfer, audience reach	Ways and methods of using the funds (resources) raised	Outcomes (returns) (income/expense) for investor/donor/ provider
Crowd sourcing	Creating voluntary interest in the people (internet users)	IT (electronic communications)	Direct financing, to create (develop and generate) new product, shaping public opinion about it	Practically zero expense on investor (zero returns to investor), investors (donors) contribute voluntarily
Fund raising	Convincing people of the need to contribute, original, effective call for assistance. Result guaranteed by the entity seeking finance	All types of mass media		In exchange for their contributions, investors acquire recognition, trust and respect of customers, with other appealing offers possible
Endowment	Endowment is a financial tool in Russia. Lacks transparency. Not suitable for reaching a broad audience	Narrowly targeted – a call for contributions from large companies and individual investors	Educational, scientific, R&D projects, scholarships and grants for students	Possible outcomes include: trained professionals, new products/ technologies developed, startups, and so on.

Social Bonds	Slow return of invested principal (duration up to 25 years) + interest.	Target audience: large businesses, affluent individuals	Various projects, including: healthcare services, immunization for children, education, social rehabilitation, etc.	Investors receve social bonds + interest as agreed at the time of issuance
Crowdfunding, including: Kickstarter	Personal interest in financing a common goal (bypassing banks and stock exchanges)	IT and electronic communications	Any projects can be financed: creative, social, software development	Without compensation (return), charitable donation. Not expecting any benefits or reputational gains Non-financial returns: generating additional business or raising finance
Crowd investing	Long-term investment of capital with a risk of losing the principal investment	A possible distribution of investment sources: 51% - financiers (professional investors), 20% - business angels or venture capitalists/funds, 29% microinvestors	Projects of different nature, in different sectors	Financial returns. Shares of stock, share in the startup assets, image/ reputational gains

Work is currently under way to expand the coverage of effective social practices to new regions, and promote the development of public-private partnerships (PPP), but the key deterrent to this is a lack of laws and regulations that would define the operating conditions for social entrepreneurs and identify the various players in social entrepreneurship, setting out restrictions and requirements (tests) by meeting which social entrepreneurs could receive certain fiscal benefits (such as tax breaks). The only regulation currently in effect is the Russian Economic Development Ministry's Order No. 223 dated 23.04.2012, which defines social entrepreneurship. It divides different types of social entrepreneurship by, for example, providing services to categories of people with disabilities, or by whether or not such companies have people with disabilities as more than half of their employees generating more than 20% of the company's total revenue. This new resource for interaction should also contain many other organizational, technological, financial and legal tools, including those linked to the establishment of special types of organizations and using corporate interaction formats. In addition, we must refine and expand laws and regulations for non-profit organizations, adding resources to motivate their internal operations and ensuring transparency of their periodic reporting.

At this point in time, as the economy continues to languish in the grip of a protracted crisis, government agencies, ministries and institutions need to support the specific initiatives and the overall proactive approach of centers for innovation in the social sphere which were intended to become the pillars for developing and expanding solutions for crucial social problems and issues, capable of providing micro finance to social entrepreneurs in the regions. In addition, government and municipal organizations tasked with defining the rules for operation of the social sector and NPOs must be assigned the following tasks, among others:

- Searching for effective and efficient partnership models in the chain linking the Government (the State) – types of NPOs – Social Entrepreneurship – society at large. Formats and models should include issues relating to legislature and law-making, standards and financial guidelines, organizational and economic, and include monitoring and statistics gathering and reporting.

- Making sure the general public and social entrepreneurs are well informed about possible ways, methods and sectors of social interaction.

- Ensuring transparent operations and regular reporting by NPOs and social entrepreneurship organizations from nationwide to municipal level.

- Sustained strong dynamism of financing for the social sector across all Russian regions.

These proposed measures should help us expand the toolset for effective interaction and achieve a balance between different socially focused organizations offering their services and the needs of population strata, groups of people and social sectors.

List of References and Further Reading:

1. Russian Economic Development Ministry's Order No. 223 dated 23.04.2012 On organizing competitive tenders for selecting Russian regions for allocation of funds in 2012 to finance measures to support small and medium-sized businesses at the level of Russian Federation regions. (In Russian). Retrieved from: http://www.economic.kurganobl.ru/ // Приказ Минэкономразвития России № 223 от 23.04.2012 г. «Об организации проведения конкурсного отбора субъектов Федерации, бюджетам которых в 2012 году предоставляются для финансирования мероприятий, осуществляемых в государственной поддержки малого и среднего предпринимательства субъектами Российской Федерации»http://www.economic.kurganobl.ru/

2. Zvereva, N. Social Entrepreneurship: Looking Into the Future. [Available online]/ Zvereva N. (In Russian) Retrieved from: http://www.nisse.ru/business/article/article_1640.html?effort // Зверева Н. Социальное предпринимательство: взгляд в будущее [Электронный ресурс] / Н.Зверева // Режим доступа: http://www.nisse.ru/business/article/article_1640.html?effort

3. Lipsett, J. Experience of Social Entrepreneurship in the UK [Available online] / Lipsett, J. Retrieved from http://www.sel.org.uk/publications.html // Липсетт Дж. Опыт социального предпринимательства на примере Великобритании [Электронный ресурс] / Дж.Липсетт // Режим доступа: http://www.sel.org.uk/publications.html

4. Distribution of Companies and Organizations by Legal Type of Organization in 2013 / 2014 Russian Regions Factbook / Available at http://www.gks.ru/bgd/regl/b14_14p/Main.htm / Retrieved from: http://www.gks.ru/bgd/regl/b14_14p/IssWWW.exe/Stg/d02/12-03.htm // Распределение предприятий и организаций по организационно-правовым формам в 2013 гг. http://www.gks.ru/bgd/regl/b14_14p/IssWWW.exe/Stg/d02/12-03.htm из сборника_Регионы_России_2014. Содержание: http://www.gks.ru/bgd/regl/b14_14p/Main.htm

5. Non-Profit Organizations With a Social Focus. Results of a Selective Survey of Non-Profit Organizations Focused on Social Issues, Based on 1 SONKO Form. In Russian. Retrieved from: http://www.gks.ru/wps/wcm/connect/rosstat_main/rosstat/ru/statistics/finance/ // Социально-ориентированные некоммерческие организации http://www.gks.ru/wps/wcm/connect/rosstat_main/rosstat/ru/statistics/finance/.Итоги выборочного исследования социально ориентированных некоммерческих организаций на основе формы №1 СОНКО

6. Strelkov I.S. International Experience of Social Entrepreneurship [Available in Russian online] / Strelkov I.S. In Russian. Retrieved from http://www.nb-forum.ru/sociallinks // Стрелков И. С. Зарубежный опыт социального предпринимательства [Электронный ресурс] / И. С. Стрелков // Режим доступа: http://www.nb-forum.ru/sociallinks

7. Say, J.-B., The Meaning of Social Entrepreneurship [Available online]. Retrieved from: https://entrepreneurship.duke.edu/news-item/the-meaning-of-social-entrepreneurship/ Сэй Ж.Б., Значение социального предпринимательства [Электронный ресурс] / Ж.Б.Сей // http://www.fuqua.duke.edu/centers/case/documents/Dees_SEdef.pdf

8. The Number of Public Associations, Political Parties and Non-Profit Organizations Registered in Russia as of 1 January 2014. / 2014 Russian Regions Factbook / Available in Russian at http://www.gks.ru/bgd/regl/b14_14p/Main.htm / Retrieved from: http://www.gks.ru/bgd/regl/b14_11/IssWWW.exe/Stg/d01/02-06.htm Число общественных объединений, политических партий и некоммерческих организаций, зарегистрированных в РФ на 1 января 2014 г. http://www.gks.ru/bgd/regl/b14_11/IssWWW.exe/Stg/d01/02-06.htm из сборника Россия в цифрах 2014 г. Содержание: http://www.gks.ru/bgd/regl/b14_11/Main.htm

CHAPTER 4

THE ORIGINS OF INTERACTION AND MEASURING EFFECTIVENESS

4.1 Values as a Source of Interaction between Management Subjects and Objects

Interaction is a philosophical category that concerns the process whereby objects and subjects influence one another, their mutual dependence and the generation of one object by another. Interaction is an objective phenomenon, a universal movement or development process that lies behind the existence and structure of any material system.[52] Bringing together all that has been said about interaction in other sections, *the serial execution of mutual economic/legal or financial/organizational managerial actions directed at a partner with the aim of prompting a concretely anticipated response, which calls forth a new response from the initiating party, may be called economic interaction, where it leads to the development or evolution of the participants.*

Since the mid-1980s the world has seen a trend away from away from administration and bureaucratic compulsion toward "cooperation and understanding"[53] in both territorial administration and other organizations, incorporating changes in management paradigms that date from the end of the 20th century. These ideas underlie the concept of public value, which gave rise to the value-oriented approach to strategic management between subjects and objects.

A management system operating between a subject and an object, and oriented toward increasing value for its participants – so-called value-oriented management – was first described in 1986 by Rappaport[54], while the term "value-based management" (VBM) was proposed by J. McTaggart. Value-based management rests on values thinking, which presupposes that all aspects of a company's management should be subordinated to a single goal; the primary goal of management is to maximize the value of the organization's (company's) capital. Value-based management requires managers and decision-makers to know what factors create value, that is, to know what variables have an impact on the organization's or company's value. These variables delineate various managerial decisions about the business in the areas of investment, finance and operations (including production, supply, marketing, personnel, etc.).

---

[52] "Взаимодействие" ["Interaction"], Wikipedia, https://ru.wikipedia.org/wiki/взаимодействие.

[53] Роберт С. Каплан, Дейвид П. Нортон, Организация, ориентированная на стратегию [Robert S. Kaplan, David P. Norton, The Strategy-Focused Organization] (Moscow: Olympus Business, 2004), 143–145.

[54] Alfred Rappaport, Creating Shareholder Value: A Guide for Managers and Investors (New York: Free Press, 1997).

At the same time, it is significant that "value" is a broader category, one widely applied in philosophical and sociological literature to designate the human, social and cultural significance of concrete actions taken by participants in events. The methods and principles applied to assessing that significance are reflected in moral principles and in normative arrangements, ideals and goals. Value is not defined by the qualities of these things themselves, but by their engagement with human activity, interests, needs and social relationships. The criteria and means for assessing significance (the extent to which such qualities are engaged) are expressed in moral principles, norms, ideals and arrangements that conflate with the concept of a "goal".[55]

In value-based management, interactions between subject and object are characterized by consensus and dialogue, informal ties, networks and contacts (rather than one-sided, unidirectional communication). For both parties, the outcome of an interaction is the creation and acquisition of value, utility arising from the interrelationship between the participants.

For a clearer understanding of economic interaction, it helps to recall that in social relationships closely related to economic relationships, interaction takes a number of possible forms. The most common is dichotomization: cooperation and competition (agreement and conflict, adaptation and opposition). In this case, both the content of the interaction (cooperation or competition) and the degree to which that interaction is manifested (successful or less successful cooperation) define the character of relationships between the participants (here, subject and object). At the same time, three types of interaction have been denoted: additive, intersecting and hidden. In an additive interaction, the partners properly perceive one another's positions. In the process of an intersecting interaction, the partners, on the one hand, demonstrate an inadequate understanding of the positions and actions of the other participant and, on the other hand, clearly reveal their own aims and actions. A hidden interaction

---

[55] A.Y. Selin, "Формирование эффективной системы регионального стратегирования" [The formation of an effective regional strategizing system] (Izhevsk, economics candidate degree thesis abstract, 2006), 10.

plays out simultaneously on two levels: one overt or explicit and the other hidden or implicit.

An interaction embraces two facets: its content (that around which or because of which it takes place) and its style (how the subject interacts with others). In economic relationships, management subjects are understood to mean direct and immediate superiors, functional management or influences (indirect and material), so the types of interaction referred to above generally fall into the economic category, although here subject-object relationships are as a rule defined by contracts, with the remainder subject to legal or administrative resolution involving third parties. The relationships between the parties are in general prescribed in writing and interactions are more transparent and predictable.

At particularly large businesses and organizations values and goals can be quite diverse. General organizational goals are formulated and affirmed on the basis of an organization's overall mission, as well as the particular values and goals that guide its senior managers. Because that orientation is defined by goals that permeate all lower levels of managerial decision-making, those goals must have certain characteristics. Fundamental goals are overt, while implicit goals are for various reasons hidden. Often an organization has several explicit (overt) goals.

In the process of formulating and working towards an organization's explicit goals, various constraints, tasks and roles become apparent, along with their duration and sequence. In this case, supplementary goals emerge, that were not initially defined, evident or known due to fluctuations in price, supply and demand, or for other reasons. In effect, such goals exist in implicit form as an inevitable consequence of the organization's declared internal goals, as well as internal and external constraints, and so on, and so are labelled "hidden". There are also distinctions in terms of achievability between critically important goals and desirable goals. For example, for any business maximizing profit is a desirable goal, while its critical goals include survival, that is, receiving a certain minimal essential income. External goals are those that facilitate interactions with partners outside the organization, while internal goals are those linked to its own particular interests and that do not directly concern other parties. If the organization is contractor that fulfils client orders, then its external goals are those that involve clients, suppliers and subcontractors, while its internal goals are those that concern business volume, profits and employee motivation.

Avoiding conflicting goals is extremely important to a company. An organization's goals must not conflict with one another, and still less with the goals and tasks that it shares with its partners. Multiple goals should be mutually supporting, that is, actions and decisions taken with the aim of reaching certain goals should not interfere with reaching others. Where goals cannot be made mutually supporting, conflicts will emerge between various subdivisions of the organization that are responsible for setting and reaching particular goals, and also in the company's relationships with its partners.

Closer analysis of relative importance and priority is required in order to prioritize goals. Two or three levels of priority should be identified. One possible hierarchy of goal priorities is proposed here (Table 7).

Table 7. Priorities and goal levels in organizations

Priority level	Preferential content	Achievemen t conditions
1	In general, assigned to goals that define the success of the organization as a whole (values orientation)	Must be achieved
2	Assigned to important goals that, where necessary, can be ignored for the sake of reaching priority level 1 goals (values support)	Should be achieved

		To be achieved under favorable internal and external conditions
3	Supplementary goals (consumption value)	

Over time and in the course of interaction, an organization's goals may occasionally change places in the hierarchy of priorities. Furthermore, goals may be assigned different priorities at different levels of management or in different subdivisions within the organization. There are a great many examples of organizations that set (for example) social goals, but whose outcomes remain focused on the economic side of their activities. Bearing in mind the analysis above, we can identify seven value areas that influence the process of managerial decision-making (Table 8).

Table 8. Value orientations and management decisions in organizations

Value area	Value category	Preferred goal types
Product	High functional value of goods to users	Increased production, improved design and product attractiveness
Economic	Practicality, utility, wealth	Expansion, profits, results
Social	Relations between organizations and subdivisions, absence of conflict	Social responsibility, climate, indirect competition, quality

Political	Power, recognition, status	Size (capital), market share, number of employees
Religious	Eternal values in various cultures	Ethics, morality, rectitude
International	Harmony and integration of views, general human values	Physical and intangible impact of goods on quality of social life, transformation of public needs
Cognitive	Truth, knowledge, rational thought	Long-term research and development

The concrete goals of commercial organizations typically involve profitability, the market, productivity, goods, finance, scale, innovation, human resources, organization, social responsibility and competitiveness.

As is well known, competitive advantages are ultimately embodied in the goods produced by this system and provided to the market. Selling goods that have a competitive advantage, or that were created with the help of a competitive advantage internal to the organization, allows it to generate an effect. Revenues from the sale of those goods, and so the effect, flow back into the system that made use of the competitive advantage. The effect is accounted for chiefly by the values (both fundamental and superimposed) that are embodied in the goods, which see constant improvement in the form of an increasingly useful product line and changes in the goods' functional characteristics. This cycle has implications for the quality of interaction between subject and object, in the case of both partnerships between producer organizations and relationships where the subject is producer organizations and the object end consumers.

Turning to interaction between businesses, the social and productive system allocates the revenues generated to various internal uses (remuneration of personnel, technical or social development of the system itself, and so on) and (or) to the acquisition/purchase of a new competitive value. This constitutes the feedback mechanism between the system of production and the company's values. It is very important for revenues to be channeled into the acquisition of effective (future) competitive values that can then be actualized as new competitive advantages for the system. Of all the values newly acquired by the system, the most effective are fundamental, global strategic values. This category includes new information technology and designs, changes in the structure or technology of a company facility, and strategic exclusive rights to the use of a particular competitive advantage. The primary difficulty here is in carrying out a comprehensive analysis, in grasping the chain of procedures by which value is transformed into effect, and then measuring the outcome resulting from that effect. From this, we may draw the conclusion that technical, social, economic or comprehensive evaluations of competitive advantage constitute a multi-faceted systemic process of interactions between organizational structures – in which case the process is bound to succeed.

The utility of an object depends on many factors, whose essence and parameters are shaped by a classification of value macro-characteristics, each of which has its own distinguishing features. This gives rise to a question: does or can an object contain a certain value or set of values? To examine this question, consider a cross-referencing of forms with their macro-characteristics (sufficient conditions) in the classification of values (Table 9).

Table 9. Correspondence between value forms and macro-characteristics of management subjects and objects

Macro-characteristics and qualities	Nature and form of values
Value content, essence	Qualitative (general utility)
	Cost-related
	Behavioral
	Synergetic
Source or basis for creation of value	Objective, natural, inherited
	Subjective, determined by the ethical conditions prevailing between partners
Values' place in system	Outside subject–object relationships
	Inside subject–object relationships
Ability to assess value	Quantitative assessment possible
	No quantitative assessment possible
Variability	Enduring, strategic
	Not enduring, tactical
Value propagation	Unlimited propagation possible in given environment
	Limited propagation in given environment
	Personal relationships

Ability to control value	Controlled by participants, deterministic
Types of consumption value	Product quality
	Product price
	Product brand and image
	Product effectiveness
	Service quality
	Competitive or egalitarian environment
	Subjective
	Intermittent acquisition

When subdivisions of an organization compete for qualified personnel, among the important factors are intelligence and qualifications, health, and the parameters of a person's psychological profile. For managers in particular, they include intelligence and culture, knowledge of various fields, the ability to set and reach goals, health, etc. Interaction between subjects and objects on the basis of shared values allows the partners to achieve the best possible outcomes. If managers and other professionals receive satisfaction from their work as a result of common and shared values, that is a solid bulwark for competitiveness. Attractive working conditions, however, do not factor into success. Subdivisions of an organization always stand in need of aspiration, a certain sense of "hunger and dissatisfaction" that encourages the appearance of new qualities in the goods produced, and so the acquisition of shared values that promote further interaction between subject and object. In that sense, other characteristics are important in technical systems: system quality as seen in the ability to satisfy needs, the cost of acquiring and operating the system, and service quality. To that end, a system of production for developing and creating technical systems must itself comprise: an advanced design system; meaningful and radical innovations; renewable equipment and technical gear; top-line personnel; and so on. In general, from the point of view of an organization's socio-economic system, a business must have competitive personnel, technologies and equipment, and a management structure that can adapt to a dynamic environment in order to interact with it.

This leads to the conclusion that interaction – including competitive advantages (competition expands the consumer market) – rests on the essence of value, which emerges as the source of those advantages (physical, intangible, financial, social and other values) and depends not only on its content, but also on its origin, the spend and scale of unfolding events, and of course synchronized support from partners in maintaining the technical components of the interaction. The process by which subject and object reach shared goals is illustrated in Figure 9, whose key features are a common definition of goals and, above all, informal feedback following on both initial and subsequent joint outcomes, which is then analyzed in order to reach top-level goals.

If we wish to define goal formation, it can be described as the process of choosing one or several goals, together with established parameters that set out allowable deviations, for the purposes of managing the process of actualizing an idea. Frequently it is understood as the practical conceptualization of a person's activities in terms of formulating (setting) and actualizing (achieving) goals by the most efficient (remunerative) means possible, or as effective management of the time resources conditioned by the person's activities. Goal formation is the initial stage of management, which involves the formulation of general goals and goal sets (goal trees) in accordance with the purpose (mission) of the system, the provisions of its strategy and the nature of the tasks being performed.[56]

---

[56] "Целеполагание в менеджменте" ["Goal Formation in Management"] Center-YF, http://center-yf.ru/data/Menedzheru/Celepolaganie.php

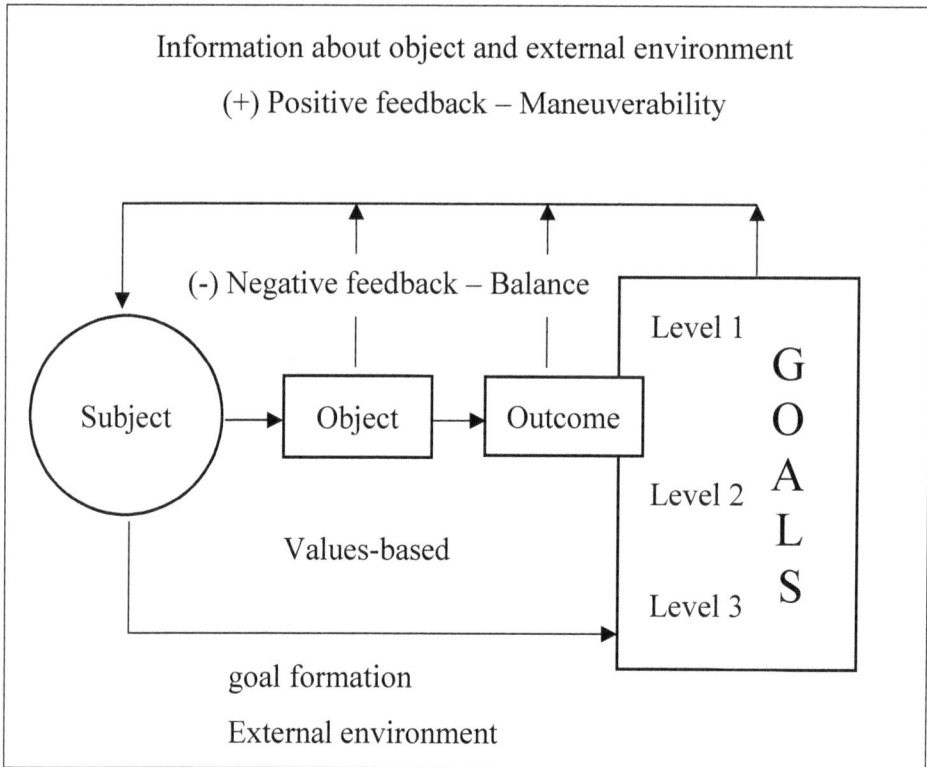

Information about object and external environment

(+) Positive feedback – Maneuverability

(-) Negative feedback – Balance

Level 1

Subject

Object

Outcome

G
O
A
L
S

Level 2

Values-based

Level 3

goal formation

External environment

Fig. 9. Reaching goals common to object and subject

As stated earlier, a value is something out of the ordinary, something possessed by a system, something contained within a subject and (or) object, which is to be preserved or obtained in future, for example: spirituality, honesty, talent, freedom to decide, health, professionalism, self-discipline, an attractive climate, competitive advantage, and so on. For a business organization, there are various specific values associated with the mission put forward by the owner–proprietor of the organization.

In that context, a company's value orientation can be classified in the following manner:

- an ideological organization follows the motto: "We have our rules, which are more important than money." Ideological companies typically seek to widen their influence over the market through the application of their own progressive work standards, and in special cases may become iconic, completely transforming the market;

- a material organization is guided by the motto "Money above all". Material organizations expand their owners' and shareholders' income and can take over a market in the absence of a strong ideological competitor;

- an emotional organization follows the principle: "Relations are more important than money." Such companies take shape around internal inter-personal relationships and invariably lose out in competition;

- an animate organization is guided by the slogan: "Our big guy knows the right thing to do today." The company functions like a family and will lose out in competition.

The levels of value in interacting organizations (subject and object) are linked together by a certain hierarchy of values. If we imagine a segmented pyramid similar to the Maslow hierarchy of needs[57], this can be presented as follows (Fig. 10):

---

[57] Абрахам Маслоу, Мотивация и личность [Abraham H. Maslow, Motivation and Personality], 3rd ed. (Saint Petersburg: Piter, 2003).

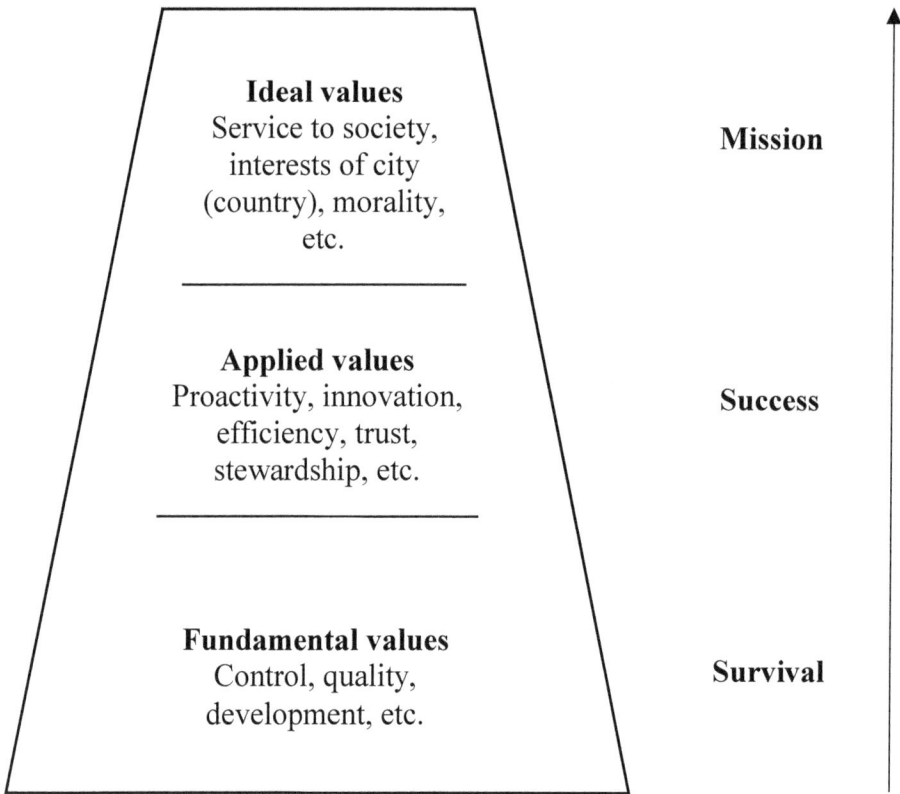

Fig. 10. Possible hierarchy of values and goal formation for organizations

One of the requisite conditions for total customer satisfaction is the formation a strong behavioral culture within a company, one where customer satisfaction is a goal for each subdivision of the management subject and object and for each employee. The organizational culture of the subject and object are important for harmonious interaction between them. The values of organizational culture include: an active orientation; fidelity to one's work; openness to customers and partners; useful (modest, not inflated) staff numbers; allowing employees to show independence and initiative; a combination of simultaneous freedom and firm action; a genuine link to real life and values guidance; and universal productivity among employees. These make it possible for values to emerge within the structure of both subject and object. It is important here that value concepts held by the subject's and object's managers and their employees coincide, and that account is taken in the workplace of competing values with the potential to affect the organizational values of subject and object. This may be illustrated with a diagram (Figure 11) that shows the mutual influence and conjunction of reference values within an organizational structure.

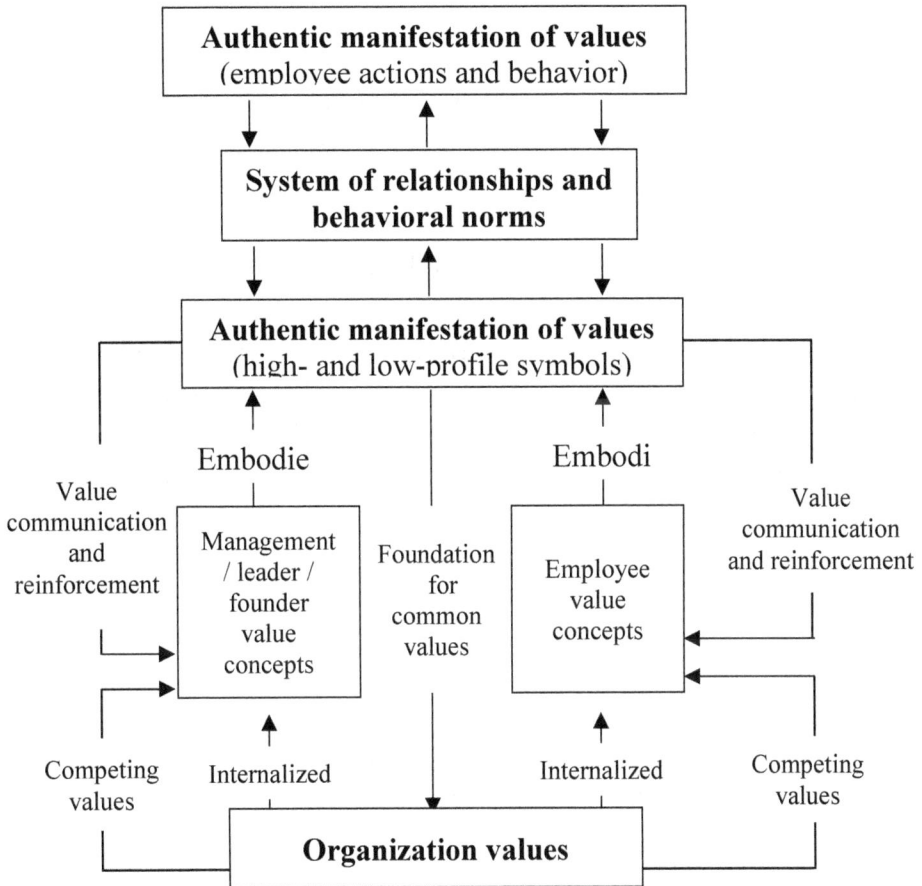

Fig. 11. Interaction of value concepts and their manifestations in an organization

If values are to serve as the motive force of interaction between management subjects and objects, it is important to give structure to the culture of employee motivation. The culture of motivation contains both material and intangible elements, specifically:

- material elements incorporating: production environment culture, work remuneration culture, and material incentive culture; and

- intangible elements incorporating: moral incentive culture, a system of responsibility, and some degree of psychological coding (corporate ideology).

These elements are formalized in documented procedures, specifically: goals and criteria; forms of recognition for work achievements (or non-performance); descriptions of the methods of statistical analysis in use; and a list of possible corrective and warning measures.

In speaking about corporate culture, which also includes the interaction of subject and object, it should be noted that it is significantly affected by the mix of fundamental values, convictions, unspoken understandings and norms shared by all participants in the corporation (subjects + objects). Where interaction is characterized by a value chain, this provides an instrument for strategic analysis and for identifying focus areas where detailed analysis of the organizations' activities can contribute to strategic planning. The value chain apportions the company's activities into strategically important types of operation that can be used to study outlays and existing or potential means of differentiation. A company's competitive advantage arises from its ability to carry out strategic operations more successfully than its competitors. To conclude this section, consider as an example the following formalized list of values compiled by the URALSIB financial corporation:

– approach to principles, values and rules of behavior – every employee of the corporation upholds its corporate values, principles and rules of behavior;

– approach to material remuneration – the corporation's incentive system is aimed at execution of a multidimensional strategic plan;

– approach to internal work regulations – every employee of the corporation voluntarily and consciously accepts responsibility for adherence to internal work regulations;

– approach to interaction and internal service – our priorities in interaction and internal service. (This point may imply neglect of value in interaction with partners and clients, but this is consistent with the corporation's self-preservation);

– approach to gifts – the corporation allows employees to accept gifts whose approximate value does not exceed 200 US dollars. If the receipt of a gift leads to special privileges for a client, the employee shall inform management.

– the levels of organizational culture in an organization can be split into three groups:

– artifacts: the superficial level seen by an outside observer;

– values and norms: a middle level, only partially visible from outside;

– behavior and archetypes: the deepest level.

Experience from other countries shows that a significant portion (if not the large majority) of small and mid-sized firms fall within the sphere of interest of major businesses. Small and mid-sized businesses are not only encompassed by a system of cooperative ties with major companies, they are an integral part of those larger corporations' production structures. Corporations take advantage of the market and structural flexibility of small and mid-sized enterprises, as well as their opportunities for innovation. This interaction between small (mid-sized) enterprises and corporations is effected in several ways: through contracts and sub-contracting; franchising, leasing and factoring; business incubators; venture financing; and industry networks (clusters).

The interaction between subject and object in state structures is also characterized by a large number of dynamic links. Academic literature on philosophy and cybernetics typically focuses on direct ties, with interactions between subject and object largely reduced to fine-tuning and processing information flows, and to making and implementing decisions. Evidently, in this case self-regulation, although it does reflect certain general cause-and-effect relationships in such systems, is more applicable to automated and technical systems. In the case of subject–object relations of an official or legal nature, information is only one form of tie, as they are further characterized by: forecasting; the active search for connections; system- and organization-building as such; conscious variations in behavior; fundamental decisions of policy; and various types of interaction (organizational, legal, technical/economic and social/psychological). It is not any one type that is subject to mutual regulation; the entire set of relationships – economic, work, psychological, and organizational, which must all be on the same platform – is governed by a system of values that defines the overall developmental thrust in their interactions.

The effectiveness of interaction between management subject and object depends to a significant degree on the extent to which they properly understand one another. The nature of interaction between subjects and objects, and the social roles that they fulfill, are among the most important factors that shape mutual cognition. At the same time, for each of the interacting parties what is important in their partners is, first and foremost, those elements of their essence, image and behavior which are most valuable in the process of reaching the goals of their joint activities.

4.2 Interaction Compatibility Levels and Assessments

Competition and cooperation (collaboration of partnership) are recognized as the main formats of economic interaction. All types of interaction are traditionally divided into two groups: partnership (cooperation), often also denoted by words such as: "collaboration," "concert," "agreement," "adjustment" and "association." In turn, competition can be described by the following terms: "rivalry," "conflict," "opposition," "disassociation." Certainly, some of these terms are subject to contentious discussion, and we propose further refining and narrowing these definitions below, reconciling the opponents and bringing them closer to a compatible solution, helping them find consensus on matters with regard to which they hold opposing views.

Interactions can be short-term or long-term by their nature, usually depending on the subject at the center of the interaction. If an interaction deals with buying and selling products or services, it would most likely be a short-term interaction. If economic relations have to do with land, natural resources generating rent, or lease (or a similar transaction) involving territory (premises), structures under construction and completed structures and buildings, they are likely to be longer-term. In turn, there are values which give rise to interactions (interconnections, mutual influences, and overall relationships) that can continue obtain for thousands of years – an example of these would be spiritual and moral interactions between ethnic groups and peoples that share the same or have similar roots of their religion. At the same time, when we talk about compatibility levels, we cannot possibly ignore the proposed hierarchy of relations: focusing on physical goods and money (commerce); finance and economic aspects; socioeconomic; sociopolitical; social and religious; cultural and pertaining to philosophy and world outlook; pertaining to science and innovation and focused on implementation of innovations. However, the most important thing is how all these seven levels interact, because in real life no separate combination of fewer than seven levels exists in a vacuum. Degree of compatibility of these (seven main) compatibility levels defines the quality of interaction in any specific area where all similar organizations that share a similar mission operate. Therefore, to make sure all efforts at each compatibility level are combined ("balled into a fist"), vectors of all events must have a similar direction and share the same purposes of their interaction.

We note further that some content aspects of interaction exist at every compatibility level. If parties in interaction represent organizations based in the same country and the same vertical power structure, we will be talking about horizontal interaction, in which two participants operate in the same environment – legal, organizational, economic and fiscal. If third (and other) parties are involved, relationships of trust (which have been built over the course of interaction) are replaced by a relationship of high mutual interdependence, in which every party depends on the others (including fiscal partners) through a multi-step chain of relations in specific areas of operation. Vertical interactions arise alongside horizontal interactions.

As multilateral interactions begin taking shape, local communication networks emerge that make it possible to group the parties in the overall interaction, which are involved in and defined by these multilateral interactions. As a general rule, these networks define and govern financial, organization, information and other coordinating flows between the parties. Direct interactions between the parties engaged in the value creation chain are minimal, as the sale or purchase transaction is seen as the end-result. However, each new interaction between the parties produces the first signs of a relationship of trust which can become the foundation for future sustainable and strong communication-based connections. Therefore, multiple interactions on the level of goods (assets) and financial, economic interactions penetrate the consciousness of the parties, their corporate culture, serving as a foundation for an ideology of interconnections based on trust (a dialogue), percolating further into the moral atmosphere of business and personal preferences of those involved in this interaction on the level of business ethics. While a simple business (commercial) relationship starts more or less in the mode of "every man for himself," by this point the parties have much in common, many things unite them and bring them closer, creating kind of a community. Certainly, risks and conflicts on the Russian markets for goods and services are capable of antagonizing anyone (and fiscal authorities only exacerbate this problem), which is a scourge of our non-democratic financial and legal system that perpetuates incompatibility, even in relationships that seems well-established on the surface. Pervasive bureaucracy, with is unprofessionalism, general mistrust of business, graft, corruption and an ossified, inflexible approach to real-life situations, makes horizontal and vertical interactions ineffectual, for example, when a new executive or a financier is hired by a large company (or a group of companies, or a government agency, or a municipality) and the existing relationships begin to fall apart. The role of a personality in interactions at different levels of management in Russia is very significant, and no rules or laws can be expected to keep a balance in interactions between two parties, as long as Russia lacks a well-developed democratic economic and legal environment for interactions between private businesses and authorities at all levels of government (on the so-called "power vertical." The current environment is not exactly conducive to democratic rivalry (competition). In the 25 years of Russia's transition to a free market, mutually beneficial interactions have begun to emerge slowly (however, they are mostly restricted to business and political clans and nepotistic relationships). Periodic international conflicts and economic crises prevent the desired progress in this area. And yet, conditions are beginning to emerge for more complex groups of organizations to take shape, groups that are connected by more than purely property-focused relations or trade in goods or services. Organizations united into free-market associations or groups are building and fostering long-term interactions that not only reflect their strategic interests, but also serve as a symbol, a demonstration of the organization's focus on sustainable long-term cooperation. Importantly, this focus on sustainable interactions promotes the emergence of a common field of knowledge and information, helping all participants to grow, reaching qualitatively new levels. The collaborative type of interaction is most efficient for this kind of development of organizations' teams (and personalities within those teams); this type of interaction is based on objective knowledge, relying on one another's strengths, realistic evaluation (or self-evaluation) of these strengths; humanistic, friendly, trusting, democratic relations, proactive attitudes and the strong contribution of all parties, jointly thought-through and approved actions, positive mutual influences – to wit, a high development level of all components of such an interaction.

Collaboration of participants in a business process requires joint goal-setting, joint planning of future activity, joint distribution of potential and capabilities, resources and workload over time in a manner that reflects the capabilities of every participant in business processes, makes possible joint supervision and evaluation of performance, generating feedback for adjustment of subsequent goals and targets. Collaboration does not allow for pointless work that brings no results. Collaboration may entail conflicts or contradictions, but all of them have to be constructive and be resolved on the basis of common efforts to achieve the ultimate goal. These contradictions should not impinge on the interests of interacting parties, opening new roads for the team and its individual members to reach qualitatively new, improved levels.

If we were to consider different aspects of directions of interaction: between the government and a business, between the government and a non-profit organization, or, for a clearer picture, at the level of relationship between two similar organizations, a unified classification of interactions between players on a market in goods and services can be presented as follows:

Table 10. Combined list of interactions between market players

Market components	Level or grade	Types of interaction
Level of competition	Free	Competition
	Moderate	Regulated competition
	Limited	Dictatorship
Type (method) of competition	On price	Price-based
	Other than on price	Not price-based
Evaluation of compatibility of player's operations	Lack of coordination (-)	Antagonistic
	Good coordination (+)	Based on trust
Strength of legal underpinnings of the market environment	High	Contract-based
	Low	Framework-based
Operating performance	Sustainable	Single-goal
	Unstable	Invariant
Business firms' involvement in takeover of market segments	Mutual reallocation	Horizontal
	Parallel reallocation	Contiguous
	Dictatorial reallocation	Vertical
Number of players	Two players	Specific
	Multiple players	Multi-aspect

Activity vector	The milieu of the players (comprising the players themselves and nothing else)	Internal
	The environment surrounding the players	External
Relationships among players	Direct	Direct / transparent
	Indirect	Circumstantial or indirect / obscured
Players' management functions	Mandatory	Regulated
	Optional	Unregulated
Time horizon	Medium-term	Technology-related
	Short-term	Procedural
Types of players' objectives	Material	Monetary, pecuniary
	Non-material	Charitable

We can also base a possible classification on the type of interaction, identifying the following three attributes: the attitudes of interacting parties to each other's interests, whether or not they have a consciously recognized common goal for their cooperation, and how "subjective" their positions vis-à-vis each other are in the interaction. Different combinations of these attributes yield specific types of interactions: cooperation, a dialogue, agreement, relationship of trust, suppression, indifference, confrontation.

After Russia's "rich man's privatization" of the 1990s, markets were built and controlled by players with money (mostly international players and domestic criminal associations and individuals) or by those who could use government funds for their own purposes with impunity, mostly high-ranking government officials and their family members and close associates. This made it possible to build very specific horizontal and vertical connections quickly (with the exception of turf wars over the juiciest parts of the markets). This represents horizontal interactions between companies within a sector, similar to interactions between partners. In a similar way, horizontal links between suppliers/contractors and principles represent associations of organizations from different sectors connected by technology processes and procedures required for manufacturing (or otherwise producing) the finished product. Vertical interactions are those arising in larger conglomerates, including industrial clusters. These can include associations, alliances and groups of organizations of different types and forms of ownership, including those controlled or completely or partially owned by government organizations, agencies or municipalities; such associations, alliances or groups can be created by their constituent organizations (or according to instructions from the government or other superior authority; a network of non-profit organizations would be an example of this).

The impact of the crisis forces changes in the market structure (level consolidation), expanding the extent and reach of monopolies and oligopolies. This is something that we observe at this time. In this connection, a greater number of short-term interactions will be replaced by relatively fewer medium-term and long-term contracts, with reductions explained by bankruptcies of many small businesses. Such interaction processes usually lead to:

- stronger cooperation between organizations within the same region and across several regions, and standardization of various aspects of their interaction and operations;

- changes in barriers to movement of the essential resources between these organizations within a single region;

- consolidation of markets of individual regions into a combined trans-regional market;
- elimination of various distinctions of economic consumer (intermediate and ultimate consumers) based in different Russian regions;
- removal of distinctive features and possible exacerbation of discrimination against players in each one of the regional economies within Russia.

Interactions between participants in the current markets create a certain system of relationships on the micro level that includes: relationships between active sellers in the market; relationships between sellers and buyers; relationships between active and potential sellers. This interaction of market participants reflects the full spectrum of measures that can affect supply and demand. If the market (environment) exerts pressure on the producers (pressure may also be exerted by the government operating as a monopoly) as a dominant type of interaction, this can be quite dangerous, because some companies tend to become more passive and opportunistic, sacrificing their efficiency and initiative, becoming indecisive and incapable of sustained operations; whereas other organizations become too despotically dominant and aggressive towards businesses they interact with, towards the environment, becoming entrenched in their (potentially delusional) sense of supremacy, even complacency. This type of interaction often leads to conflicts and confrontation.

Market interactions can also be indicative of an organization's strategic behavior. Strategic behavior is commonly defined as comprehensive behavior in the course of which a business picks one of the possible alternatives for its actions (deciding on the price, quantity and quality of its products) taking into consideration possible reactions by its competitors. Strategic behavior implies that an organization can influence the market, affecting the equilibrium market price. The degree of this influence would depend on the business organization's strategic power: its market share, its public image and access to market information. Only when organizations are relatively evenly matched in power (influence) can they influence each other, on the one hand, and do they have to make allowances for reciprocal influence by competition, on the other. The degree of market competitiveness is a key criterion for categorizing interactions of a certain organization. There are three market categories: perfectly competitive markets with a maximum degree of competitive interaction at one end of the spectrum, monopolistic markets with minimal (or non-existent) competition at the other, and imperfectly competitive markets in the middle, with some competition present, while its effects are diluted by the actions of some extraordinarily powerful players.

The available literature on the subject covers quite extensively the categorization of market players depending on the degree of competition. Therefore, when discussing types of interaction, we only note that interaction can take the shape of the following actions in different types of markets:

- competitive behavior, with players highly dependent on one another in a perfectly competitive market;

- market behavior categorized by medium inter-dependence of market players upon one another in an oligopolistic market;

- monopoly behavior where a player can act independently of all other players in a monopolistic market.

Interaction among market participants enables them to make a market highly competitive, while changes in economic environment and passive response to such changes weakens interaction among market players, undermining the condition of producers and, as a result, their consumers and partners in this market. In practical terms, this means that oligopoly (regulated by the government and/or municipalities) is currently the prevailing format of interaction in countries with a developed free market (mixed) economy. In this case, competition on price and other factors invites attention from the government (federal, regional or local) which can dampen price fluctuations and ensure consistent product quality.

Compatible coexistence of competitors and partners can result in either adversarial (competitive) or independent behavior in the market, or, alternatively, in coordinated (collaborative) actions by partners involved in marketing a product (moving it from producers through intermediate to ultimate consumers). Staying within the legal boundaries of economic activity offers some degree of protection and comfort to market players provided that relations and interactions between organizations are strictly and unambiguously defined; such interactions and the overall situation would be typical of a well-developed free market economy. The alternative would be for relations and interactions between market players to be based mostly on informal agreements (arrangements) rather than on properly drafted and executed paper contracts. If the legal environment were more institutionalized, market relations and conditions would be more stable and predictable; the opposite is also true. Typical features and factors of stable markets include minimum efficient production, producer diversification, demand elasticity and growth, foreign competition and product diversification.

In this context, interaction through integration is especially important. As research into different approaches to integration (there are more than 24 different integration strategies) indicates, 30% of all cases in the US tend to benefit from development without integration (without control over all assets needed for production/operation). However, a majority of businesses that proceed with integration resort to partial integration (in 75-85% of all cases), while only 15-25% of businesses implement full integration. Quasi integration accounts for around 25% of all cases when businesses decide whether or not to control their assets, but this is the most promising option for business integration. Factors that make quasi integration especially relevant (for Russia, with its vast territory, among other countries) include irreversible globalization processes and concomitant qualitative changes not only in the competitive situation in the market, but also in consumer needs. In addition, integration into business groups is a logical outcome of evolution in interactions of regional organizations and companies (organizations active in their local environment). Therefore, we need to take a look at different possible business associations of market players (organizations).

Any study of unstable markets would indicate that to be compatible with this dynamic environment, a business organization has to respond not only to strong, but also (and most importantly) to weak market signals from the entire market. An organization's behavior is largely spontaneous, triggered mostly by its decisions. This can manifest itself through efforts of organizations to enter into vertical/horizontal or mixed contracts, and join an industry-specific or a regional industrial association or group. In other words, the high costs associated with signing contracts reduce the stimuli for an organization to engage in competitive interactions, encouraging it instead to choose cooperative interactions. An organization can become part (or a subsidiary) of another company, or it can split into two or three organizations if it was originally active in several areas, to avoid additional costs. An organization may transcend its industry, exit it and move entirely to a similar (or different) industry, for example, a dining establishment can enter the hotel or travel industries. In other words, an organization's refreshed interactions presume its higher compatibility with different aspects of its environment, from new accounting requirements to a radical push to advance its culture for producing a completely new and different type of goods. Essentially, compatibility is defined by the development of institutional, systemic, evolutionary, global and information economies, with the direct involvement of those sociopolitical, social and religious organizations and institutions that define the ideology and cultural values of peoples, that in turn define entire countries and states.

This is why a staggered (rather than instantaneous) privatization in Russia, with its large territory, spanning many different sectors as well as the large-scale reorganization of many sub-sectors in the resource production and processing economies have turned a stable market into an amorphous one (with weak or otherwise lacking institutions), reducing the compatibility of this environment, and making it largely unsuitable for the sustainable operation of various companies and interactions between them. As it turns out, the more active that a market participant is by using a range of different interaction formats, the more compatible it can be with this (constantly changing) environment, as well as with other cross-sectoral environments that it may find appealing. To achieve this, all subsystems of a business organization (there seven key subsystems of this kind) must be operating "at full capacity."

Let us take a look at how key subsystems in an organization can be matched with subsystems within the environment of social needs by overlaying one type of structure over the other. Table 11 indicates that every subsystem in a business organization finds a correspondence, that every level in one substructure corresponds to a compatibility level (meso system) in the other macro environment (society).

Table 11. Providing an example of functional correspondence: compatibility between macro and micro systems:

Subsystems in which the society (community) develops	Formative subsystems of an organization (within a community)
Cognitive/learning (scientific) and spiritual level	Cognitive subsystem
Level of culture and philosophy (world outlook)	Mental subsystem
Level of religion and theology	Cultural subsystem
Political level	Historical subsystem
Social level	Institutional subsystem
Financial and economic level	Imitation subsystem
Level of products and assets	Organizational, technological, asset-based subsystem

As we can see, a harmoniously compatible environment for the development of society comprises seven levels, but most importantly, this environment should be compatible, ensuring that society would not be stuck in a recurring scenario of monotonous socioeconomic and sociopolitical crises, following instead the path of development through innovation, which requires all the levels to interact with one another. The table above shows compatibility levels for a business organization on the right and compatibility levels of its environment on the left. Interactions of these levels determine the environment's compatibility structure to support human development (as a personality and vis-à-vis one's family), development of the organization and various communities which ultimately unite to span 7 billion people.

It follows from the above, as we go back to market interactions, that this process is about more than just operation of companies manufacturing and otherwise producing all the goods, including fixed assets for other companies. Business technologies also rely on operations of financial and economic organizations that create and ensure effective operation of the securities markets. These organizations have been carried away with financial and political speculation in recent years, operating largely for their own benefit, creating financial bubbles and reducing Karl Marx's famous formula of money – goods – money to money1 – money2...

Since the end of the 1990s, the sociopolitical environment has mostly aimed to address strategic goals and become based on partnership. For the full-year 1999, hostile takeovers accounted for less than 5% of the combined value of corporate takeovers, representing less than 0.2% of the total number of such deals. However, in line with the cycle theory, in 2015 artificially created hotspots of political discord flared up again in many African countries, in the Middle East and Ukraine, as a result of renewed redistribution of global resources and spheres of influence and the USA's redoubled efforts to recover and maintain its erstwhile geopolitical influence. Back to square one. Achieving compatibility requires interaction by all organizations comprising more than just the level of products and physical assets and the financial/economic level. This would require the involvement of organizations that shape the social, political, religious and theological, cultural and philosophical, and scientific and educational (innovational and creative) levels. The main path for transition to other, more productive types of interaction relies on engagement in collaborative creative activity, which serves to create conditions for shared emotional spiritual experiences, requiring every participant to make a significant contribution to the overall result, generating relationships that do not involve material (financial) dependence. In turn, indifferent, detached, emotionless type of interaction can lead to conflict and even escalate into confrontation if the work and interactions are not organized properly, and if the interacting parties were to start boasting by exaggerating their unilateral past success or achievements. Here we need to identify conflict as a type of interaction, because it may accompany all other kinds and types of interaction. Conflict usually has a temporary, intermediate nature, becoming transformed into a different, usually constructive and productive type of interaction. Conflict is a consequence of risk, resulting from a clash of diverging, sometimes opposite objectives, interests, positions, opinions or views of the parties to interaction. At the core of every conflict lies a situation that comprises opposing views of the parties on any aspect of the situation, or their opposing goals and ways to achieve them under the given circumstances. The root cause of conflict can also lie in a mismatch of interests and desires of partners. Conflicts can arise from contradiction: from a search for a solution which usually creates a clash of innovation and conservatism; from diverging group interests, when groups or individuals advocate only the interests of their side, completely ignoring any different or common interests in the process at hand; self-serving or mercenary motives of an individual, when monetary gain overrides all other motivation.

Conflict may be triggered when an individual impinges on the interests of another individual. If the other individual responds with a similar reaction, the situation may unravel towards a non-constructive or constructive conflict. Non-constructive conflict arises and comes to a head when one of the parties is driven by purely materialistic, amoral interests, picking amoral methods of pressure (fighting), often resorting to discrediting and publicly humiliating the other party (on other compatibility levels). As a rule, conflict triggers head-on resistance from the other party, and dialogue continues with additional refusals to agree on a compromise and pressure of different kinds. Constructive conflict is only possible when both parties follow the rules of logical reasoning and persuasion, without demeaning the honor and dignity of the opponent, using real facts or formal business analytics to support one's arguments. Conflict initially slows the development of events, creating mistrust, while understanding and internalizing conflict (which involves all compatibility levels) is accompanied by psychological distress (at the understanding stage), but then conflict can quickly transform the situation for both parties, enabling them to find a way to resolve the situation quickly. This enables the parties to conflict, despite any mutual concessions, to continue their common development in a more harmonious and efficient manner not only in narrowly materialistic terms of financial and economic interests.

Vertical interaction is known to determine development cycles in practical terms. Politicians tend to focus predominantly on financial and economic tasks these days, because many of them are trying to maximize their personal gain in this game. This craving for celebrity status and money, often found in politicians latching themselves onto power, comes at a high cost to their countries and fellow citizens. When the political elite finally looks up from the money, it may help to increase significantly the share of realistic moral and ethical scenarios for the development of nations, peoples and ethnic groups in interactions alongside consumerist values, finally emphasizing the communities' spiritual, creative, scientific and educational interaction which actually define compatibility at all levels for each and every one of community members. Interactions in practical operation, work and living are categorized by how optimal they are, as well as by their efficiency, frequency and sustainability.

Different approaches to classifications of interaction types are not mutually inclusive; rather, they emphasize the multi-aspect, multifaceted nature of these processes in achieving a cohesive compatibility of the environment, and individuals and organizations living and operating within it.

All the interaction types reviewed here are interconnected. Most often they operate alongside one another, and when environmental conditions change, they can morph into one another. Collaboration or dialogue should hardly be considered as universal types of interaction. In specific situations, some individuals (organizations) require, when working multi-stage contracts and agreements, fiduciary care, financial due diligence and economic support; some have developed a business relationship based on a oral agreement that is satisfactory to both parties thereto, while tough conditions may be justified at a given time in respect of someone else. Certainly, a dominant, optimal type of interaction can be identified with regard to specific conditions. However, the great variety of all possible situations, and the high speed at which they tend to replace each other tend to define the dynamics of interaction between the process participants. It may be through the turbulence of interaction methods and by maintaining a relatively balanced economic and legal environment that we can maintain some degree of compatibility at all levels of the vertical of needs that define the development of society and its members.

As we consider formally the question "What should the interaction be between participating organizations to take them to a higher degree of operating compatibility?" we have to review the model of societal development (Fig. 12), which represents constructive and destructive processes in the life and progress of a society.

As we divided interactions above into two key groups: interactions that unite participants (partnership and cooperation) and divide them (conflict and rivalry/competition).

Fig. 12. Life of society – a compatible multi-level multifunctional macro system.[58]

The main purpose of levels within the structure:

- (7) – Shaping and accumulation of integrative knowledge;

- (6) – Globalization (and analysis) of universal human values;

- (5) – Combination of values of religious institutions;

- (4) – Combining ideological behavioral formats;

- (3) – Development of social institutions;

- (2) – Development of financial and economic institutions;

- (1) – Use of physical products produced by manufacturing companies/physical assets.

C – input/output; C^1 – processes (signals) from the external environment.

H – harmonizing (including morphogenic) processes create and reinforce a compatible environment.

E – evolutionary processes help the system to self-organize by levels (clockwise), involutionary processes (counterclockwise)

R – reproductive processes temporarily "insure" (protect) the lower adjacent levels

---

[58] Morozov V. EXPLORING COMPATIBILITY Foundations of a Theory. Published in England by QUICKSTONE PUBLISHING UK 2014.

M_2 – catabolism (metabolism) processes that destroy integrative structures of cycles development (similar to evolutionary processes, counterclockwise by levels)

M_1 – anabolism (metabolism) processes that shape products by level:

K_1 – material cone (Cycle 1); K_2 – non-material (cognitive
K_3 – material cone (Cycle 2)   and spiritual) cone of the
                                   Cycle

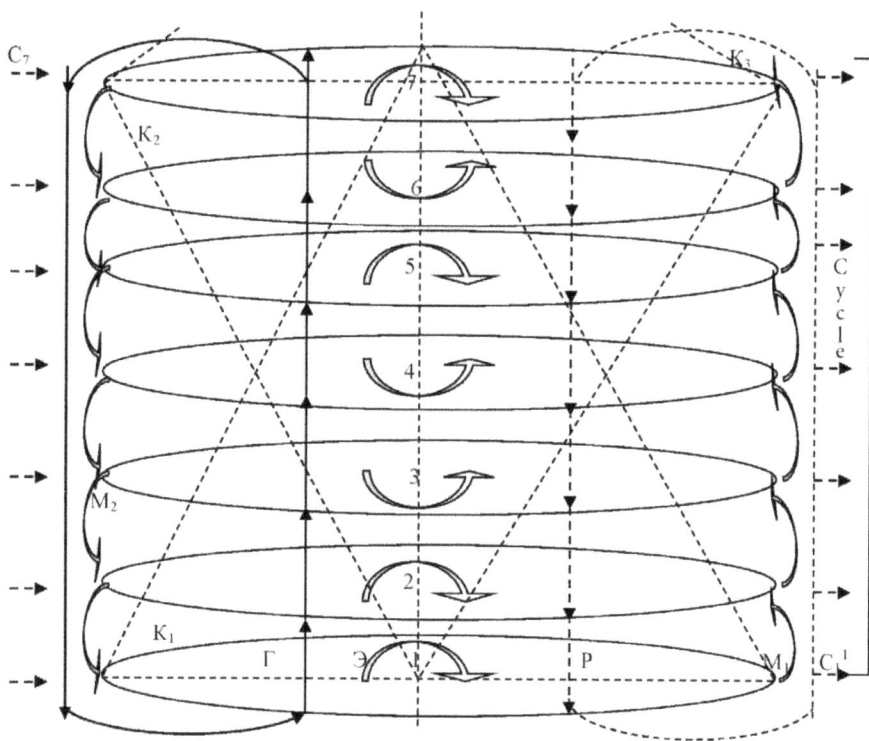

Fig. 12.

After reviewing this structure – the model of societal development and interaction of environmental players, we can make the following assumptions that, for the model of compatible operation (of human being – organization – community – society):

-the existing formats of interaction should incorporate the best interests of all the seven subsystems shown for participating organizations that have equal rights and obligations;

-participants that are government agencies and intergovernmental organizations should establish transparent (open) conditions to establish, sustain and achieve results of interaction for upper and lower compatibility levels (government contracts, grants, competitive bidding tenders; public discussion of preparation of draft laws and bills; reporting by all organizations of all types, levels and sizes, and so on);

-conflict-driven – competitive interactions should be only constructive through the mutual requirements, rights and obligations of the parties;

-hierarchy of compatibility levels (non-material links and mutual influences of parties from higher compatibility levels – from Level 7 to Level 1) should be seen as a key priority principle of interactions of all kinds and formats;

-comprehensive nature of interaction – unity of interaction when more than two participating organizations are involved;

-regular, systematic operating reports by participants at all levels (for interactions with the government and society)

-refreshing/introducing new interaction formats if the current ones are ineffective in specific circumstances.

We propose a generalized expanded format for increasing compatibility through development of inter-relationships between members of interacting parties (see Table 12):

Table 12. Formats and types of compatibility depending on interactions between parties

#	Formats of developing compatible relations	Types of compatibility
1	SELF-IMPOSED ISOLATION, ISOLATIONISM State of non-antagonistic isolation; each player for himself	Mutual isolation
2	MEDIATED DIALOGUE Recommendation to use the products made/sold/delivered by a nearby player with which one has no direct relations	Mediation, intermediary role
3	DIALOGUE Negotiations necessary for joint survival of both parties The state in which negotiations on different aspects and at different compatibility levels are in the best interests of both parties, with parties trained to behave in certain ways and assume certain responsibilities	Mutual influence
4	COOPERATION The state in which parties engage in delivery of products and services of different kinds at specific compatibility levels The state in which parties engage in multifunctional long-term exchange of products and services	Interconnection

5	PARTNERSHIP The state in which parties engage in multifunctional long-term exchange of products and services that involves all compatibility levels	Interaction
6	ASSOCIATION An overall state of comfortable conditions for participants, giving them equal privileges within the association vis-à-vis the external environment and any players that operate outside the association	One person in control
7	MERGER Gradual elimination of differences at all compatibility levels while preserving a formally distinct cultural and historical status (as a nation, an ethnic group or a people)	Unity

A majority of contemporary economists are staunch proponents of synthesizing (or combining) externality and interval theories. Economics of interaction is essentially a material projection of the compatibility (interaction) theory. Factors that drive changes in interactions include: biotech innovations; unregulated population growth dynamics, spontaneous migration of cultures; conflict-riddled development of new resource-rich regions.

Let us try to describe the structural and functional relation – what the interaction (Veda) of organizations should be like to result in a high degree of their operational compatibility:

$$Vd = f(E, P, I, K, R, Of)/Rc,$$

Where E is the commonality of interaction interests for all the seven subsystems of interaction participants;

P is transparency and openness of operation of the parties/participants;

I – hierarchical (top down) influence of interaction levels;

K – comprehensive use of interaction formats with a view to mutual influences of the human factor (leaders of the interacting parties);

R – regular and systematic nature of reporting by the participants in interaction;

Of – allowable/forced (constructive conflict) format refreshment needed to keep interaction efficient;

Arc – risk to allowable compatibility[59].

We believe that the recent crisis of interactions, including its allowable and forced aspects should be more amenable to regulation, which means that spontaneous and planned quantitative and qualitative changes to it should be achieved as planned.

$$C_{AR} = \text{Material changes} / \text{Spiritual transformations} \Rightarrow 1$$

This would enable us to delay or prevent the next potential crisis, or at the very least reduce its depth and duration, limiting its effects to a few local conflicts at lower compatibility levels.

List of References and Further Reading:

1. Balabanova, A.V. Managing Economic Growth: Models and Strategies. – Moscow: Russian Academy of Entrepreneurship, 2004.

---

[59] Морозов В.А. Совместимость социально-экономических систем. Основы теории совместимости.М.: ЗАО «Издательство «Экономика»,2013.С-253.

240 p. (In Russian) // Балабанова А.В. Управление экономическим ростом: модели и стратегии.- М.: Российская Академия предпринимательства, 2004.- 240с.

2. Belyakov, S.A., Klyachko, T.L. Russian Higher Education: Development Models and Scenarios. – Moscow: Delo, RANEPA Publishing House, 2014. – 316p. (In Russian) // Беляков С.А.,Клячко Т.Л.Российское высшее образование: модели и сценарии развития.- М.: Издательский дои «Дело»РАНХиГС, 2013.- 316с.

3. Volgina, O.A., Golodnaya, N.Yu., Odiyako, N.N., Shuman, G.I. Mathematical Modeling of Economic Processes and Systems. – Moscow: KNORUS, 2012. – 200 p. (In Russian) // Волгина О.А., Голодная Н.Ю., Одияко Н.Н., Шуман Г.И. Математическое моделирование экономических процессов и систем. – М.: КНОРУС, 2012.- 200с.

4. Морозов В.А. Совместимость социально-экономических систем. - М., Экономика, 2013.- 334с. Morozov V. EXPLORING COMPATIBILITY Foundations of a Theory. Published in England by QUICKSTONE PUBLISHING UK 2014.

5. Shakhmalov, F. State and Economy. Basis for Interaction: Textbook. Moscow: ZAO Ekonomika Publishing House, 2005. – 727 p. (In Russian) // Шахмалов Ф. Государство и экономика. Основы взаимодействия: Учебник.- М.: ЗАО «Издательство «Экономика», 2005.-727с.

4.3 Conditions for Effective Interaction between Organizations

The concept of compatibility is currently undergoing active exploration, not only in the fields of technology and psychology, but also in medicine, biology, cybernetics and other academic disciplines. In systems theory, compatibility is understood to mean "a relationship between two systems in which their similarity or commonality in essence or on certain parameters becomes apparent, making possible interaction between the systems."[60]

In the area of technical sciences, the concept of compatibility offered by A. L. Gorelik[61] is worthy of note: technical compatibility is described as the ability of technical devices (systems) to function effectively in interaction with other devices.

In our view, the classification scheme applied to technical compatibility[62] can – naturally, subject to certain additions and modifications – be applied to classifying types of compatibility in a more fundamental sense (for the purposes of sociology, economics and other social sciences). This is possible because compatibility in social processes may be examined in several dimensions:

- by the type of objects brought together, for example, compatibility between systems of the following types: social (human being – family – society); socio-political (human being – organization – state); financial, economic, market (consumer – business / entrepreneur – state); socio-economic (human being – (non-)

---

[60] N. N. Obozov, "Три подхода к исследованию психологической совместимости" ["Three approaches to research on psychological compatibility"], Voprosy psikhologii, no. 6 (1981).

[61] A. L. Gorelik and V. A. Skripkin, Построение систем распознавания [Building Recognition Systems] (Moscow: Sovetskoye Radio, 1974).

[62] A. A. Nosenkov and V. I. Medvedev, "Теория технической совместимости как новая дисциплина системного анализа" ["Technical compatibility theory as a new discipline in systems analysis"], Vestnik SAA, no. 2 (2001): 231–236.

commercial organization – state); socio-cultural (human being – religion – state); scientific and ecological (human being – nature – society), etc.;

- by the fundamental nature of the compatibility: psycho-physiological, organizational, physico-mathematical, biochemical, etc.;

- by the factors brought together: property, economic, financial, legal, social, political, religious, artistic/creative compatibility (the number of such factors is large and here only levels of correspondence for the listed factors are presented);

- by life cycle stage: birth, growth, maturity, senescence, death/renewal;

- by "place": external, internal and transitional compatibility;

- by the nature of its manifestation: overt – covert, stable – unstable, physical – intangible;

- by degree of realization: complete, core, partial;

- by degree of randomness: deterministic, stochastic;

- by degree of predictability: predictable, unpredictable;

- by degree of self-sufficiency: autonomous, dependent;

- by degree of assimilation: personal – social, native – foreign, substantive – ostensive, current – future;

- by the arena where it is realized: international, governmental, religious;

- by the nature of ties between objects: intermediated, direct, mixed compatibility.

Having thus broken down compatibility into types, we will start by considering human and interpersonal compatibility, given that the human factor is fundamental and decisive for our purposes. To use the dictionary definition of psychological compatibility, by this we mean "an effect of interaction between people characterized by the maximum possible satisfaction with one another."63 In other words, the existing biorhythms (biological compatibility) between individuals and their chakra lines of communication are aligned in order to permit voluntary interaction between them, much in the manner of interaction between technical devices that we spoke of earlier. Chakral lines of communication are, of course, much more diverse and complex than technical devices, and this is true to an even greater degree of interpersonal interactions: in the case of interactions between groups, it is difficult to apply the term "maximum possible satisfaction". Academic researchers A. N. Sukhov and N. N. Obozov propose examining compatibility from two perspectives: as a process and as a result of interaction. "Compatibility as a result is the degree of the partners' satisfaction with one another (their thoughts, feelings and behavior). Viewing compatibility as a process, we note the processes of adaptation and of 'fitting' characters, needs, and behavioral motives to one another."64

In principle, we can say with reasonable confidence that: 1) compatibility is a result of interactions; 2) externally, compatibility is manifested in the aspiration and ability of people to voluntarily associate with one another; 3) internally, compatibility is a coherence in behavior and mutual influences, although not only that; 4)

---

63 "Коллектив. Личность. Общение." ["Collective. Personality. Association."] in Y. S. Kuzmina and V. Y. Semyonova, eds., Slovar sotsialno-psikhologicheskikh ponyatii [Dictionary of Socio-Psychological Concepts] (Leningrad: Lenizdat, 1987).
64 A. A. Bodaleva and A. N. Sukhova, eds., Основы социально-психологической теории [Fundamentals of Socio-Psychological Theory] (Moscow: International Pedagogical Academy, 1995).

internally, compatibility is a coherence in emotions and interactions, although not only that; 5) internally, compatibility is accompanied by mutual cognition and understanding, although not only that; 6) it arises from a certain combination of personal qualities; and 7) compatibility is a cause of other psychological phenomena (love, friendship, closeness, psychological climate, etc.).

The satisfaction criterion in interaction is subjective and contextual (compatibility is a long-term phenomenon, while satisfaction may change from one day to the next). Indeed, it might be better seen as a result of compatibility, one that characterizes the socio-psychological climate in a group of people rather than their compatibility.[65] Satisfaction with an interaction and with relationships is simultaneously a criterion for effective teamwork, friendship and group cohesion (via emotional attraction).[66] Minimal conflict, too, is a less than precise criterion for compatibility, inasmuch as it can be a consequence of both teamwork and indifference, and to a large extent is again a criterion for psychological climate.

All criteria for compatibility may be classified into three groups: 1) behavioral (the choice of a partner or relationship, effective interaction, minimal conflict, harmonization of behavioral roles, etc.); 2) emotional (satisfaction with the result and process of interaction and with interpersonal relationships, positive mutual feelings, etc.) and 3) cognitive (a high degree of mutual understanding, positive perceptions of the interaction, etc.).

We will take compatibility between groups of people – specifically, organizations, the subject of this book – to mean their ability to interact in a coordinated manner for an extended period of voluntary joint development predicated on an optimal mix of

---

[65] Y. S. Kuzmina and V. Y. Semyonova, eds., Социальная психология: история, теория, эмпирические исследования [Social Psychology: History, Theory and Empirical Research] (Leningrad: Leningrad State University Publishing, 1979).
[66] Y. S. Kuzmina and V. Y. Semyonova, eds., Социальная психология: история, теория, эмпирические исследования [Social Psychology: History, Theory and Empirical Research] (Leningrad: Leningrad State University Publishing, 1979).

mutually-reinforcing qualities. By "coordinated" we mean free of contractions and where there is a correspondence between the expectations and actions of the participants (and their technologies).

Approaches to studying compatibility include: structural (focused on the search for an optimal combination of various parameters and qualities of the partners at various levels – or in various forms – of interaction); adaptive (focused on improving interpersonal relationships and communication processes in groups); and functional (focused on the study of group dynamics, functions, goals and tasks).[67]

There are certain regular patterns in transitions from: less ideal to more ideal variants of direct dependence; direct to intermediated compatibility; intermediated to direct compatibility (where the intermediary has exhausted its function); and from less ideal to more ideal variants of intermediated compatibility.

Three more regularities (the fifth, sixth and seventh) constitute a complete set of variants for changes in the number of distinct types of compatibility. The fifth concerns transitions to a smaller number of compatibility types. The sixth concerns transitions to a wider range of compatibility types, where the physical or intangible essence of the new (product, material, service, management decision, etc.) arises from a new principle of action. The seventh regularity is to be found in transitions to a different set of compatibility types, with no change in their number. In other words, the physical or intangible essence of the new arises from a new action principle that has the same number of functions as the action principle of the preceding decision, but where some types of compatibility have been supplanted. Any effect is possible. The same economic or social logic applies to the fifth and sixth regularities. It should be noted here that it is impossible as a matter of principle to supplant the entire set of compatibility types. For example, system compatibility (in economics, sociology and other social sciences) is

---

[67] N. N. Obozov and A. N. Obozov. "Три подхода к исследованию психологической совместимости" ["Three approaches to research on psychological compatibility"], Voprosy psikhologii, no. 6 (1981): 98–101.

present in any organizational space (much as constructional compatibility, a form of technical compatibility, is present in any technical device). Only its degree of perfection can change. Table 13 examines corresponding levels of compatibility in systems that differ in their origin and purpose: the human being, family, organization and society.

Table 13. Possible functional correspondence between subsystems (7 levels of compatibility)

№	External environment (levels)	Enterprise (subsystems)	Human being (subsystems)	Family (values subsystems)
1	Cognitive (scientific) and intangible level	Cognitive subsystem	Control of the thinking mind (inspired, intuitive, supra-mental)	Absence of issues
2	Cultural and worldview level	Mental subsystem	Control of the will and direction of mental activity (subtle perception – third eye)	Mentoring, patronage
3	Religious and theological level	Cultural subsystem	Control of all forms of mental expression	Self esteem

4	Political level	Historical subsystem	Control of emotional life: love, hate, etc.	Care and protection
5	Social level	Institutional subsystem	Control of authoritarian impulses (to rule, possess, conquer) and ambition	Daily life
6	Financial and economic level	Imitation subsystem	Control of vibrations: jealousy, envy, desire, greed, anger	Money
7	Product and property level	Organizational / technological and property subsystem	Control of physical being and sexual impulses	Sexual relations

From the table we can see a correspondence between the energy levels of the participants. This implies the existence of a common denominator that can be used to act on and regulate the overall development and betterment of society.

Over time, compatibility in various spheres of life tends to move in the direction of decline, senescence and other retrograde processes that flow from human evolution, regardless of the best possible efforts to preserve it. In the case of goods and services, the loss of physical compatibility has often been treated by academics as a random phenomenon, one that emerges from the laws of random processes that have been thoroughly investigated in probability theory. Yet we noted at the start of this section that this kind of compatibility is naturally transient.

In a system of governmental relationships (as in technology) we typically see the actualization of a *single principle for ensuring a certain adequate degree of internal and external compatibility between the creators and users of the system*, between federal subjects and municipalities (as between technical devices).

Inasmuch as this **principle of adequate compatibility** is characteristic of society as a whole, *we may suppose that its dialectical origin is present* from the moment that the general laws of dialectics become manifest in society. In order to examine this hypothesis, consider the law of the unity and conflict of opposites. The essence of this law lies in the proposition of certain contradictions coupled with the proposition of a dialectical conflict between those contradictions. Examples of such contradictions, broader and more individual, might include:

1) interaction and non-interaction between the constituent elements of a community (society);

2) the positive and negative impacts of contradictions, conflicts and similar phenomena on social life;

3) the existence of various religious systems and, accordingly, civilizations that unite nations and ethnic groups who share a common faith.

The principle of adequate compatibility may be classified as a methodological principle, i.e. it can serve as a methodological basis and reference point for the theory of compatibility.

Because the second law of dialectics is closely related to the first law and draws on many of its categories and concepts, it must also have an impact on the process that gives rise to compatibility in a society. We may surmise that *the principle of adequate compatibility and the **principle of maximum perfectibility** together belong to the category of methodological principles in the theory of compatibility.* The principle of maximum perfectibility applies only to the structural stage of the formation of social relations. In fact, each new institution embodying economic or legal relationships is intimately bound up with the processes surrounding its introduction and functioning, which themselves undergo creative development in accordance with the second law of dialectics.

Taken together, the basic dialectic laws govern the development of the world around us, including its natural, financial and economic, socio-political, socio-cultural, and scientific and ecological innovations and relationships in general. It follows that the third law of dialectics also plays a role creating compatibility. To continue, then, *the principle of rational continuity belongs, together with the principles of dialectic compatibility and maximum perfectibility, to the category of methodological principles in the theory of compatibility.*

Relationships of unity are closely tied to relationships of compatibility, both between the elements of the system, and between each element and the system itself. As V. G. Afanasiev writes: "The quality of compatibility is particularly characteristic of social systems, whose principal components are people. Above all, compatibility between components ensures rational interaction between them, without which a system is inconceivable."[68]

In M. I. Setrov's view, compatibility is the first and most important prerequisite for any interaction between objects and phenomena.[69] Furthermore, correspondence is one form of compatibility between real phenomena and reflects the compatibility between a system and its environment, as well as the compatibility between the structure or functions of the system and the conditions in which it exists. "In order for a system to be organized," Setrov notes, "two types of compatibility must both be present: compatibility between elements of the same order, a necessary condition for interaction, and compatibility between a given element and all other

---

[68] V. G. Afanasiev, Системность и общество [Systems and Society] (Moscow: Politizdat, 1980), 83.

[69] M. I. Setrov, Организация биосистем [The Organization of Biosystems] (Leningrad: LGK, 1971).

elements of the whole, i.e. between the element and the system of which it is a part."

The success and development of an organization, as a rule, depend critically on the impact of outside forces. An organization is an open system that relies on a supply of resources, energy, personnel and, of course, clients. An organization's external environment can be characterized as the set of factors that impact on its activities, including: clients, competitors, government institutions, suppliers, financial organizations and sources of labor, as well as scientific and technical progress (the scientific and intellectual breadth of the environment and of individual people); culture (theological and national developments, as well as global processes); the state of society (political and social events); and natural phenomena.

Table 14 presents one way of arranging of classes of organizations with analogous functions in accordance with the above-mentioned levels of compatibility vis-à-vis the external environment.[70] For a more substantive examination of the interaction between an organization and its environment, it is important to examine them in one context, which depends on the intended object of the development compatibility and, accordingly, the mutual influences. Looking at factor compatibility in the course of executing a given project, we see that the actors are confronted with constraints on their reach in both space and time. If those actors fall into the category of system processes, such constraints will arise with respect only to time, and not to space.

---

[70] V. A. Morozov, "Предприятие и внешняя среда: уровни взаимодействия" ["The enterprise and its external environment: levels of interaction"], Rossiiskoye predprinimatelstvo 206, no. 8 (4.2012).

Table 14. A multi-level external environment and types of functional object

№	Level of external environment	Primary functional organizations
1	Product – property	Shareholder companies with various degrees of liability involved in the production of goods, services and trade. Research and innovation "startup" companies. Individual entrepreneurs. WTO. Inter-industry planning and management associations. Business incubators and multinational technology companies. Corporate universities.
2	Financial – economic	Banks, exchanges, investment structures, IMF, financial and economic organizations (authorities), etc.
3	Social	Social groups (voluntary, national, territorial, special-purpose, professional, youth, women's and men's organizations), social strata (classes, castes), etc.
4	Political	Political organizations, parties. State structures (territorial, regional, municipal). Inter-governmental organizations with coercive powers.
5	Religious – theological	Religious institutions, including sects, distinct fraternities and orders, religious organizations of specific nationalities and ethnic groups. Atheist organizations. Inter-confessional organizations, etc.

| 6 | Cultural – worldview | Organizations related to culture, history and art. Educational and health organizations. Voluntary societies and associations that promote cultural integration. |
| 7 | Scientific (cognitive) and intangible | Global and national (state) scientific research institutes and laboratories, research centers and universities, institutions of higher learning, private research institutes and personal research. |

In our case, which involves the functioning of enterprises, both the external environment and the organizations themselves are seen as objects (types of systems) and, in the language of system economics, there are constraints in space but not in time.

Inasmuch as various forces in the external environment act on an organization, we may distinguish between direct and indirect factors, as well as between direct and indirect action in the external environment as a whole.

If an enterprise has clients, then even when faced by the severest competition (and subject to aggressive influences from financial, economic, social, political, theological and general cultural factors), it will have some minimal capacity to cover its costs. These are minimal conditions for the organization's viability, the minimum consistent with its functioning at a given point in time.[71]

Society, conceived of as a collection of individuals, may be broken down into components with varying purposes and whose members experience needs on varying levels, in accordance with a range of social forms such as enterprises, institutions, exchanges and associations. It is worth examining here a situation where the social

---

[71] V. A. Morozov, "Предприятие и внешняя среда: уровни взаимодействия" ["The enterprise and its external environment: levels of interaction"], Rossiiskoye predprinimatelstvo 206, no. 8 (4.2012).

development framework we propose (in the form of seven levels or circles, each of which corresponds to a level in Table 10) becomes disengaged from its central developmental axis at all compatibility levels, in response to an insufficient degree of organization (evolutionary economy) at each level. In other words, those levels are not located directly below one another, as is required for full compatibility, but have to some extent been displaced, even breaking down altogether at certain levels (much like the Earth's ozone layer). This can be illustrated in a Venn diagram, as used in symbolic logic to clarify relationships between groups. Imagine we are viewing the above-mentioned structure from below. If the seven levels coincide, we will see just one circle. If the axis has become misaligned, the picture will be different. The structure now appears as a set of overlapping circles, such as might be seen in a circus arena. This proposition is illustrated in Figure 13.

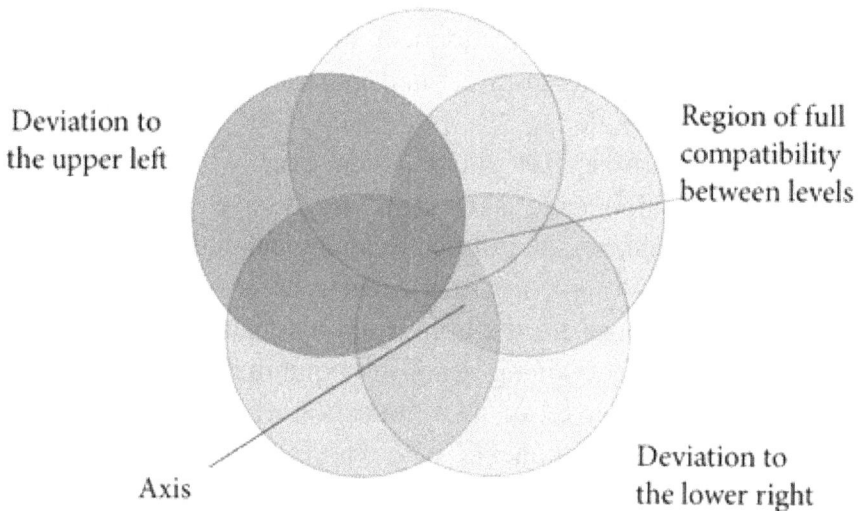

Deviation to the upper left

Region of full compatibility between levels

Axis

Deviation to the lower right

Fig. 13. Overlapping circles – levels of compatibility

The first level is accordingly the product – property level and the last (seventh) the (cognitive) scientific and intangible level. When the circles are aligned, the development process will be all-embracing: all organizations are taking part, each making its own specific contribution and drawing on the contributions of other levels. If one compatibility level circle is not aligned with the others, then the process is incomplete, inasmuch as the given level – which represents many individuals and organizations – is not playing its full part in the civilizing process of renewal. There is a failure of integrate, including the given level into other levels, and so the system is not enriched by the product of that level, leading to deficiencies. This in turn leads to a large number of non-constructive local conflicts, possibly even to deliberate counteraction and mutual destruction.

Table 15 looks at what is required for mutual compatibility and interaction if both are to function effectively, not forgetting (as stated above) that interaction is the outward manifestation of compatibility, that is, in the visible environment.

Table 15. Requirements for participating organizations, prior to and during interaction

Requirements during interaction	Requirements prior to and following interaction
Nature of the interaction between the systems required to preserve their potential (compatibility)	Required condition of the systems prior to (after) the start (conclusion) of relationships between the participants
Common interest in interaction on the part of all seven subsystems of the participants	Readiness to choose another participant as partner, in accordance with assessed mutual complementarity between potentials
Transparency and openness in the participants' operations	Readiness to coordinate role (functional) behavior in order to avoid conflict

Hierarchy of influence (top to bottom) in levels of interaction, with forms of interaction revised as needed	Readiness to carry out detailed assessment of a prospective partner's potential across all seven (1–7) compatibility subsystems
Integrated application of all forms of interaction, allowing for the human factor (leaders of the respective participants)	Readiness to assess the personal compatibility of the leaders on the basis of cognitive – intangible and emotional – psychological parameters
Regularity and systematization in reporting by the participants	Compatibility of specific subsystems between participants and between a given subsystem and other subsystems
Acceptable or enforced renewal (constructive conflict) of forms of interaction, in order to raise compatibility between the participants' operations	Acceptance of long-term relationships, yielding a minimum satisfaction for all subsystems and an effective overall outcome for all participants

To sum up what has been said so far, we may describe interaction as the ability of participants to voluntarily associate with one another over an extended period: to prepare joint projects; to create products in the form of goods and services; and to erect structures of various types. This includes products and structures of an intangible, charitable, artistic and moral nature. At the same time, compatibility is an acquired capacity of a participant (the result of previous interactions) that is manifested in the coordinated functioning of its seven subsystems with those of a another potential participant, along with a certain combination of qualities.

A system's fitness for compatibility prior to entering a relationship with another participating system can be expressed mathematically in the following functional form:

$$S(st) = F (Z, R, C, P, S7/S1, E); \qquad (1)$$

Where

Z is a system for evaluating a partner prior to interaction;

R is a procedure for coordinating the behavior roles (functions) of each participant prior to interaction;

C is a multi-faceted analysis of top-level compatibility between the given and prospective participants;

P is the personal compatibility of the two sides' leaders, on cognitive and emotional parameters;

S7/S1 is the compatibility of the two sides' subsystems, as well as the compatibility of each subsystem with other subsystems; and

E is elasticity (operational compatibility) during long-term interaction.

st is the current state of the system being examined.

st* is the current state of the partner system.

Formula (1) thus allows for an assessment of compatibility in interaction between systems in a given state. In assessing the effectiveness of interaction, the following asymptotes may be defined:

$$S(st) + S(st^*) = \begin{cases} 0, & \text{no compatibility} \\ < 1, & \text{degenerate compatibility} \\ = 1, & \text{stable compatibility} \\ > 1, & \text{developing compatibility} \end{cases} \qquad (2)$$

It is important to note that $S(st) \neq S(st^*)$, meaning that compatibility and fitness for cooperation are not symmetrical. One system may force interaction and partnership on another. If that proves unproductive, fitness for cooperation will decline in both systems and their mutual compatibility will decline further.

The fitness of each participant's compatibility state and the state of effective interaction (Vd) between the two sides must be balanced if each system is to find itself in an ideal condition and if they are to achieve exemplary interaction:

$$S(st) + S(st^*) = Vd; \tag{3}$$

This equilibrium condition allows us to describe the evolution of interrelationships between two participating systems by examining their compatibility, $F(st, st^*)$ (for further details see Morozov, Exploring Compatibility: Foundations of a Theory). If the participating systems' initial states are st and st*, then after interaction they will have transitioned to the new states $st(t=1)$ and $st^*(t=1)$, where 1 represents the time frame under consideration (whether a month, quarter or year). Then we can say that:

$$F(st(t=1), st^*(t=1)) = F(st, st^*) + Vd(st, st^*) \tag{4}$$

This is a significant result, because it allows us to forecast the development of the relationships between the participating systems even where their interrelationships are asymmetrical. With the help of sequential analysis of the systems at each point in time, we can estimate their fitness for interaction $S(st)$, the effectiveness of the interaction Vd and, given those values, by iteration calculate the compatibility of the two systems.

Now, having examined this question, we can surmise that *compatibility is the set of tolerant developing interrelationships within a society, including issues of interconnectivity, mutual influence, interaction and the combination of parts into a whole through a voluntary smoothing of each side's distinguishing features, in order to create a new shared quality of relationship (which over time is renewed, feeding from the general to the particular and vice versa, while maintaining compatibility) that is needed for overall development.*

To draw some conclusions at this point, it should be noted that:

- the economy of each functional compatibility level, which embraces a vast number of organizations, must place an identical (or mutually intelligible) emphasis on various qualities in establishing operating conditions for that environment;

- all subjects – organizations within the compatibility levels must have as a primary goal (in additional to economic benefits) intangible and creative development that harmonizes with values and the needs of the human being, organization and society;

- the operating principles of organizations (including federal and local governments) with respect both to their internal subsystems and to external antagonists must include mutual respect for the interests and needs of all participants in an interaction, based on the creative and innovative development of those participants.

A whole originating in contradictions will, in any case, be preferable to an accumulation of differences. A society formed around democratic principles, mutual respect and trust, allows for constructive (synergistic) conflict, accelerating the pace of change at each compatibility level.

CONCLUSION

Why the interaction economy? Interaction, as an objective form of enterprise (subject) development, is shaped by the state and structure of the organization. An enterprise will always experience the effects of the external environment and its own internal organization, which are manifested in greater or lesser disturbances. An appropriate response changes the internal state of the organization's subsystems. This results in a deformation of the organizational structure and a clarification of goals and tasks not only for the subsystems, but also for the enterprise as a whole. Disturbances in the environment can originate with competitors, partners or consumers, and may therefore vary in nature and form. Where an organization has potential, that is, where it is able to respond promptly and correctly, this is evidence of compatibility in its constituent subsystems, with certain subsystems able to compensate for a lack of resources needed to counter the environmental impacts. Examples can be found at the micro, meso and macro levels. The macroeconomic level may be a national economy (section 2.3) and the micro level an organization with a family72 of subsystems, while an industry cluster is a meso-system with the same family of subsystems.

What constitutes the interaction economy? We have repeatedly referred to seven subsystems that derive from levels of human need and intangible value (section 1.2), taking into consideration Maslow's hierarchy of physical needs.[73] Taking as a basis for discussion a model of social development, and all of the elements that flow from that, we develop a model of the interaction economy (section 2.3) that incorporates various economy types.

---

[72] G. B. Kleiner, Стратегия предприятия [Enterprise Strategy] (Moscow: Delo, 2008).

[73] Абрахам Маслоу, Мотивация и личность [Abraham H. Maslow, Motivation and Personality], 3rd ed. (St. Petersburg: Piter, 2003)

These constituent economies represent the environment, objects, processes and (so) projects that drive social development. There are so many sectors in the economy that their functions sometimes overlap, but the seven compatibility levels define a hierarchy of economies. If economies on the level of physical compatibility are taken as a foundation for the model, then interactions will be brief and lacking trust, mechanical in nature, shaped by pragmatism and dry intellect. On the one hand, this excludes disturbances arising from the human factor. On the other, it leaves no place for the seven billion human beings and the purpose behind those economies. In our opinion, there is only one solution. The foundation must rest on a synthesized intellectual – intangible (innovation and cultural – worldview) economy, one that is partially expressed in "green economics", and which we call the vital – mind economy. This incorporates the economies of human health, organizations and society. In a model of multiple economies, it must play a decisive role at all levels and in all combinations. Only then will the vector of development and states' values fall into line with the resources available for interaction between them.

What do we need to know in order to apply it? To take advantage of the interaction economy, we must become acquainted with all of its constituent economies and with their correspondence to the structures of various types of organizations, in order to discover, in that correlation, how compatible your particular enterprise is in the situation where has until now found itself (the areas where it operates and the nature of its mission). Given the priorities laid out here, we can then build a development program based on a combination of indicator sets. These sets are described in the previously-mentioned sections (3.2 and 3.3). You need to examine the relationship between your indicators and their relationship to the organization's subsystems and compatibility levels. Each indicator is of value to another indicator in some appropriate combination, and that relationship helps in reaching the right decisions as an organization interacts with outside entities in the pursuit of its own client-oriented projects. Evaluating those indicators also makes it possible to effect the necessary adjustments to interconnections between enterprise subsystems, allowing for the human factor, i.e. noting where subdivision leaders influence an existing interaction for better (+) or worse (–).

What does the interaction economy help us to understand? What do we need to grasp? The interaction economy, based on a model of social development, helps us grasp how to regulate intercommunication and commutability not only with respect to an organization's external and internal environment, but also in the actions of every participant in those interactions, that is, in the personalities of individuals and the subdivisions of the organization. The table in section 4.3 presents an arrangement of compatibility levels for all subjects participating in an event: the human being, family, organization and society. The table shows where the capacities of these participants can be directed and what instruments can be used to reexamine actions (compatible interaction indicators for each level) in order to mesh successfully with the actions of a partner. Furthermore, the hierarchy of values makes it possible to determine the appropriate sequence for resolving issues that arise from changed priorities and sequence of moves aimed at maintaining the organization's strategic course.

What drives close interaction and strong performance in organizations? Such outcomes are driven by a harmonious correspondence between goals and the instruments used to achieve them in all spheres where an enterprise operates, taking into consideration the actions of each employee, which arises if we bear in mind the interaction economy model and the established set of features with which it operates. Moreover, an extended period of interaction can trigger a change in the nature of the enterprise's own operations and the conditions under which they take place, given the emergence of new relationships that create new conditions for interaction. By sustaining subsystem functions and amassing their potential, it is possible to improve internal and external compatibility, leading to better interactions between the enterprise and other entities, including fiscal authorities. Compatibility allows an enterprise to set up new lines of business while retaining its existing ones. The compatibility potential of an organization (driven by diversity) extends the life cycle of its operations and, where needed, can give rise to separate, independent enterprises. All of this, moreover, equally benefits meso- and macro-systems (of organizations); in other words, it acts with identical effect on all vertical power structures (although the model is significantly differentiated at the macro-level).

Where does the interaction economy fit in with other types and forms of economy? Its place, most likely, is to serve as an umbrella that brings together all the others, a sort of common home. True, it cannot exist by itself. The interaction economy is a collection or generalization, one that cannot itself yield unequivocal results. A permanent invisible presence, it is like a stadium on whose track each kind of economy in turn takes the lead without ever leaving the facility. Essentially, the interaction economy sets the rules of the game (in concert with institutional, system and some other kinds of economy) and so either widens the track or, on the contrary, limits the scope for new activity. Its primary distinguishing feature is that it is dominated by the moral and intangible characteristics present in all subject interrelationship, which play a decisive role in decision making by the participants in any interaction. Whereas the institutional economy is bound by a framework of laws and rules, here we are dealing with unwritten laws and boundaries drawn from the profound and subtle moral, ethical, creative and intangible principles inherent to its subjects and their composite elements.

What does the interaction economy mean for each of us? Reading this work and coming to a personal understanding – which is what should happen – will make its significance apparent: it is in its comprehensive embrace of all fundamental issues in the life and activities of a subject. Possibly its complex description will prompt us to investigate issues of compatibility – we are, after all, speaking of an "interaction" economy. Knowing our capacities – and in general we lack objective knowledge in this area – moves us to act quickly. After several successful and unsuccessful attempts at interaction, we reevaluate ourselves, and this is where the interaction economy begins, even though the interaction proper has not yet started. As is sometimes said, "A halt is part of the route". At times it may be more important than moving ahead, as when we continue to reevaluate ourselves and adjust various elements as needed. In essence, compatibility is a path of interaction that leads from one idea to the next idea of interaction. Unfortunately, as Confucius said, it was only at the age of sixty that his hearing became obedient; before that he listened without always hearing all that was important. Perhaps for that reason it has been said that every traveler should be seen as a teacher. This is where we see the significance of the interaction economy, in which physical and intangible scenarios for future developments (intended or otherwise) are formulated in partnership with others. In any case, the interaction economy becomes necessary as we seek to physically embody all of our emotional and intangible understanding. It allows us, without watering down the content of a subject's emotional and intangible aims, to go on pursuing those visions, goals and tasks that physically embody our destiny, a destiny whose richness and duration will only be increased by our ability to exercise reliable control over the life vector that we are walking.

BIBLIOGRAPHY

1. Alford, John and Janine O'Flynn. "Public Value: A Stocktake of a Concept." Paper presented at the twelfth annual conference of the International Research Society for Public Management, 2008, 8.

2. Amable, Bruno. "Institutional complementarity and diversity of social systems of innovation and production." Review of International Political Economy 7, no. 4 (2000), 645–687.

3. Aoki, Masahiko. "The Contingent Governance of Teams: Analysis of Institutional Complementarity." International Economic Review 35, no. 3 (1994), 657–676.

4. Boehm-Bawerk, Eugen von. Grundzude der Theorie des wirtschaftlichen Gutenwerts in Conrads Jahrbucher für Nationalökonomie und Statistik, 1886. Translated from the German by A. Sanina, in Менгер, К., Е. Бём-Баверк и Ф. Визер. Австрийская школа в политической экономии [The Austrian School in Political Economy]. Moscow: Ekonomika, 1992, 243–426.

5. Chang, Ha-Joon. "Understanding the Relationship between Institutions and Economic Development." UNU World Institute for Development Economics Research Discussion Paper No. 2006/05, 14 pp., http://www.wider.unu.edu/stc/repec/pdfs/rp2006/dp2006-05.pdf

6. Crouch, Colin, Wolfgang Streeck, Robert Boyer, et al. "Dialogue on 'Institutional Complementarity and Political Economy.'" Socio-Economic Review 3, no. 2 (2005), http://ser.oxfordjournals.org/cgi/reprint/3/2/359.pdf.

7. Deeg, Richard. "Complementarity and Institutional Change: How Useful a Concept?" Wissenschaftszentrum Berlin Discussion Paper SP II, 2005–21, 39, http:// bibliothek.wzb.eu/pdf/2005/ii05-21.pdf.

8. Economist Intelligence Unit. "Рейтинг стран мира по уровню продовольственной безопасности в 2016 году." ["Countries of the world ranked by food security in 2016."] Center for Human Technologies, http://gtmarket.ru/news/2016/01/29/7291, accessed 29.01.2016.

9. Hall, Peter A. "An introduction to varieties of capitalism," in Hall, Peter A. and David Soskice. Varieties of Capitalism: the Institutional Foundations of Corporative Advantage. Oxford: Oxford University Press, 2001, 1–68.

10. Höpner, Martin. "What connects industrial relations and corporate governance? Explaining institutional complementarity." Socio-Economic Review 3, no. 2 (2005), 331–358.

11. Lane, Jan-Erik and Svante Ersson. The New Institutional Politics: Performance and Outcomes. London and N.Y.: Routledge, 2000.

12. Lichtenstein, P. "Post-Keynesian Theories of Value and Price," in An Introduction to Post-Keynesian and Marxian Theories of Value and Price. N.Y.: M.E. Sharpe, 1983, 54. 90.

13. Moore, Mark and Sanjeev Khagram. "On Creating Public Value: What Business Might Learn from Government about Strategic Management." Corporate Social Responsibility Initiative Working Paper No. 3, March 2004, 224–225.

14. Müller-Armack, Alfred. "Soziale Marktwirtschaft," in Handwörterbuch der Sozial-wissenschaften, Bd. 9. Stuttgart u.a., 1965.

15. North, Douglass C. Institutions, Institutional Change and Economic Performance. Cambridge: Cambridge University Press, 1990. Translated by A. N. Nesterenko. Институты, институциональные изменения и функционирование экономики. Moscow, 1997. Center of Human Technologies, http://gtmarket.ru/laboratory/basis/6310, accessed 07.09.2013.

16. North, Douglass C. "The Role of Institutions in Economic Development." United Nations Economic Commission For Europe Discussion Paper Series No. 2003.2, 2.

17. Putnam, Robert D. "Bowling Alone: America's Declining Social Capital." Journal of Democracy 6, no. 1 (January 1995), 65–78.

18. Rappaport, Alfred. Creating Shareholder Value: A Guide for Managers and Investors. N. Y.: Free Press, 1997.

19. Renshaw, Vernon. "Organizing work in an information age." Post-Keynesian Economics 10, no. 4 (1988).

20. Solow, Robert M. "The Economics of Resources or the Resources of Economics." The American Economic Review 64, no. 2, Papers and Proceedings of the Eighty-sixth Annual Meeting of the American Economic Association, Richard T. Ely Lecture (May 1974), 1–14.

21. Science and Society. N.Y., 1984. no. 4., 428.

22. Smith, Vernon L. "experimental methods in economics." [1987] The New Palgrave Dictionary of Economics, 2nd edition, 2008. Abstract.

23. The Heritage Foundation and The Wall Street Journal, Index of Economic Freedom 2016.

24. Transparency International. "Индекс восприятия коррупции 2015 года." ["Corruption Perceptions Index 2015."], Center for Human Technologies, http://gtmarket.ru/news/2016/01/27/7287, accessed 27.01.2016.

25. Агафонов К. П. Единство физической картины мира. Неоклассическая концепция. – М.: Изд-во ЛКИ, 2007.

26. Андерсон Б. Воображаемые сообщества. – М., 2001.

27. Анохов И. В. Игровой аспект экономики. Известия ИГЭА. 2013. №2 (88).

28. Антонович А. Я. Теория ценности. Критико-экономическое исследование. – Варшава. 1877. – С. 58.

29. Асаул Н. А. Теория и методология институциональных взаимодействий субъектов инвестиционно-строительного комплекса. Монография. – АНО Институт проблем экономического возрождения: 2004. – 255 с.

30. Аузан А. А. Социокультурные коды в экономическом анализе // Журнал Новая экономическая ассоциация. №1(17), 2013. С. 174.

31. Афанасьев В. Г. Системность и общество. – М.: Политиздат, 1980, С. 83.

32. Байтурганов Х. Н. Основы теории единого информационного поля. – СПб., 1998.

33. Балабанова А. В. Управление экономическим ростом: модели и стратегии. – М.: Российская Академия предпринимательства, 2004. – 240 с.

34. Балицкий Е. Ментальные контуры, стратификация общества и цивилизационные волны. 19.05.2010 kapital-rus.ru>articles/article/177327

35. Бартенев С. А. Экономические теории и школы (история и современность). Курс лекций. – М.: БЕК, 1996. С. 74.

36. Беляков С. А., Клячко Т.Л. Российское высшее образование: модели и сценарии развития. – М.: Издательский дои «Дело» РАНХиГС, 2013. – 316 с.

37. Бентам И. Введение в основания нравственности и законодательства / И. Бентам // Микроэкономика: в 2 т. / под ред. В. М. Гальперина. – СПб. Экономическая школа, 1994. - Т. 1. – 349 с.

38. Бессонова О. Раздаточная экономика России / О. Бессонова. – М.: РОССПЭН, 2006. – 144 с.

39. Бессонова О. Траектории и современный вектор развития цивилизационной матрицы России // Мир России. – 2008. - № 2. – С. 108–138.

40. Блауг М. Методология экономической науки, или Как экономисты объясняют. – М.: МП «Журнал Вопросы экономики», 2004.

41. Блауг М. Экономическая мысль в ретроспективе. – М.: Изд-во "Дело Лтд", 1994. С. 285.

42. Блауг Марк. Методология экономической науки или как объясняют экономисты. – М: НП «Журнал Вопросы экономики», 2004. С. 49.

43. Блауг, М. Экономическая мысль в ретроспективе [Текст] / М. Блауг. – М.: Дело, 1996. – 583 с.

44. Блэкуэлл Д., Миниард П., Энджел Дж. Поведение потребителей. Изд. 9-е. – СПб.: Питер, 2002.

45. Бодрийер Ж. Общество потребления. – М., 2006.

46. Бодрийяр Ж. Система вещей. – М., 1999.

47. Болдырев И. А. Методология экономических исследований. Национальный исследовательский университет Высшая школа экономики, М., 2010.

48. Большая Советская Энциклопедия. М.: «Советская энциклопедия», 1969-1978.

49. Бондаренко О. Философия единства (серия книг). – Бишкек, 2000.

50. Бондаренко О. Я. Сборник докладов по теории и философии единого поля. – Бишкек, 2000.

51. Буайе Р. Демократия и социал-демократия перед лицом современного капитализма: «регуляционистский» подход / Р. Буайе // Прогнозис. – 2009. – № 1. – С. 91–130.

52. Василенко И. А. Государственное и муниципальное управление. – М.: «Издательство ООО Юрайт», 2014. С. 92.

53. Васильева Т. В. Афинская школа философии. Философский язык Платона и Аристотеля. – М., 1985. С. 134.

54. Вебер М. Основные социологические понятия // Вебер М. Избранные произведения. – М., Прогресс, 1990.

55. Вебер М. Протестантская этика и дух капитализма // Вебер М. Избр. произв. – М.: Прогресс, 1990.

56. Вебер М. Хозяйственная этика мировых религий // Вебер М. Избранное. Образ общества. – М.: Юрист, 1994.

57. Великая трансформация Карла Поланьи : прошлое, настоящее, будущее : [сборник] / [сост. Р. М. Нуреев] ; под общ. ред. Р. М. Нуреева. – М.: Изд. дом ГУ ВШЭ, 2006. – 65 с.

58. Взаимодействие – Википедия, ru.wikipedia.org

59. Винер Дж. Концепция полезности в теории ценности и ее критики / Дж. Винер // Вехи экономической мысли. Теория потребительского поведения и спроса / под ред. В. М. Гальперина. – СПб.: Экономическая школа, 2000. - Т. 1. – 380 с.

60. Владиславлев А. П. Идентичность и культурное многообразие: можно ли ими управлять. – М., 2007.

61. Внедрение сбалансированной системы показателей / Horvath & Partners; Пер. с нем. 2-е изд. – М.: Альпина Бизнес Букс, 2006. С. 19.

62. Волгина О. А., Голодная Н. Ю., Одияко Н. Н., Шуман Г. И. Математическое моделирование экономических процессов и систем. – М.: КНОРУС, 2012. – 200 с.

63. Восканян С. С. Практика политического менеджмента в России: состояние, проблемы, сценарии развития // Власть. 2015. № 5. С. 29–34.

64. Всемирный индекс счастья. Гуманитарная энциклопедия [Электронный ресурс] // Центр гуманитарных

технологий. - 20.01.2010 (последняя редакция: 07.07.2014). URL: http://gtmarket.ru/ratings/happy-planet-index/info

65. Гадамер Х.-Г. Истина и метод: Основы философской герменевтики. – М., 1988. С. 319.

66. Гармония хозяйственных отношений. – СПб., 1860; – 38 с.

67. Гаспаров М. Л. Историзм, массовая культура и наш завтрашний день // Вестник истории, литературы, искусства. Т.1. – М., 2005.

68. Геец В. М. Общество, государство, экономика: феноменология взаимодействия и развития. Издательство «Экономика», 2014.

69. Гидденс Э. Социология. – М.: Эдиториал УРСС, 1999.–704 с.

70. Гидденс Э. Устроение общества. С. 45–46.

71. Голованов А. И. Методология современной экономической науки: определение общего вектора. Вестник ТГУ Экономика №3/2012.

72. Горелик А. Л. Построение систем распознавания. // А. Л.Горелик, В. А.Скрипкин. – М.: Сов. Радио, 1974.

73. Гуляев Г. Ю. Проблемы и пути развития конкуренции в России. // Экономика и социум №2 (15), 2015. www iupr.ru

74. Давыдов В. М., Ладанов И. Д. Психологическая совместимость в трудовых коллективах. – М., 1985. С. 31–45.

75. Данилин О. Принципы разработки ключевых показателей эффективности (КПЭ) для промышленных предприятий и

практика их применения // Управление Компанией. 2003. №2(21).

76. Дель Пи. От успеха к удовлетворению. – Ростов-на-Дону: Феникс, 2005.

77. Деминг У. Э. Новая экономика. – М.: Эксмо, 2006.

78. Джевонс, У. С. Краткое сообщение об общей математической теории политической экономии / У. С. Джевонс // Вехи экономической мысли. Теория потребительского поведения и спроса / под. ред. В. М. Гальперина. – СПб.: Экономическая школа, 2000. - Т. 1. – 380 с.

79. Джевонс, У. С. Об общей математической теории политической экономии / У. С. Джевонс // Вехи экономической мысли. Теория потребительского поведения и спроса / под. ред. В. М. Гальперина. – СПб. Экономическая школа, 2000. - Т. 1. – 380 с.

80. Доклад академика С. Ю. Глазьева в РАН «О внешних и внутренних угрозах экономической безопасности России в условиях американской агрессии» 29.10.2014 г. С. 3.

81. Дубко В. Г. Проблемы объединения наук. (Фонд «Достижения естествознания для решения проблем общества»). – СПб, 2010.

82. Дюпюи, Ж. О мере полезности гражданских сооружений / Ж. Дюпюи // Вехи экономической мысли. Теория потребительского поведения и спроса / под ред. В. М. Гальперина. – СПб: Экономическая школа. 2000. - Т. 1. – 380 с.

83. Егоров Е. В. Политика развития здравоохранения в современной России // Вестник Московского университета. Серия 6: Экономика, 2009. № 6.

84. Ельмеев В. Я. К новой парадигме социально-экономического развития и познания общества. – СПб, 1999.

85. Ершов П. М. Потребности человека. – М.: Мысль, 1990.

86. Жакунова Т. С. Политика и мораль. – М., 1992.

87. Жеребин В. М. Уровень жизни населения – как он понимается сегодня / В. М. Жеребин, Н. А. Ермакова // Вопросы статистики. 2008. № 8. С. 3–11.

88. Жильцов Е. Н., Егоров Е. В. Экономика и управление социальной сферой. – М: Издательско-торговая корпорация «Дашков и К», 2015.

89. Заманская Е. Витальная саморегуляция – что это такое? 2006. library.by> portalus/modules/psycholgy/redme.php/?

90. Зверева Н. Социальное предпринимательство: взгляд в будущее [Электронный ресурс] / Н. Зверева // Режим доступа: http://www.nisse.ru/business/article/article_1640.html?effort

91. Адизес И. К. Управляя изменениями. – М.: Питер, 2011.

92. Индекс глобальной конкурентоспособности. Гуманитарная энциклопедия [Электронный ресурс] // Центр гуманитарных технологий. - 09.09.2010 (последняя редакция: 30.09.2015). URL: http://gtmarket.ru/ratings/global-competitiveness-index/info

93. Индекс развития человеческого потенциала. Гуманитарная энциклопедия [Электронный ресурс] // Центр гуманитарных технологий. - 10.10.2009 (последняя редакция: 15.12.2015). URL: http://gtmarket.ru/ratings/human-development-index/human-development-index-info

94. Кайсарова В. П. Ценностно-ориентированный подход в стратегическом управлении крупным городом // Вестник С.-Петерб. ун-та. Сер. 5: Экономика. 2008. № 4. С. 129.

95. Каплан Р., Нортон Д. Организация, ориентированная на стратегию. – М.: Олимп-Бизнес, 2004. С. 143–145.

96. Каплан Роберт С., Нортон Дейвид П. Сбалансированная система показателей. От стратегии к действию. – М.: ЗАО «Олимп-Бизнес», 2003.

97. Каплан Роберт С., Нортон Дейвид П. Стратегические карты. Трансформация нематериальных активов в материальные результаты. – М.: ЗАО «Олимп-Бизнес», 2004.

98. Каткова Л. М. Совместимость персонала в организациях. – М.: МОСУ, 2002. С. 23–48.

99. Кениг В. Ремесленные организации в системе институтов / В. Кениг // Проблемы современной политической экономии. - 2003. - № 1-2. - С. 61.

100. Кирдина С. Институциональные матрицы и развитие России / С. Кирдина. – Новосибирск: ИЭиОПП СО РАН, 2001. – 308 с.

101. Китов А. И. Психология хозяйственного управления. – М.: Профиздат, 1984. С. 150–154

102. Клейнер Г, Петросян Д. Взаимодействия государства и общества при формировании экономической политики // Общество и экономика. - 2005. - № 4. - С. 49.

103. Клейнер Г. Б. Рациональность, неполная рациональность, иррациональность: психологические факторы // Человек институциональный. – Волгоград: Вол ГУ, 2005. С. 222.

104. Клейнер Г. Б. Системная экономика - новое направление в экономической теории. – Казань: КФУ, 2012. – 62 с.

105. Клейнер Г. Б. Стратегия предприятия. – М.: Дело, 2008.

106. Козлов А. А. Организация эффективного взаимодействия государственных органов и предпринимательских структур. Docme.ru>doc/235124/organizaciya.. gosudarstvennyh…

107. Коллектив. Личность. Общение. Словарь социально-психологических понятий / под ред. Е. С. Кузьмина, В. Е. Семенова. – Л.: Лениздат, 1987.

108. Кондратьев Н. Д. Большие циклы конъюнктуры и теория предвидения. Избранные труды. 2002. С. 527.

109. Кропоткин П. А. Анархия: Сборник. – М.: Айрис-пресс, 2002. С.47–113.

110. Кругман, П. Международная экономика: теория и политика [Текст] / П. Кругман, М. Обстфельд. – СПб.: Питер, 2005.–832 с.

111. Кузнецов В. Ю. Мир единства. – М.: Академпроект, 2010.

112. Кузнецов Ю. В. и др. Государственное стратегическое управление. – С-Пб.: Питер, 2014. С-180.

113. Кузык Б. Н., Яковец Ю. В. Цивилизации. – М.: Институт экономических стратегий, 2006.

114. Куликов Л. М. Основы экономической теории. – М.: Кнорус, 2015.

115. Леонтьев В. В. "Избранные произведения в 3-х томах. Том 2. Исследования на основе методологии «Затраты-выпуск». – М.: Экономика, 2007.

116. Либман А. М. Современная экономическая теория: основные тенденции // Вопросы экономики. 2007. № 3. С. 3.

117. Лилеев И. Основные начала политической экономии. СПб., 1860. – 273 с.

118. Липов В. Институциональная комплементарность в формировании и развитии национальных социально-экономических систем стран мира / В. Липов // Terra Economicus. Экономический вестник Ростовского государственного университета. – 2009. – Т. 7.–№ 4. – С.51–67.

119. Липов В. В. Институциональная комплементарность, как фактор формирования социально-экономических систем // Журнал институциональных исследований. Том 4. №1, 2012. – С. 38.

120. Липсетт Дж. Опыт социального предпринимательства на примере Великобритании [Электронный ресурс] / Дж. Липсетт // Режим доступа: http://www.sel.org.uk/publications.html

121. Логический словарь: Совместимость http://www.slovarik.kiev.ua/logic/s/128241.html>Совместимость<

122. Лосев А. Ф. Комментарии к диалогам Платона. Компиляция из четырехтомного издания диалогов Платона. – М.: Мысль, 1990–1999. К.: PSYLIB, 2005.

123. Маевский, В. О рациональном поведении реального потребителя / В. Маевский, Д. Чернавский // Вопросы экономики. - 2007. - № 3. - С. 71–85.

124. Макконнелл К., Брю С. Экономикс: принципы, проблемы и политика. – М., 1993. – С. 23.

125. Малинова О. Ю. Гражданство и политизация культурных различий // Политические исследования. 2004. № 5.

126. Малый экономический словарь / под ред. Л. Н. Азрилияна. – М.: Институт новой экономики, 2000. - 783 с.

127. Маркс К. Теория прибавочной стоимости у физиократов. В кн.: Классики политической экономии от XVII до середины XIX века // Сборник извлечений из сочинений экономистов с пояснительными статьями. М. - JL: Госиздат, 1926. С. 102.

128. Маршалл, А. Принципы экономической науки / А. Маршалл. – М.: Прогресс, 1993. – 374 с.

129. Маслоу А. Мотивация и личность. 3-е изд. – СПб.: Питер, 2003.

130. Мельков С. А. Какие ценности предстоит защищать России // Власть. 2015. № 2. С. 94–97.

131. Микульский К. и др. Социально-экономические модели в современном мире и путь России. – М.: Экономика, 2003.–758 с.

132. Минакир, П. А. Пространственная экономика: эволюция подходов и методология [Текст] / П. А. Минакир, А. Н. Демьяненко // Пространственная экономика. – 2010. – № 2. С. 29– 30.

133. Михеев В. В. Глобализация и азиатский регионализм. Вызовы для России. М., 2001, С. 11.

134. Морис Алле. Экономика как наука. Современная экономическая мысль. М.:1995.

135. Морозов В. А. Механизмы экономики взаимодействия // Креативная экономика. -2014. - №9 (93).

136. Морозов В. А. Предприятие и внешняя среда: уровни взаимодействия // Российское предпринимательство, № 8 (206)/4.2012.

137. Морозов В. А. Совместимость социально-экономических систем. – М.: Экономика, 2013. – 334 с. Morozov V. Exploring Compatibility: Foundations of a Theory. – Quickstone Publishing UK, 2014.

138. Морозов В. А. Совместимость социально-экономических систем. Основы теории совместимости. – М.: Экономика,2013. С. 20–35.

139. Морозов В. А. Совместимые показатели экономики взаимодействия // Креативная экономика. -2014.-№10(94).

140. Морозов В. А. Экономика взаимодействия (введение) и теория совместимости // Креативная экономика. -2014.-№8(92).

141. Науманн, Ф. Срединная Европа [Текст] / сост. Б. А. Исаев. – СПб.: Питер, 2007. – 512 с.

142. Национальная промышленная политика конкурентоспособности: опыт Запада – в интересах России. М.: ИМЭМО РАН, 2002. – 278 с.

143. Ненасилие: философия, этика, политика. – М.: Наука, 1993.

144. Нещадин А. Общество, бизнес и власть: условия цивилизованного взаимодействия // Общество и экономика. - 2005. -№10, 11. - С. 5–41.

145. Нонака И., Такеучи Х. Компания – создатель знания. Зарождение и развитие инноваций в японских фирмах / Пер. с англ. – ЗАО «Олимп-Бизнес», 2003. – С. 86–101.

146. Носенков А. А. Теория технической совместимости как новая дисциплина системного анализа / А. А. Носенков, В. И. Медведев // Вестник СAA имени академика М. Ф. Решетнева. Вып. 2. – Красноярск, 2001. С. 231–236.

147. Носенкова А. А., Медведева В. И., Муллина А. М. Совместимость технических систем. – Красноярск, 2005. – 376 с.

148. Обозов Н. Н. Три подхода к исследованию психологической совместимости / Н. Н. Обозов, А. Н. Обозов // Вопросы психологии. – 1981. - № 6. – С. 98–101.

149. Обуховский К. Галактика потребностей. Психология влечений человека. – СПб.: Издательство «Речь», 2003.

150. Олейник А. Модель сетевого капитализма / А. Олейник // Вопросы экономики. - 2003. -№ 8. - С. 144.

151. Основы социально-психологической теории / под общей ред. А. А. Бодалева и А. Н. Сухова. – М.: Международная педагогическая академия, 1995.

152. Панов П. В. Институты, идентичности, практики: теоретическая модель политического порядка. – М.: РОССПЭН, 2011.

153. Парсонс Т. Понятие общества: компоненты и их взаимоотношения // THESIS. 1993. № 2. С. 102.

154. Пилипенко, В. И. Конкурентоспособность стран и регионов в мировом хозяйстве. Теория, опыт малых стран Западной и Северной Европы [Текст] / В. И. Пилипенко. – М.: Ойкумена, – 86 с.

155. Плотковский А. А. Учение Гегеля о праве и государстве. Гос-ное изд-во юрид. литературы, М. – 18 с.

156. Поланьи Карл. «Великая трансформация»: прошлое, настоящее, будущее [сборник] / [сост. Р. М. Нуреев] ; под общ. ред. Р. М. Нуреева. – М.: Изд. дом ГУ ВШЭ, 2006. – 406 с.

157. Политэкономический словарь [Текст] / под ред. О. Ожерельева, А. Улюкаева, И. Фаминского. – М., 1990. – 570 с.

158. Портер, М. Конкурентное преимущество. Как достичь высокого результата и обеспечить его устойчивость [Текст] / М. Портер. – М.: Альпина Бизнес Букс, 2005. – 715 с.

159. Постановление Правительства РФ от 17 декабря 2012 г. № 1317.referent.ru>1/ 207820

160. Постановление Правительства РФ от 3 ноября 2012 г. № 1142 «О мерах по реализации Указа Президента Российской Федерации от 21 августа 2012 г. № 1199 "Об оценке эффективности деятельности органов исполнительной власти субъектов Российской Федерации". Garant.ru>Продукты Прайм>Документы ленты прайм >70154132

161. Прайснер А. Сбалансированная система показателей в маркетинге и сбыте. М., 2009.

162. Приказ Минэкономразвития России № 223 от 23.04.2012 г. «Об организации проведения конкурсного отбора субъектов Федерации, бюджетам которых в 2012 году предоставляются для финансирования мероприятий, осуществляемых в государственной поддержки малого и среднего предпринимательства субъектами Российской Федерации» http: //www.economic.kurganobl.ru/

163. Программа развития ООН: Индекс человеческого развития в странах мира в 2015 году. [Электронный ресурс] // Центр гуманитарных технологий. - 16.12.2015. URL: http://gtmarket.ru/news/2015/12/16/7285

164. Радюкова Я. Ю., Бушуева Е. Н. Совершенствование конкурентной политики как инструмент развития предпринимательства в России. // Социально-экономические явления и процессы №1 (035), 2012.

165. Райнерт Э. С. Как богатые страны стали богатыми, и почему бедные страны остаются бедными. М., 2011. С. 68.

166. Рамперсанд Х. Универсальная система показателей: Как достигать результатов, сохраняя целостность. – М.: Альпина Бизнес Букс. 200

167. Распределение предприятий и организаций по организационно-правовым формам в 2013 гг. http://www.gks.ru/bgd/regl/b14_14p/IssWWW.exe/Stg/d02/12-03.htm из сборника Регионы России 2014. Содержание: http://www.gks.ru/bgd/regl/b14_14p/Main.htm

168. Рахаев Б. Витальные ресурсы, ментальная среда и организационные циклы бизнеса. 31.01.2010. finanal.ru>001

169. Рейтинг стран мира по уровню процветания. Гуманитарная энциклопедия [Электронный ресурс] // Центр гуманитарных технологий. - 10.06.2011 (последняя редакция: 03.11.2015). URL: http://gtmarket.ru/ratings/legatum-prosperity-index/info

170. Рейтинг стран мира по уровню экологической эффективности в 2016 году. [Электронный ресурс] // Центр гуманитарных технологий. - 29.01.2016. URL: http://gtmarket.ru/news/2016/01/29/7292

171. Рикардо Д. Начало политической экономии и налогового обложения [Текст] / Д. Рикардо. – М.: Директ-Медиа, 2007. – 327 с.

172. Роббинс Л. («Предмет экономической науки») in L. Robbins. An Essay on the Nature and Significance of Economic Science. 2nd ed. London: Macmillan, 1935, 12.

173. Россияне адаптировались к бедности. Светлана Бороздина, Газета.GZT.Ru. http://www.gzt.ru/rubricator_text.gzt?rubric=novosti&id=64054900000047762

174. Рубочкин В. А. Современная этика: Учебное пособие. / Под редакцией проф. Бражник Г. В. – М.: Московский университет потребительской кооперации, 2003.

175. Фишер С., Р. Дорнбуш, Р. Шмалензи. Экономика. – М.: Дело, 2001.

176. Савельев, Ю. В. Теоретические основы современной межрегиональной конкуренции / Ю. В. Савельев // Журнал экономической теории. – 2010. – № 2. С. 94.

177. Сальвиоли Д. Капитализм в античном мире: этюд по истории хозяйственного быта / Г. Сальвиоли; пер. с фр. Р. Гальперина. – Екатеринослав. – Харьков: Всеукраинское государственное издательство, 1922. – 187 с.

178. Светлов В. А. Конфликт: модели, решения, менеджмент / В. А. Светлов. – СПб.: Питер, 2005.

179. Селин А. Ю. Формирование эффективной системы регионального стратегирования: Автореф. дис. канд. экон. наук. Ижевск, 2006. С. 10.

180. Семенов Н. Н. Наука и общество. Статьи и речи / Н. Н. Семенов. – М.: Наука, 1973. – 358 с.

181. Сетров М. И. Организация биосистем. – Л.: ЛГК, 1971.

182. Словарь логики. «Толковый словарь Ефремовой». enc-dic.comSovmestimost-348

183. Словарь логики. Logic/Sovmestimost-348.html.

184. Смит А. Исследование о природе и причинах богатства народов. – М., 1962. С. 28.

185. Соколов А. Б. Влияние политических и социально-экономических факторов на здоровье населения в постсоветской России «Российская академия правосудия. С-К филиал. 2001.

186. Сорокин П. А. Заметки социолога. Социологическая публицистика [Текст] / П. А. Сорокин. СПб, 2000. С. 48.

187. Сорокин П. А. Человек. Цивилизация. Общество / Общ. ред., сост. и предисл. А. Ю. Согомонов: Пер. с англ. [Текст] / П. А. Сорокин, А. Ю. Согомонов. – М., 1992. – 211 с.

188. Социальная психология: история, теория, эмпирические исследования / под ред. Е. С. Кузьмина, В. Е. Семенова. – Л.: Изд-во ЛГУ, 1979.

189. Социальное партнерство в субъектах РФ в 2005 году. Сибирский федеральный округ [Электронный ресурс]. - режим доступа: http://www.mzsrrf.ru.

190. Социально-ориентированные некоммерческие организации http://www.gks.ru/wps/wcm/connect/rosstat_main/rosstat/ru/statistics /finance/. Итоги выборочного исследования социально ориентированных некоммерческих организаций на основе формы №1 СОНКО

191. Социальные конфликты и партнерство / Под ред. А. В. Глухова, В. С. Рахманина. – Воронеж: ВГУ, 2004. – 372 с.

192. Стиглиц Д. Ю. "Крутое пике: Америка и новый экономический порядок после глобального кризиса". – М., 2014.

193. Стрелков И. С. Зарубежный опыт социального предпринимательства [Электронный ресурс] / И. С. Стрелков // Режим доступа: http://www.nb-forum.ru/sociallinks

194. Струве П. Б. Основная антиномия трудовой теории ценности. Жизнь. 1900. Кн. 2. – 306 с.

195. Структура национальной экономики. Реформы в экономике России.qrandars.ru>struktura-nacionalnoy-ekonomiki.html

196. Суслова С. В. Социальный капитал современной фирмы / С. В. Суслова // Экономика. Вопросы школьного экономического образования. - 2003. -№ 2. - С. 37–39.

197. Суханова Т. В. Теоретические подходы к исследованию полезности экономического блага как объекта потребительского спроса / Т. В. Суханова // Известия высших учебных заведений. Поволжский регион. Общественные науки. -2012. - № 4 (24). - С. 91–100.

198. Сэй Ж. Б., Значение социального предпринимательства [Электронный ресурс] / Ж. Б. Сей // http://www.fuqua.duke.edu/centers/case/documents/Dees_SEdef.pdf

199. Темплтон Джон. Всемирные законы жизни. – М.: АСТ, 2005.

200. Терборн Г. Принадлежность к культуре, местоположение в структуре и человеческая деятельность: объяснение в социологии и социальной науке // THESIS. 1994. Вып. 4.

201. Титов, Л. Ю. Особенности сетевой экономики как новой формы организации экономической деятельности / Л. Ю. Титов // Транспортное дело рOCCU ZL -2008. -№ 3.

202. Туган-Барановский М. И. Периодические промышленные кризисы. Общая теория кризисов. – М.: Наука-РОССПЭН, 1997.

203. Фишер. С, Дорнбуш Р., Шмалензи Р. Экономика. – М: Дело, 2001.

204. Франтов Г. С. Единство мира природы. – СПб, 2004.

205. Фромм Э. Психоанализ и религия; Искусство любить; Иметь или быть. Киев: Ника-Центр, 1998.

206. Ханингтон С. Столкновения цивилизаций. – М., 1998.

207. Хантингтон С. Политический порядок в меняющихся обществах. – М.: Прогресс-Традиция, 2004.

208. Ханттингтон. Столкновение цивилизаций. 2002.

209. Хейне Пол. Экономический образ мышления: [перевод с английского] / Пол Хейне, Питер Дж. Боуттке, Дэвид Л. Причитко. – Москва [и др.]: Вильямс, 2007. – 530 с.

210. Хикс Дж. Р. Стоимость и капитал. – М.: Издательская группа "Прогресс", 1993. – 127 с.

211. Хикс Дж. Р., Аллен Р. Г. Д. Пересмотр теории ценности // Вехи экономической мысли. Теория потребительского поведения и спроса. Т. 1. Под ред. В. М. Гальперина. – СПб: Экономическая школа, 2000. – 106 с.

212. Целеполагание в менеджменте. http://center-yf.ru/data/Menedzheru/Celepolaganie.php

213. Чекмарёв, В. В. Экономическое пространство и его сотово-сетевая организация / В. В. Чекмарёв. – Кострома: КГУ им. Некрасова, 2002. – 120 с.

214. Черемисинов Г. А. Теоретико-методологические и духовно-нравственные проблемы формирования российской модели экономики // Изв. Сарат. ун-та. Нов. серия. 2009. Т. 9. Сер. Экономика. Управление. Право. Вып. 2. С. 3–19.

215. Число общественных объединений, политических партий и некоммерческих организаций, зарегистрированных в РФ на 1 января 2014 г. http://www.gks.ru/bgd/regl/b14_11/IssWWW.exe/Stg/d01/02-

06.htm из сборника Россия в цифрах 2014 г. Содержание: http://www.gks.ru/bgd/regl/b14_11/Main.htm

216. Чичерин Б. Курс государственной науки. Ч1: Общее государственное право. – М.: Типо-лит. т-ва Н. Н. Кушнеров и К, 1894.

217. Чугин-Русов А. Е. Единое поле мировой культуры. Кижли-концепция – М.: Прогресс-Традиция, 2002.

218. Шаститко А. Е., Павлова Н. С. О сбалансированности инструментов конкурентной политики. МГУ. Бюллетень конкурентной политики №7. 06.2012. – 12 с.

219. Шахмалов Ф. Государство и экономика. Основы взаимодействия: Учебник. – М.: ЗАО «Издательство «Экономика», 2005. – 727 с.

220. Шилз Э. Общество и общества: макросоциологический подход // Американская социология: Перспективы, проблемы, методы. – М.: Прогресс, 1972.

221. Широкова Г. В. Управление изменениями. Хрестоматия. – С-Пб: Издательство «Высшая школа менеджмента», 2010.

222. Шлёцер Х. А. Начальные основания государственного хозяйства, или науки о народном богатстве. 1-е изд. Ч. 2. - С. 11.

223. Шумпетер Й. А. Теория экономического развития. – М: Директмедиа Паблишинг, 2008. – с. 148.

224. Щеглова Л. В. Культурология: единство и многообразие форм культуры. – Волгоград: Перемена, 2009.

225. Эволюция экономической теории: воспроизводство, технологии, институты. – СПб.: Алетейя, 2015.

226. Экономическое мышление: философские предпосылки: учебное пособие для высших учебных заведений по экономическим специальностям / Е. Н. Калмычкова, И. Г. Чаплыгина. – Москва: Инфра-М, 2005.

227. Энгельс Ф. Наброски к критике политической экономии. Газета «The Northern Star» №340, 18 мая 1844г.

228. Якимова Н. Н. Дыхание Вселенной (Единство мира). – М.: Дельфис, 2010.

www.ingramcontent.com/pod-product-compliance
Lightning Source LLC
Chambersburg PA
CBHW061927190326
41458CB00009B/2680